Language and Globalization

Series Editors
Sue Wright
University of Portsmouth
Portsmouth
United Kingdom

Helen Kelly-Holmes
University of Limerick
Castletroy Limerick
Ireland

In the context of current political and social developments, where the national group is not so clearly defined and delineated, the state language not so clearly dominant in every domain, and cross-border flows and transfers affects more than a small elite, new patterns of language use will develop. This series aims to provide a framework for reporting on and analysing the linguistic outcomes of globalization and localization.

More information about this series at
http://www.springer.com/series/14830

Jennifer Dailey-O'Cain

Trans-National English in Social Media Communities

Jennifer Dailey-O'Cain
Modern Languages and Cultural Studies
University of Alberta
Edmonton, Canada

Language and Globalization
ISBN 978-1-137-50614-6   ISBN 978-1-137-50615-3 (eBook)
DOI 10.1057/978-1-137-50615-3

Library of Congress Control Number: 2017936963

© The Editor(s) (if applicable) and The Author(s) 2017
The author(s) has/have asserted their right(s) to be identified as the author(s) of this work in accordance with the Copyright, Designs and Patents Act 1988.
This work is subject to copyright. All rights are solely and exclusively licensed by the Publisher, whether the whole or part of the material is concerned, specifically the rights of translation, reprinting, reuse of illustrations, recitation, broadcasting, reproduction on microfilms or in any other physical way, and transmission or information storage and retrieval, electronic adaptation, computer software, or by similar or dissimilar methodology now known or hereafter developed.
The use of general descriptive names, registered names, trademarks, service marks, etc. in this publication does not imply, even in the absence of a specific statement, that such names are exempt from the relevant protective laws and regulations and therefore free for general use.
The publisher, the authors and the editors are safe to assume that the advice and information in this book are believed to be true and accurate at the date of publication. Neither the publisher nor the authors or the editors give a warranty, express or implied, with respect to the material contained herein or for any errors or omissions that may have been made. The publisher remains neutral with regard to jurisdictional claims in published maps and institutional affiliations.

Cover image © Chantal van Doreen

Printed on acid-free paper

This Palgrave Macmillan imprint is published by Springer Nature
The registered company is Macmillan Publishers Ltd.
The registered company address is: The Campus, 4 Crinan Street, London, N1 9XW, United Kingdom

Acknowledgments

Like any book, this one could not have been written without the financial, intellectual, and emotional support of others. First, I would like to say how indebted I are to the participants of the *unserekleinestadt* and *vragenuurtje* communities who not only welcomed me into their respective digital spaces, but ultimately gave me permission to use their conversations for the purposes of linguistic analysis. I would especially like to single out the participants who later went on to meet with me in person so that I could interview them about their language practices. I enjoyed every minute of the time I spent with them, and I feel privileged to continue to have several of them in my life on an ongoing basis.

Second, I acknowledge the support of the University of Alberta for two internal grants (allowing me to hire research assistants and to travel to collect data and give conference papers) and two separate sabbatical leaves (allowing me first to carry out the interviews and ultimately to write the manuscript). None of those privileges can be taken for granted in these lean times, and I am extremely grateful. I would also like to thank the research assistants who helped with the coding and/or transcription of data: Artem Medvedev, Richard Feddersen, Jessika Wrobel, Cathlelein Aaftink, and Jolien Witte.

Next, I would like to thank the colleagues who contributed to this book through everything from the discussion of core concepts to concrete feedback. There were many of these, but I would like to single

v

vi   Acknowledgments

out five. First, Roel Vismans' influence on the early stages of my analysis of the language use in the *vragenuurtje* community cannot be underestimated: my great thanks to him. Second, Susan Wright's commentary regarding the role of nationalisms was very helpful as I was revising the paper that became Dailey-O'Cain (2013) and which ended up comprising parts of each of Chapters 2, 3, and 4 of this book, and similarly, Selma Sonntag's input following a paper I gave at the Multidisciplinary Approaches to Language Policy and Planning conference in Calgary helped point me in the right direction on how to approach the influence of the state. Also, Grit Liebscher deserves a huge thank you both for helping me tighten up the initial proposal for this book and for being so supportive of me striking out on my own with this project, and Kristine Horner deserves another not just for inviting me to join the WUN network on Multilingualism and Mobility (and thereby affording me the opportunity for a great many helpful conversations), but also for being a never-ending fount of knowledge on so many fronts. All remaining errors and inconsistencies are, of course, my own.

Finally, my never-ending gratitude to my photographer and friend Chantal van Dooren for conceiving and executing the photograph on the front cover based on my attempts to explain my research, and to Ben Farnell for his expert figure-making skills. And last but never least, one more huge thank you to Christie Lutsiak for her constant support and encouragement, especially during the final phase of the project. <3

Contents

1	Introduction	1
2	Language Ideologies, Multilingualism, and Social Media	23
3	The Who and the What: Amounts and Types of English	61
4	The How: Interactional Functions of English	89
5	The Why: Ideology, Positioning, and Attitudes toward English	135
6	English as a Trans-National Language	279
	Bibliography	291
	Index	309

List of Figures

Fig. 1.1	A post in the community *unserekleinestadt* and one of its comments	9
Fig. 3.1	Percentages of English use in the two communities	81
Fig. 3.2	Percentages of use of the four identified categories of switching	81
Fig. 3.3	Percentages of flagged vs. unflagged switches in the two communities	83
Fig. 3.4	Percentages of different languages in usernames	85
Fig. 6.1	The influence of a language regime on informal language practices	286

List of Tables

Table 1.1 Interview participants' ages and genders: *unserekleinestadt* (German)   12

Table 1.2 Interview participants' ages and genders: *vragenuurtje* (Dutch)   12

1

Introduction

(1) ich bin echt so **happy** mit meinem schnäppchen! (*i really am so happy with my bargain!*)

(2) Het is zo gaaf om lekker met z'n allen te **worshippen** en samen **fellowship** te hebben! **#GodIsAwesome** (*It's so cool to just kick back and worship and have fellowship together! #GodIsAwesome*)

(3) Er zit veel... nou, "toneelspel" is een beetje een zwaar woord, maar er zit veel **performance** bij. (*There's a lot of... well, "toneelspel" is a little bit of a heavy word, but there's a lot of performance in it.*)

(4) **Day 02: your favourite song in a foreign language (not Dutch or English)**

Although English is my native language, the German language has been a central part of my life since I was a teenager. So whenever I say that I grew up with the kind of casual English borrowing seen in example 1 above, that is literally true. That particular example is from the Instagram account of a young German of my acquaintance (where it was accompanied by a picture

© The Author(s) 2017   **1**
J. Dailey-O'Cain, *Trans-National English in Social Media Communities*, Language and Globalization,
DOI 10.1057/978-1-137-50615-3_1

2   1 Introduction

of the new scarf she'd just bought), but if you were to surf over to any online space where German is used and have a look around, it wouldn't take long for you to notice this sort of thing yourself: an English lexical item in the place of where a similar German lexical item might otherwise be, used in order to make the thing they're talking about sound cooler, younger, and just more fun. And like I said, this sort of thing isn't especially new, either; I'm well into middle age by this point, and I got used to the idea many years ago that sliding words from my own native language into German sentences would have this effect. As a young learner of the language in the country for the first time all those years ago, I eventually even found myself doing it too (because when in Germany, I wanted to do as the Germans do, even if this sometimes paradoxically meant using English).

As I grew more and more interested in Dutch, though, and started paying more attention to the way *that* language tended to be used in casual contexts, I encountered different kinds of uses of English that were unfamiliar to me from my personal history with German. The English in Example 2 (from Facebook, from a young Dutch evangelical Christian of my acquaintance, and accompanied by a picture of her with three smiling friends) brought me up short when I saw it—in part because there's just so much of it ("worship," "fellowship," and the hashtag "#Godisawesome" are all rendered completely in English), and in part because the notion of *lekker worshippen* was an amusing mental image to me, as if what Christians did with other believers were somehow analogous to *lekker relaxen* (kicking back and relaxing) or *lekker chillen* (kicking back and chilling out). In thinking about it further, though, I could see why the English terms had been used. The Dutch term *aanbidden* ("to worship/ praise"), as well as possible Dutch equivalents of the other English words in my young friend's Facebook status update such as *kameraadschap* for "fellowship," and *God is groots* for "God is awesome," would have instinctively seemed to transfer the church context to a more traditional Calvinistic Dutch one that wouldn't have conveyed my young friend's evangelical environment properly at all. It seemed as if the English words "worship" and "fellowship" and the English hashtag "#Godisawesome" were not just cooler and more fun, but also somehow more *authentic*, as if those terms had managed to retain some element of the American origins of those forms of evangelical Christianity in being transferred to Dutch.

Once I started paying attention, I found myself seeing different kinds of new-to-me Dutch uses of English everywhere. Example 3 was striking because it came from a more formal context than social media: a radio interview from then-criminology Ph.D. student Robby Roks from the Erasmus University of Rotterdam, as he was being interviewed about the behaviour of a criminal gang from The Hague in July of 2014 on the Dutch public radio programme *Met het oog op morgen*. In trying to describe the performative aspects of the aggressive way the gang communicates, he proposed and immediately explicitly rejected the Dutch term *toneelspel*, opting instead for the English term "performance." In doing this, he gave a reason for why the Dutch word wouldn't really fit: the word is too "heavy." The English term brings with it a sense of *lightness*, in other words—leaving any baggage the Dutch term would have had behind by decoupling it from its specific cultural environment. Finally, Example 4 is arguably the most interesting of all. It's taken from the personal blog of a young Dutch woman, and it's the second day of what people in her wider community of personal bloggers call a daily "meme"—on the first day, everyone posts their responses to one prompt, on the second day, everyone reacts to a different prompt, and so on. This prompt for the second day is entirely in English, which is at least somewhat interesting in and of itself (though it should be said that this is not necessarily unexpected, as many such memes originate among Anglophones). More intriguing, however, is what the prompt is asking for: everyone is invited to say what their favourite song is "in a foreign language," which is specified as meaning "not Dutch or English." Dutch is not "a foreign language" by virtue of being the native language of this young woman and her friends/presumed audience, while English is also not "a foreign language," either, by virtue of . . . something else, something unspecified.

It was these kinds of observations—among many other similar ones—that prompted this book. In taking a closer look at how Dutch young people were using and talking about English in their conversations with other Dutch people, I found myself noticing a lot of phenomena that were mostly unfamiliar to me from the way I'd always noticed English being used together with German by young Germans, and a lot of implied or even directly expressed attitudes toward that usage that were different from the ones I'd seen Germans express, as well. As a result, I couldn't

4   1 Introduction

help but ask myself how those kinds of phenomena might be studied systematically, applying the tools of sociolinguistic discourse analysis I use in my work, but in a specifically *comparative* way, a way that might be able to uncover both what those differences in use might be and the reasons for those differences. The study that makes up this book attempts to do just that through a comparative analysis of the use of English in two social media communities, one German and one Dutch, hand in hand with an analysis of interviews with community members about their perceptions about that use.

In this chapter, I provide a broad sketch of the two social media communities and the project from which my data stems, as well as a short discussion of the research questions I will address in the analysis. I begin by introducing the notion of computer-mediated spaces as *communities* and give a broad overview of the role such communities have come to play within the social lives of European young people. Moving beyond this, I then introduce the two specific communities that provide the data analyzed in this book, and talk about the methodologies I will use to carry out the analysis of them. Finally, I end with the argument that an analysis of the language use in these kinds of communities goes beyond studies of so-called "internet language," and can in fact serve more broadly as a close look at how globalization phenomena (in the form of "international English") play out in the practices of everyday life.

Computer-mediated Spaces as Communities

Early research into computer-mediated spaces struggled with the extent to which the groups of people who populated these spaces could be described as *communities* (cf. Baym 2015: 81–100, Angouri 2016: 324–6). However, Jones (1995: 23) argued that many such groupings of people are in fact in line with what sociologist and communities scholar Amitai Etzioni (1991) defines as primary criteria for community, such as the ability to create, maintain, and control (virtual) space, and a linkage through that control to issues of authority, dominance, submission, rebellion, and cooptation. In fact, the main distinction between these kinds of communities and face-to-face ones is the fact that the "space" community members control is metaphorical (cf. Baym 2015: 86).

Because of the metaphorical nature of these spaces, Herring (2004: 351–2) proposes that we claim the term *virtual community* for such groups as long as they can be said to conform to six sets of observable criteria. These are:

1. active participation and a core of regular participants
2. shared history, purpose, culture, norms, and values
3. solidarity, support, reciprocity
4. criticism, conflict, means of conflict resolution
5. self-awareness of group as entity distinct from other groups
6. emergence of roles, hierarchy, governance, and rituals.

Together, these criteria seem to sum up what Rheingold (1993: 5) seemed to be describing when he stated that such virtual communities are "social aggregations that emerge from the Net when enough people carry on those public discussions long enough, with sufficient human feeling, to form webs of personal relationships." Kytölä (2016: 376)—who terms these communities *translocal* rather than *virtual* but certainly seems to be discussing the same phenomenon—further distinguishes three types of such communities. The first of these are "old" or "new" diasporic communities that have been shaped by patterns of migration and mobility, and which share either an ethnocultural or linguistic affiliation, or both. The second of these are what Wenger (1998) might term computer-mediated *communities of practice*, i.e. groups of people sharing common goals and acting together towards them (in non-virtual space, two common examples of communities of practice are classrooms and workplaces). Finally, the third group consists of digital *affinity spaces* (cf. Gee 2004), i.e. online spaces where people gather because they share interests, causes, lifestyles, activities or cultural products with short lifespans or passing popularity. Parks (2011: 105) argues that this does not make social media sites like MySpace, Facebook, and livejournal into communities in their own right, but it does allow them to function as social venues in which many different communities may form.

6 1 Introduction

Throughout this book, I have chosen to refer to the two social media spaces chosen for this study as communities in part because they conform to Herring's six criteria as discussed above (in that they have active participation and a core of regular participants, a shared culture, solidarity and reciprocity, criticism and conflict, self-awareness as a distinct entity, and distinct roles). However, I have also chosen that term because the site on which they are located—livejournal.com or just *livejournal*—refers to them in precisely that way, and because it is therefore the way both groups refer to their own spaces (exclusively—as it turns out—using the English term *community* rather than any local-language equivalent). Livejournal is "a large hosting website with social networking and blogging functionalities that allows users to exchange information and advice, as well as engaging in other types of communication" (Kouper 2010: 1). Similarly to other social media sites such as Facebook, photosharing sites such as Flickr or Instagram, or the comments sections of YouTube, livejournal is a site that can be described as a *web 2.0* environment, or a "web-based application that allows users to create and publish their own content online" (Barton and Lee 2013: 9). The site enables users to create their own journaling blogs similar to those found on other blogging platforms such as Blogger or WordPress, i.e. frequently updated websites with *posts* arranged in reverse chronological order and *comments* below each post (Herring et al. 2004, Rettberg 2008).

But livejournal blogs are also different from conventional blogs in two ways that make them more similar to social networking sites like Facebook: *interconnectivity* (i.e. bloggers can *friend* other livejournal users and read all of their friends' recent posts by clicking on a single page), and *social spaces* (i.e. alongside their own blogs, users can create *communities* that anyone who keeps a blog at livejournal.com may join and participate in). This means that while all participants in the broader world of livejournal maintain their own blogs (or *journals*, in the site's terminology), everyone also has the option to create and/or participate in one or more of these communities, which are often centred around particular common interests. In these communities, authors' identities are represented by sets of thumbnail pictures called *userpics* or *icons* that are appropriated from elsewhere on the internet and creatively modified to suit users' identification purposes, and by usernames that link back to the authors' own blogs and information pages. The interface on these

Computer-mediated Spaces as Communities 7

communities organizes the conversations that result from posts into *threads* that are easy to follow and which allow for side conversations to develop, and the site also sends users email notifications about any responses they receive to their posts or to the comments they make. These features promote back-and-forth interactivity to a degree that many other blogging services do not, and as a result, these threads are more analogous to spoken types of conversation than much other online interaction. Although livejournal's origins are in the United States, at the time of the retrieval of the data (and still now, at the time of this book's publication) it was owned by a Russian company called SUP (Kouper 2010: 1). While English remains the dominant language on the site as a whole, it is nonetheless decidedly international in scope, with users from a great many countries keeping blogs and participating in communities in their native languages (Herring et al. 2007).

This book's two communities will be identified by pseudonyms: *unserekleinestadt* (or "ourlittletown") for the German community and *vragenuurtje* (or "questiontime") for the Dutch one. In discussing them, I will always refer to them by these names in their local languages rather than with the English translations, in order to serve as a reminder that the livejournal users who originally started the two communities each chose a name in their local language—a decision that is not necessarily automatic, as we will see. The two communities exist entirely independently of each other (in fact, until I began my first inquiries to community members about how they might feel about me engaging in this sort of work in their communities, no one from either group knew of the other group's existence) but they can still be easily compared, as they both centre around the asking, answering, and discussing of questions. It should be said that there is one difference between the two communities in this respect: the Dutch community *vragenuurtje* is specifically designated for question-asking and question-answering (to the point where it is explicitly forbidden within community rules to make a new post that does not contain a question unless it is a *vraagvrije vrijdag* or "question-free Friday" post), while the German community *unserekleinestadt* does not have such a rule. In practice, however, there is little difference, because even in *unserekleinestadt*, most new posts are in fact centred on the posing of a question to the group. The content of these questions runs the gamut of everything that could be asked

8   1 Introduction

in a question, in that some are posted purely to promote member interaction (e.g. "What are you making for dinner tonight?"), some are informational (e.g. "Does anyone know where I might be able to buy a shirt that looks like this? [picture attached]"), and some are requests for advice (e.g. "My boyfriend is driving me crazy, here's what he's doing, how can I get him to stop?").

While the excerpts of interaction presented for analysis in Chapters 3 and 4 will be highly simplified for ease of reading, it seems useful to get at least one look at what such a conversation actually looks like on the livejournal site itself. An example of such a conversation can be seen in Fig. 1.1 below. All identifying information has been obscured or changed to protect users' privacy (see the section on ethics below for details), but everything else has been left as it looked in the original conversation. At the top of the page we have the post's author, in this case someone with the username of "weltall," and the name of the community, i.e. *unserekleinestadt*. Below that is the title of weltall's post—*outdoor-schuhe & -kleidung* (or "outdoor shoes and clothing")—and then the post itself. Below that is an indicator of how many comments in total the conversation comprises, followed by the comments. In this case, we're only looking at the post plus one of the comments, though you can see that a total of seven comments were made in the original discussion. The pieces of text that are bright blue are *hyperlinks,* i.e. links that you can click on in order to go to other pages within the livejournal site. Clicking on weltall's or captain_jenny's usernames takes the reader to their own livejournal blogs, while clicking on the name of the community takes the reader to the main community page. The various hyperlinks in the date display pages with lists of posts that were made in a given day, month, or year. Clicking on "Post a new comment" allows the reader to make an additional comment, which is automatically added to the bottom of the list of comments already made, but clicking on 'Reply to this' in response to the comment threads the new comment immediately beneath that one.

A point that needs to be underscored here is that the precise demographics of these two communities are not—and in fact cannot be—known. There are two main reasons for this. One is that while both communities do have a steady core of regular participants, the boundaries of the community are necessarily fluid due to the architecture of the

Computer-mediated Spaces as Communities 9

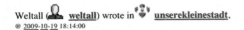

Weltall (<u>weltall</u>) wrote in <u>unserekleinestadt</u>,
@ 2009-10-19 18:14:00

outdoor-schuhe & -kleidung
ich bin auf der suche nach sogenannten outdoor-schuhen, in erster linie wohl für geocaching, spaziergänge, 'light'-wandern, im grunde also nicht sehr anspruchsvoll - wasserfest, warmhaltend, eine ordentliche, griffige sohle. mir ist klar: ohne anprobieren geht das nicht, aber: welche marken - evt. auch modelle - könnt ihr empfehlen, womit habt ihr keine guten erfahrungen gemacht? ähnliches für (3in1-)jacken.
danke im voraus!

(7 comments) - (<u>Post a new comment</u>)

<u>captain_jenny</u>

2009-10-19 09:00 pm UTC (<u>link</u>)

Ich hab ein paar "Boots" von Landrover (wird über Deichmann vertrieben).

3in1-Jacken
Da hab ich mich ja in die Columbia-Jacken verliebt, damals während meines Aupairjahres.
Sind hier aber sauteuer.

(<u>Reply to this</u>)

Fig. 1.1 A post in the community *unserekleinestadt* and one of its comments

livejournal software. It is possible, for example, for any livejournal user to join a community, read (i.e. "lurk") or even participate for a bit, decide it isn't really his or her cup of tea, and then leave the community a day or two later. It is also possible to leave livejournal altogether by deleting one's own journaling blog (though posts and comments made in communities then remain behind). The second reason is that because these are virtual spaces, it is impossible to be absolutely certain that the identity any given community member presents with on the group is precisely the same as that person's identity on for example his or her government ID card or even in his or her workplace. Indeed, one of the challenges of doing research in social media environments has to do with identity, in the sense that identity online—to an even greater extent than identity in face-to-face environments—"is not just about *who we are,* but also *who we want to be to others,* and *how others see us*" (Barton and Lee 2013: 68, emphasis in the original). For this reason, it is impossible to say with absolute certainty exactly how many members either community has, whether those members are primarily male or female, where they live, or any other specific identifying information.

There are, however, things that *can* be known, albeit with a somewhat lesser degree of certainty than would be possible in a study of participants the researcher saw and met face-to-face. First of all, livejournal regularly publishes very rudimentary statistics about the information it has regarding its users (as provided by users themselves). This was the information the site was providing in January of 2010, at the time the data was retrieved:

Are males or females more likely to maintain journals?

- Male: 3997185 (38.1%)
- Female: 6504000 (61.9%)
- Unspecified: 4321286

The following are the 15 most popular countries livejournal is used in:

- United States – 4954504
- Russian Federation – 1650225
- United Kingdom – 459787
- Canada – 441745
- Ukraine – 271262
- Singapore – 214609
- Australia – 209143
- Philippines – 130646
- Germany – 97982
- Brazil – 85284
- Japan – 80299
- India – 77773
- Belarus – 63963
- Finland – 57263
- France – 54488

While we of course cannot assume that the demographics of *unsereklei-nestadt* and *vragenuurtje* are identical to the demographics of the site as a whole, this information still tells us that at least for that snapshot in time, a large majority of overall livejournal users were female, that users from native English-speaking countries were strongly dominant on the site as a whole, and while Germany made the list of top countries, the Netherlands did not (perhaps unsurprising, given the difference in population between the two countries). A great deal of other information can also be gleaned from publicly visible conversations in each community alongside these official statistics. It is clear, for example, that most of the participants in the German community are in fact Germans living in Germany (with a few occasional Austrian and Swiss users) and that most participants in the Dutch community are in fact Dutch people living in the Netherlands (with a few occasional Belgian users), because in both groups it is common to refer to locally specific items (e.g. media, shops, holidays) without any sort of explanation (something that would not be done, at least not commonly, in explicitly international livejournal communities). Furthermore, it can be said impressionistically based on stereotypes that are commonly voiced/jokes that are made by community members that the majority of each community's core group of users is believed to cluster within comparatively powerful and urban regions within their respective countries (within the German community this would be western Germany, especially the Ruhr region and the Cologne area, and within the Dutch community this would be the *Randstad*, or the grouping of major cities in the northwest of the country that includes both Amsterdam and Rotterdam). Perceptions also exist that most community members are female, in their twenties, disproportionately well educated, middle class, and ethnically German/Dutch, though there are known prominent exceptions to each of these generalizations in both communities.

Finally, there were ten participants from *unserekleinestadt* and 12 participants from *vragenuurtje* who were interviewed for this book, and of course I have more precise demographics about that subgroup. These participants were chosen based on a combination of criteria: their participation in the community (for example whether it would be possible to ask them specific questions about their own practices, or whether I would be limited to asking them only about generalities), their availability during the period of time

12   1 Introduction

I had to do the interviews, and their willingness to participate in an interview. Charts with information about their ages and genders can be seen in Tables 1.1 and Table 1.2 below:

Although obviously no conclusions can be drawn based on such a small subsection of each community, in general it can be said that the interview participants at least skew slightly older in *unserekleinestadt* than in *vragenuurtje*, though all can generally be said to be of "student age" (most interview participants did, in fact, turn out to be students, either at universities or at other kinds of schools). Both groups also clearly fall within livejournal's stated demographic of predominantly female users.

These two communities cannot be seen as fitting neatly into any of Kytölä's (2016) three proposed types of translocal communities, but instead as having elements of each of them. First, while they are certainly not classic diasporic communities, as nearly all participants do seem to reside within their countries of origin, they can still be seen as a sort of digital diaspora within the wider world of livejournal (which is overall quite English- and Russian-dominant, and culturally strongly influenced by Anglophones). These types of communities are often regarded as spaces—and for many participants, the only such spaces online, including their own journaling blogs—where German or Dutch culture and German or Dutch language are ordinary and expected. They therefore have the same unifying ethnocultural and linguistic element that more conventional digital diasporic communities do. Second, while they are certainly not full-fledged communities of practice

Table 1.1 Interview participants' ages and genders: *unserekleinestadt* (German)

	21–23	24–26	27–29	30–32
female	1	1	2	4
male	0	0	0	2

Total participants = 10

Table 1.2 Interview participants' ages and genders: *vragenuurtje* (Dutch)

	21–23	24–26	27–29	30–32
female	2	7	2	0
male	0	0	1	0

Total participants = 12

analogous to classrooms or workplaces, the tradition of their use as a place to ask questions frequently means that they serve as a way of asking for and getting help with some problem, and community members do share the common goal of providing that help and regularly act together in order to do so. Third, while they do not meet the requirement for being affinity spaces in the sense that there is no single passion that unites them and which is each community's reason for existence, the collective enthusiasm in both communities for certain common interests, activities, or cultural products is both recurring and palpable to all members, and often does serve as a way of tying the community together.

As one last thought before we leave the world of livejournal, because this book is being published some time after the data was first retrieved, it seems relevant to mention that there have been important developments in these communities in the years since then. While the communities do both still exist at livejournal now, the number of active users there has dropped dramatically (a development that reflects trends in the life of the livejournal site as a whole). Segments of both communities continue to interact regularly on Facebook and in person—*vragenuurtje* in particular has a very active presence on Facebook now, including many of the same core group of users from the heyday of the livejournal community—but in terms of the original two livejournal communities, neither can be said to occupy anything close to the central position in the online social lives of most of their members that they used to enjoy. However, at the time of the retrieval of the data in January 2010, both livejournal communities were active and vibrant, with daily posts on all kinds of topics.

Data and Analysis in this Book

In order to investigate not just the language practices in each community, but the way differing language ideologies might be affecting those practices, the research in this book involved not just two communities, but also two distinctly different types of data. The first type is written interactional data drawn from each of the respective social media communities, and the second is a set of in-person interviews with

14   1 Introduction

community members about language practices and conceptions of, beliefs about, and attitudes toward those practices. This is in keeping with the need for what Androutsopoulos (2008: 2) calls a *discourse-centred online ethnography,* which combines the analysis of data drawn from a computer-mediated community with in-person interviews with participants. The social media data consists of a total of 1000 online conversations, while the interview data involves a total of 22 conversations, of between one and two hours, with participants about issues concerning their use of English-origin practices. The research questions addressed in the analysis then focus on an examination of the amount of such practices in each community and what they are used for interactionally, as well as what the attitudes are among the members of each community toward that usage, and how these might be reflective of broader ideologies.

Social Media Data: Methods of Collection and Analysis

The data for the first phase of this project is drawn from the 500 most recent publicly available posts and discussions resulting from those posts in each community ("most recent" at the time the data was retrieved, in January of 2010), for a total of 1000 online conversations. In the analysis, all instances of English in both data sets were coded with the help of the qualitative analysis software NVivo. "English" language items are defined here conservatively as any words that are not sufficiently integrated into monolingual language use to appear in the most recent editions of the dictionaries *Duden: Das große Wörterbuch der deutschen Sprache* (for German) or *Van Dale groot woordenboek van de Nederlandse taal* (for Dutch). While an approach that asked participants to define for themselves which English-origin words and phrases still qualify as English to them and which have become part of the local language might arguably have been preferable (see Chapter 3 for a more in-depth discussion of the potential pitfalls of this conservative approach), the unbounded and ever-changing nature of livejournal communities unfortunately would have made such an

Data and Analysis in this Book   15

approach impossible here. In any case, since this aspect of the research is primarily contrastive in nature, a conservative approach should be acceptable for measuring differences between the two communities as long as similar sorts of dictionaries are used as the final authority in each of them.

While I begin my analysis with general information about how much English there is in each community, the bulk of it will consist of the analysis of individual data excerpts, using the approach to analyzing language alternation in interaction proposed by Auer (1998, 2007). This approach focuses on the ways in which speakers alternate between languages in order to alert others to the social and situational context of the conversation. In this approach, switches from one language to another are regarded as *contextualization cues* (cf. Gumperz 1982) that are used either to structure conversation (by highlighting elements of it such as asides or topic shifts), or as a tool for identity construction (by drawing on the social meanings of different languages) (cf. Hinrichs 2006: 86–127). As an additional layer, the analysis will take not only linguistic and interactional features into account, but also images— such as the aforementioned user icons—whenever they are made relevant in the analysis. Unfortunately I am not able to get permission to reproduce the images here (it is impossible to obtain copyright permission to reproduce images that were themselves used and modified without permission), but whenever the use of images is relevant to the analysis, I will provide descriptions of them. These elements of *multimodality* are important for any analysis of social media interaction, as computer-mediated ways of representing intonation and gesture can serve to compensate for the loss of non-verbal cues and an absence of audiovisual context in a written medium (Baym 1998, Benwell and Stokoe 2006: 252). In some cases such material must be analyzed non-sequentially (van Leeuwen 2004), which adds an additional dimension to a form of analysis that was originally based on the sequential order of talk (cf. Auer 1998). My analysis will focus first on the different types of language alternation found in each community, comparing the practices in each, and then move on to an analysis of the different functions that can be identified for English, focusing again on any differences that emerge between the two communities.

Interview Data: Methods of Collection and Analysis

The data for the second phase of the project results from a series of audiotaped conversational interviews with between one and three participants each (10 individuals in total from *unserekleinestadt* and 12 from *vragenuurtje*), carried out by me throughout 2012 in each of the two local languages (German and Dutch, respectively). These interviews each lasted between one and two hours, depending on the number of participants and how much they found they had to say. I did begin each interview with general questions about participants' overall attitudes toward the use of English, as is common in most interview-based language attitude research (cf. O'Hara-Davies 2010), and common examples of such questions included whether participants had noticed influence from English in their own language practices and how they felt about that influence. However, in each interview I also provided examples of their own and other community members' use of English, which participants were prompted to discuss their reactions to. The samples used in this part of the interview emerged from the first phase of the project, and whenever possible they were individually tailored so that the reflection could be based not only on generalities, but also include discussion of the structures and functions of each interviewee's own language alternation. This part of the interview can be viewed as a sort of adaptation of the stimulated recall technique (cf. Gass and Mackey 2000), an introspective method that was originally conceived as a way of gaining access to the mental processes that accompany second-language use, but which can also be used to provoke reflection on previous language use in the context of interviews regarding attitudes toward language (e.g. Parmegiani 2008).

The purpose of such an interview is to gain access to participants' language attitudes and ideologies of language as they emerge within the local interaction. The method of data analysis for this component will therefore be an approach to *language attitudes in interaction* first introduced by myself and my co-researcher (Liebscher and Dailey-O'Cain 2009), which interprets expressed language attitudes within their interactional context as forms of *positioning*. Positioning is a process by which interactants make their orientations toward social categories relevant (Harré and van Langenhove 1991), and interpreting language attitudes in light of it can reveal both the ways in which social categories are evoked in the expression of attitudes and the ways in which the conversational context affects their expression (Liebscher and Dailey-O'Cain 2013). While the surface meanings of the responses to the interview questions are of course taken into account, an analysis of language attitudes in interaction is not limited to the *direct* expression of language attitudes, but is also able to analyze turn-internal semantic and pragmatic information (such as adjective choice or presuppositions) and interactional information (such as conversational laughter or the switch to a code another participant is using), that allows indirect expressions of attitudes to be analyzed as well.

Research Ethics

In the online world, much computer-mediated interaction is completely publicly accessible and would therefore seem to be simply there for the taking for any linguist who wanted to take advantage. However, Deumert (2014: 27–8) argues that because the physical and virtual worlds are in fact deeply entangled, the basic ethical principles for offline research that sociolinguists take for granted should also apply to online research. These principles include the right to informed consent, the protection of privacy, and even anonymity. The concept of anonymity might seem strange in an environment where participants already do not go by their own names, but because usernames are linked to livejournal users' specific virtual identities (just as personal names point to specific identities in the physical world), the possibility of an additional layer of anonymity should at least be entertained. Barton and Lee (2013: 174–5) make reference to the *Ethics Guide* published by the Association of Internet Researchers, which provides examples of informed consent forms that have been used in actual projects and outlines key ethical concerns that need to be taken into account when doing research in online environments. They argue, though, that there are still unsolved

18   1 Introduction

problems when it comes to researching multimodal content, and using screenshots, images, and public comments. Remaining ethical questions that still do not have clear, pat answers include the following (Barton and Lee 2013: 174):

- What kind of public space is the online world and who owns and has rights over the use of publicly available texts online?
- When and to what extent should anonymity be assured? When should screen-names of participants be preserved as they appear online? When do faces need to be censored?
- When is it ethical to *lurk* unannounced or observe without participating in publicly available sites?
- In what situations can freely available online content be used for research purposes without seeking permission?
- If permission is needed, what kind of permission is needed and whose permission should be sought?
- In what way can researchers seek consent from strangers online?

What is clear from the very fact that we are still asking these questions after more than a solid decade of research in virtual communities is that these questions have no one-size-fits-all answers, and that different online environments will likely require different kinds of solutions. For example, research on language use in YouTube comments, where participants are not part of a particular identifiable community, would instinctively seem to be different from research on language use in livejournal communities like *unserekleinestadt* and *vragenuurtje*, because the latter sort of data involves a core group of participants who all come to know each other over time and work together to establish the boundaries of the community. What we can hopefully agree on, however, is that it is important to be guided in our procedures by general accepted principles of research ethics, that it is important to take steps to make participants feel as safe and protected online as they would offline, and that we should take community norms and practices into account as we come up with project-specific approaches to things like informed consent, privacy, and anonymity.

When I was first considering doing this project, I made the decision that I did not want to do it without enthusiastic assent and participation

Data and Analysis in this Book 19

from the communities as a whole. In order to gauge reaction, I therefore made introductory "protected" posts in the two communities (i.e. posts that were not publicly available, but visible only to community members) that introduced me by name and title, linked back to my university website, and explained what I was hoping to do both in terms of informed consent and in terms of an eventual analysis. In these posts I also told community members that the name of the community would receive a pseudonym so as not to invite unwanted attention from outsiders, and that any publications would obscure any identifying information from any user (such as the names of cities and towns). Finally, I mentioned that their data would be compared with another livejournal community, though I did not link to or mention the name of that other livejournal community. Members of both communities were then able to ask questions about the project, as well as offer up suggestions for different ways of approaching how I'd proposed doing things. (One change I made at this stage of the process is that while I had originally said I would give each user a pseudonymous username, some users stated that they preferred to be quoted under their own actual usernames instead, so I made a change to my ethics procedures to allow for either of these options depending on individual users' preferences.) After a long discussion, then, most of which was generally approving, I decided to proceed with the next step of obtaining consent to use the data.

Although most conversations that take place within these communities are publicly available to anyone who cares to read them, and any livejournal user is able to join in the discussion at any time, it nonetheless seemed paramount that I take into account the fact that the members of these communities were never expecting any special outside attention from either researchers or members of the public, and none of their conversations had occurred with the possibility of such attention in mind. Therefore, in order to make sure that no additional undue and potentially unwanted attention would be paid to community members after the research was published, I took an approach that was governed by the principle of privacy both for the communities themselves and for any individual who might potentially be identified. This principle suggested that any data that I was only ever going to use in aggregate (such as the quantitative analyses in Chapter 3 of the amounts of English used by the

20   1 Introduction

two communities) would not require me to obtain informed consent, since such an analysis would not permit any individual users to be singled out and identified. On the other hand, it seemed important to treat any conversations that I might want to quote from directly in the same way that I have always treated audiotaped and videotaped spoken-language data—by obtaining informed consent for use, and also by making use of pseudonyms for any users who decided they would prefer an additional layer of privacy (as well as additional pseudonyms for the two communities themselves). Of course, the sheer number of conversations I wanted to be able to analyze—stretching back some time in both communities—meant that consent could only be obtained retroactively, after the conversations had already occurred. This is an important difference from general practice for spoken-language data, where consent is always obtained before any data is recorded. However, most members of both communities were amenable to the idea, so I decided to proceed.

After those initial feelers, informed consent proceeded in two phases: the social media data phase and the interview data phase. The social media data phase involved getting permission from each participant in any conversation where English-origin language practices were used, in order to allow me to potentially quote from that conversation in future presentations and publications. In order to do this, I made a list of each instance of English use and got in touch with everyone who was involved in each conversation by sending them private messages through the livejournal site. In these messages, I first asked whether they were 18 (the age of majority in both countries), and stated that I would not use their data if they were younger than that. Next, I linked to each conversation they had participated in that I might potentially want to cite in my analysis, asking them whether they would be willing to give blanket permission for all conversations or whether they would perhaps prefer to deny permission for some conversations and give permission for others. In these private messages, I also linked back to the post and the ensuing discussion where I had initially introduced the project, and reminded them that I would protect their privacy in the ways I had mentioned there. Once a participant had granted consent, I also asked in a second private message whether they would prefer that I give them a pseudonym (and if they wanted that, what their preferred pseudonym would be) or whether I should simply use their existing username. I then kept track of all approvals and requested pseudonyms through a detailed spreadsheet. An enormous benefit of such an approach to a discourse-centred online ethnography is that although it was sufficiently rigorous to make most participants feel safe enough to enthusiastically participate in the project, at no point was I required to ask for their official legal names, as all of our interaction was carried out through the livejournal site, under our respective usernames.

Finally, about a year and a half after the initial inquiry, consent for the in-person interviews was obtained through a somewhat more conventional informed-consent process. This involved again getting in touch with potential participants through livejournal private messages, asking whether they would be interested in meeting me for an in-person audiotaped interview about their language practices (and specifying that I would be willing to come to the town where they live and meet with them in a café or restaurant of their choice over a meal that I would pay for). In these private messages, I also provided sample questions involving the kinds of things I might want to ask about, so that they would know what to expect. Those who agreed were then given formal consent forms at the beginning of the ensuing interviews, and the recorder was not turned on until they had signed. At the end of each interview, participants were also asked to fill out a questionnaire that asked for their legal name, gender, age, occupation, their native language or languages, information about the circumstances under which they normally spoke English, and whether they had ever lived in an English-speaking country. When referring to the interview participants in this book, I use the same pseudonymous username (or actual username, depending on the individual's preference) that was chosen for them for the initial analysis of the computer-mediated data.

The Structure of this Book

Following this introductory chapter, the remainder of this book will be structured as follows: Chapter 2 outlines my theoretical framework by reviewing and synthesizing the background literature on such central concepts as language ideologies and language policy, language use in social

22   1 Introduction

media, and multilingual language use in interaction. Chapters 3 and 4 are a detailed analysis of the different kinds of multilingual practices found in the data, addressing the amounts and types of English and the interactional functions of English, respectively. Chapter 5 is an analysis of the interview data, using the interaction-based approach to an analysis of language attitudes that was outlined above. Finally, Chapter 6 summarizes and ties together my findings, but also goes beyond them to further explore and underscore their implications for a theory of global English and for language policy.

This last observation brings me to an important point that should be underscored again here. Though this book draws its conclusions from data from two specific social media communities, I would like to argue that the phenomena analyzed in the data have important implications for language practice beyond Germany and the Netherlands on the one hand, and beyond social media on the other. I will therefore analyze these two communities not just as examples of social media conversations in Germany and the Netherlands, but also more generally as examples of how issues of globalization directly impact language practice. In the next chapter, I will make the case for proceeding in this way.

2

Language Ideologies, Multilingualism, and Social Media

The foundation of this book is the intersection of three areas of sociolinguistic research: language ideologies and language policy, language use in social media, and multilingual language use in interaction. Though these often tend to be regarded as largely separate and unrelated fields of inquiry, they need to be woven together in order to form a sufficiently robust theoretical framework within which to interpret the analysis in Chapters 3, 4, and 5. In this chapter I will attempt to do just that by outlining the relevant research within each subfield, by pointing out the places where these bodies of research intersect, and by explaining the implications these linkages have for the analysis in this book.

This chapter focuses first on the relationship between ideology and language, including a discussion of common ideologies regarding the position and status of English within Europe and the rest of the world, the ideology of nationalism and the role of the state, and the concept of ideology within a theory of globalization. I then move on to talk about language use in social media discourse, both in terms of the linguistic and interactional features that are typical of social media language and in

© The Author(s) 2017
J. Dailey-O'Cain, *Trans-National English in Social Media Communities*, Language and Globalization,
DOI 10.1057/978-1-137-50615-3_2

terms of the provenance of different languages on the global internet. Finally, I end with a discussion of multilingual language use in interaction both in conventional spoken discourse and in social media, before coming back around again to the specific research questions I alluded to in Chapter 1.

Language Ideologies in a Globalizing Europe

The concept of *language ideology* draws attention to the way that language use always has a political dimension. However, one crucial aspect of language ideologies is the fact that while they are formulated as being entirely about language (Seargeant 2009: 349), they in fact "envision and enact links of language to group and personal identity, to aesthetics, to morality, and to epistemology" (Woolard and Schiefflin 1994: 55–6). As such, moral judgments or public discussions that appear on their surface to be exclusively language-specific are often at their core simply *using* language to stand in for moral judgments and public discussions about other aspects of society and culture. In this book, I therefore define language ideology as "sets of beliefs articulated by users as a rationalization or justification of perceived structure and use" (Silverstein 1979: 173) that are regarded as being universally true (Seargeant 2009: 348–9). Despite such claims to universality, however, it is not at all uncommon for groups from geographically close societies (or even different ethnic groups within the same society, as in Barrett 2006) to have entirely different language ideologies about the same language, especially when the two groups have had markedly different ideological traditions. In this book, the language ideologies that are most central are the ones participants in the *unserekleinestadt* and *vragenuurtje* communities hold about appropriate roles, use, and provenance of both the English language and their own languages, as well as the mixing of the two. I will be addressing not just what these ideologies are, but what traditions have contributed to their existence throughout German and Dutch history, and what effects they have on what people do with their languages.

Of course, the element of language ideology that most comes into play in a book like this one is that last part: the inherent relationship between language ideology and language practice. This relationship implies that the things people believe to be *right* and *true* and *normal* about the languages they have access to will tend to have an influence on not just how they believe those languages *should* be used, but also on how they *actually* use them. So, for example, the extent to which a given German or Dutch user of English feels he or she is permitted to use that language in new and creative ways may well depend on whether that particular user tends to conceive of the language as primarily the possession of Anglophone countries such as the United Kingdom and the United States or instead as a more "neutral" international language that belongs to no one in particular (cf. Callahan 2005: 284, Park and Wee 2012: 147–8, Kelly-Holmes 2013: 135). As such, language ideologies can be seen as forming "a mediating link between social structures and forms of talk" (Woolard 1992: 235). This relationship is a *dialectical* one, meaning that language practice not only is affected by, but also in turn affects, language ideologies. Furthermore, because language ideologies are fundamentally not exclusively about language, they affect and are affected by not just language practice, but also the hierarchies and power relationships that exist within a given society (Seargeant 2009: 248).

Through an analysis of a combination of data from language practices in social media and language attitudes as expressed in interviews, I will attempt to show in this book that the different language practices found in the *unserekleinestadt* and *vragenuurtje* communities are not accidental, but fundamentally related to the different sets of ideologies about English and local languages that have developed within the two countries over their histories. As I will argue below, these differing conceptualizations of the role of English are rooted in a combination of factors: different broader societal ideologies such as types of national identities, different state traditions, different traditions of language policy, and even differing semi-institutionalized practices such as traditions of subtitling vs. dubbing in the translation of English-language television and film to a local audience.

26 2 Language Ideologies, Multilingualism, and Social Media

The Position of English: Ideologies and Practice

The European youth who make up the *unserekleinestadt* and *vragenuurtje* communities are coming of age in a world where English is playing an important and ever-increasing role. Within this world, communication for EU governance (Phillipson 2004), business (Nickerson 2000, Hilgendorf 2010, Edwards 2014: 49–55, Holden 2016, Björkman 2016a), and higher education (Ammon 1998: 227–52, Coleman 2006, Erling and Hilgendorf 2006, Phillipson 2006, Jenkins 2013, Wilkinson 2013, Edwards 2014: 43–5, Björkman 2016b) are all increasingly taking place in English, even among speakers of the same non-English local language. In addition, the advertising these young people see and hear around them (Gerritsen 1995, Gerritsen et al. 2007, Hilgendorf and Martin 2001, Kelly-Holmes 2013, Edwards 2014: 51–4), the various media they consume in the form of books, television, film, and magazines (Hasebrink 2007: 89–101, Hilgendorf 2013, Edwards 2014: 62–4) and the music they listen to (Hasebrink 2007: 101–10, Edwards 2014: 65–8) are all increasingly influenced by English as well. In light of all of these changes, it is perhaps inevitable that English would also be coming to occupy an ever more central position in the communication that takes place in these young people's daily lives, and research tends to bear this out as well (cf. Edwards 2014: 77–9). In fact, Preisler (1999: 244) goes so far as to argue that an informal use of English "has become an inherent, indeed a defining, aspect of the many Anglo-American-oriented youth subcultures which directly or indirectly influence the language and other behavioural patterns of young people generally."

It should come as no surprise that the debate currently taking place within sociolinguistics about the position of English (cf. Seargeant 2009: 217) is itself highly ideological. It centres on whether the role of English is best understood as a tool of American-led neoliberalism, an increasingly denationalized lingua franca, a set of varieties spoken all over the world as either a native or a non-native language, or perhaps something else altogether. One view, characterized as *linguistic imperialism* (e.g. Phillipson 1992, 2006, Skutnabb-Kangas and Phillipson 2010) sees

English as a part of global capitalism and draws parallels between the English language and other global homogenizing trends, focusing on the ways that English contributes to the respects in which the world is becoming ever more similar. Another view, that of *English as a lingua franca* (e.g. Seidlhofer 2005, Jenkins 2009, 2013, Kirkpatrick 2006, Breiteneder 2009), suggests that English has become a culturally neutral language that is the possession of all its users around the world, native speakers or not. As a counterpoint to both of these, a third view refers not to a singular English but to *world Englishes* (e.g. Kachru 1985, 1992, Saraceni 2010, 2015), envisioning users of the language as falling within a set of concentric circles with the traditional bases of English in the inner circle, countries from the so-called "second diaspora" like India and Nigeria in the outer circle, and countries (like Germany and the Netherlands) where English plays no historical or governmental role in the expanding circle. Finally, Pennycook (2007) argues that each of these perspectives is flawed as a result of approaching the issue within too simplistic a theory of globalization. Instead, he argues that English must be understood as a *translocal*, fluid language that "moves across, while becoming embedded in, the materiality of localities and social relations" (Pennycook 2007: 6, see also Park and Wee 2012: 83–4). I will discuss this theory in more detail toward the end of the chapter.

Of course, the changing role of English in a globalizing Europe has not gone unnoticed outside of sociolinguistics, whether in the public sphere or in the academic one. In both Germany and the Netherlands, there has been a great deal of discourse about the extent to which English represents a threat to the respective local languages. These different discourses differ ideologically in key ways, however. Within *academic* discourse in Germany, linguists have taken steps to reassure the public that the effect of English on the German lexicon has been a part of a normal and understandable process of contact (Spitzmüller 2005, Barbour 2005, Onysko 2009), and perhaps as a result, the main concern among their fellow academics seems to be about domain loss and the fact that German is no longer a major language of wider communication (cf. Ammon 1998). The German *public* discourse, on the other hand, has been overwhelmingly characterized by purism (Spitzmüller 2005, Barbour 2005, Onysko 2009, Dodd 2015), particularly about the effects of individual lexical items or *anglicisms*. Throughout German history such public criticism has tended to come in waves, the most recent of which began in the 1990s (Spitzmüller 2005, Dodd 2015), and while the type of argument presented within this discourse has been largely unchanged since then, ever more people have joined the debate and the sharpness of their arguments has only grown. Barbour (2005: 159) also noted that within public discourse in Germany, concerns about domain loss on the one hand and the influence of anglicisms on the other have been conflated to the point where these two very different issues are insufficiently distinguished.

The Netherlands is another story. While there was in fact a public debate in the Netherlands about lexical borrowings from English in the 1980s (Edwards 2014: 203–4), by the late 1990s one non-academic book about the lexical influence of English and other languages on Dutch (van der Sijs 1998) clearly regarded that influence as more of a curiosity than a threat. De Vries (2008) also mentions a parliamentary report to the Dutch Language Union about the detrimental effects of high-tech English on Dutch in 1997, but the debate it sparked shifted very quickly from lexical influence to domain loss. Indeed, the primary emphasis in the Netherlands concerning potential negative influence from English in recent years—in *both* popular and academic discourse—has been much more on domain loss than on any perceived effects of widespread lexical borrowing. In fact, the use of English as the primary language in domains like business and higher education has increased to the point where concern has indeed been voiced that Dutch could eventually be reduced to a language of the home (de Bot 1994: 11–12, de Swaan 2000, Van Hoorde 2013: 15), but even so, there is considerable ambivalence about whether that situation should be resisted or simply accepted, and if it should be resisted, how. In a newspaper article from the start of the current millennium, it was reported that a majority of Dutch speakers seem "more or less indifferent to" this situation (Van Hoorde 2013: 14), and around the same time even the head of the Dutch Language Union concluded that "fighting English as a lingua franca makes no sense" (Van Hoorde 2013: 23), arguing instead for a plurilinguistic approach to international communication that makes room for both Dutch and English. Given the very different traditions of nationalism and state institutions in Germany and the Netherlands (discussed in the following section), these ideological differences between the two countries regarding the influence of English may be mostly unsurprising, but they certainly have enormous implications for the way the use of English in social media is perceived in the different countries.

Another common way some non-academics have conceptualized the position of English is by adopting what amounts to the polar opposite ideology to purism: the notion of English as a "neutral" language. This perspective builds on the *English as a lingua franca* position mentioned above in that it involves a sense that the position of English in today's world is such that it is no longer a mere "foreign" language that is inextricably bound up with particular foreign countries and cultures, but this version goes further than that in asserting that English cannot possibly be a threat to anyone because it belongs to everyone equally (Kelly-Holmes 2013: 135–6). As a result of the widespread status of English as an international lingua franca, it is often perceived as "a code that can be used to avoid whatever implications may result from choosing a more identity-laden language" (Callahan 2005: 284). Such an attempt to avoid any ideological connotations of language practice has of course been critiqued on the grounds that the extent to which English actually is "everyone's language" is still deeply contested, and because it has different meanings and associations depending on who its users are and where they are located (Park and Wee 2012: 113, Kelly-Holmes 2013: 136). However, these implications seem to have mostly gone unnoticed outside of the academy.

There also seems to be disagreement among users about what the idea of a "culturally neutral" language implies. At the very least, the notion would seem to contain the implication that the form of English no longer needs to be bound to norms of use associated with the countries where it is spoken as a native language, and that the role of gatekeeper of the norms for the language's use no longer needs to be reserved for native speakers. However, findings from Germany and the Netherlands suggest there may be differences between the two countries in terms of how far people are willing to take that. Two survey studies, one in Germany (Gnutzmann et al. 2012) and one in the Netherlands (Edwards 2014) both inquired about the idea of European norms of use for English

30   **2 Language Ideologies, Multilingualism, and Social Media**

separate from those of native speakers. The Germans were overwhelmingly critical of this idea, and insistent upon the native speaker norms as paramount (Gnutzmann et al. 2012: 79–81). The Dutch, on the other hand, were more likely to think of their target model of English as "a neutral variety of English that does not represent one culture or country," with that option coming second only to a British English model and ahead of a US English one (Edwards 2014: 109–13). In fact, there is some evidence that some Dutch are increasingly "willing to act as 'language builders' rather than as passive recipients, actively shaping the English used in their own environment" (Edwards 2014: 206–7). This corresponds with work done on actual informal interaction in other northern, smaller-language European contexts such as Finland (Peuronen 2011: 158), where one social media community was found to be "engaging in the dynamic processes of appropriation and creation of cultural and linguistic forms" in order to "index their sense of connectedness between different locales," and Iceland (Jeeves 2014), where exposure to English has become so pervasive and young people's usage of the language so much a part of everyday life that it is now regarded as something other than a foreign or second language.

Complicating these matters further still is the fact that while the role of English is indeed changing all over Europe, the amount of contact that people tend to have with the language is anything but uniform across the continent (Soler-Carbonell 2016). For example, we know that English-language media is dubbed in Germany, while it is subtitled in the Netherlands (Berns et al. 2007: 32–3, Hilgendorf 2013), and the two countries also differ with respect to how much English is used as a medium of instruction in higher education (Berns et al. 2007: 27–30, Erling and Hilgendorf 2006, Wilkinson 2013). Survey research also suggests that these differing opportunities are correlated with higher English proficiency in the Netherlands than in Germany (Hasebrink et al. 2007: 115). One conclusion of this last study that is particularly compelling for this book states that English tends to be seen as "a necessary professional qualification which has to be learned like other formal qualifications" by German youth, and as "one means to express themselves and their cultural orientation" by Dutch youth (Hasebrink et al. 2007: 115). This distinction seems to be supported by the aforementioned findings of Gnutzmann et al.

(2012) and Edwards (2014). However, it is essential to keep in mind that all of these findings are from survey research, which are of course limited to inquiring about habitual and suspected practices and can therefore say little about the effects of these ideological stances on actual language practices.

One area where a great deal of work has in fact been done on language use is that of lexical borrowing from English into different European languages. In a study of Austrian, German, and Swiss newspapers from 1949 to 1989, Schelper (1995) finds a slight general rise in the number of English borrowings into German over time, and more recently Onysko's (2007, 2009) study of one German news magazine found a continued increase, due particularly to the growing frequency of English terms for technology-related items. Glahn (2002) also reports similar findings for the language of the spoken news media in Germany, while also finding evidence of influence on the grammatical and phonological levels. In the Netherlands, Claus and Taeledeman's (1989) study of Dutch dictionaries suggests that the number of English borrowings has increased there as well, particularly in the areas of technology and music, and findings from a rudimentary study of one Dutch newspaper suggests that an average page with 500 words of text contains approximately seven English loanwords (van der Sijs 2012). A much larger study using a corpus of Dutch newspapers from 1999 to 2002 (Zenner et al. 2012) reports on the linguistic criteria the Dutch seem to be using in either accepting or rejecting a potential new English borrowing (one of these being whether the word is used to express a concept originating in Anglo-American culture). Of course, one result of the aforementioned preoccupation with anglicisms in Germany is that far more work of this type has been done on German than on Dutch, but it can still be said that a comparison of quantitative findings seems to point toward a slightly greater overall lexical influence on Dutch than on German. In a cognitive interpretation of the impact of these influences, Thelen (2005: 245–6) even provides evidence that widespread competence in English in the Netherlands has left "apparent mental traces" on the Dutch language, yielding situations in which educated native speakers of Dutch need to borrow from their English lexicon in order to fill gaps in Dutch syntactic structures. However, nearly all of this body of work in both countries has focused on formal domains such as the language of the media, which tells us little about the ways English may be being used within everyday, informal interaction.

This book therefore builds on existing bodies of research by venturing into an area of inquiry that has been missing from the debate on the position of English thus far: a systematic and empirical examination of how European youth incorporate English into their everyday, otherwise local-language interactions, and a comparison of the language's scope, its functions, and the ideologies that influence that use among youth from two different European countries. By going beyond survey research and print-media corpora to investigate actual language use in informal interaction, and by also incorporating an investigation of attitudes and ideological stances as they emerge naturally within interactional contexts, I will be able to situate the abstract concept of *language* within actual practice. Before I move on from the ideologies that have been taken up by others regarding the position of English, however, I'd like to say one last word about one clear ideological stance of my own. While I have taken pains not to bias my findings by making judgments about which uses of English are and are not "appropriate" (either in my interview conversations or in my analysis), I have been clear throughout the project that I do regard the participants in *unserekleinestadt* and *vragenuurtje* first and foremost as legitimate users of the language, regardless of their lack of native speaker status (cf. Peuronen 2011). As such, I hope that this project has helped make room for these young people to decide for themselves which practices and ideologies concerning the use of English they would like to take up and which ones they would prefer to leave aside (or behind).

Nationalisms and the Role of Official State Policies

Of course, none of the different ideologies concerning the position of English discussed in the previous section appeared out of thin air and within a vacuum, but instead arose under the influence of various national historical and institutional traditions. Because of this, it is important to take a closer look at the role that national ideologies and state institutions have played in Germany and the Netherlands throughout their histories, and consider how these have influenced (and may be continuing to influence) the way the position of English is framed within those societies. The most readily apparent ideological differences between the two countries are the rather different traditions of *ethnic nationalism* in Germany and *civic nationalism* in the Netherlands, which can be seen as stemming from two opposing models for how European states should attempt to fit the ideal of equating its people with its territory. The first of these models is what Wright (2004: 19) terms the *state nation*, in which a polity first delimits a territory through the acquisition of land and only retro-actively attempts to try and mould the group into one people. The Netherlands is one example of this ideological tradition (Wright 2004: 26–7, Yaǧmur 2009), although the separate ideological tradition of *pillarization*—in which various religious and political communities were kept separate-but-equal through separate institutional arrange-ments—can be seen as having equally strong and lasting effects on that country's particular variant of civic nationalism (Entzinger 2006: 123–4). By contrast, Wright (2004: 19) refers to the second of these two models, in which a group first comes to see itself as a cultural and linguistic entity and only retrospectively attempts to acquire territory exclusively for that group, as the *nation state*. Germany is a classic—and arguably *the* classic—example of this model (Wright 2004: 32–3, Vihman and Barkhoff 2013: 6, Sériot 2013: 258).

The relationship between these two nationalist ideologies and the languages within their societies can again be seen as a dialectical one in that the two nationalisms both affect and are affected by language use. In fact, taking a historical perspective, language was the principal tool each of the two emerging states originally used to promote its ideology of nationalism: in the Netherlands, the language of the dominant group spread after the state's formation because of institutions that used it and laws that promoted it, while in Germany, a common language was the most powerful argument the elite used as a justification for the existence of the ethnic group as an entity and therefore of the creation of the state in the first place (Wright 2004: 43–5). Since the nineteenth century

34   2 Language Ideologies, Multilingualism, and Social Media

there has been a shift in both countries away from these respective "one nation, one language" ideologies toward a "language and commodity" model that sees language-related skills such as communication and literacy as marketable tools to be used by individual citizens (Bjornson 2007: 67, Stevenson 2015: 80), but the respective centuries-old ideological traditions have certainly still left their mark in both countries.

While sociolinguists have spent a great deal of energy analyzing the relationship between language, ideology, and policy, to date the role of the state has largely been ignored in those analyses (Sonntag and Cardinal 2015: 3–5). And yet phenomena such as language ideologies and language policies are not just socially constructed, but also influenced by state institutions (such as the legal or educational systems) and their historical traditions. The concept of the *language regime* was developed to address this missing piece of the analytical puzzle (Sonntag and Cardinal 2015, see also Stroud 2007 for the related concept of *linguistic citizenship*). By incorporating the political science concept of *state traditions* (cf. Dyson 1980), an analysis of language ideologies and policies within their broader language regimes allows sociolinguists to view them as historical and institutional constructs alongside the ways in which we have already been viewing them as social constructs. Within this model, state traditions influence and frame language practices and ideologies, and then language users act on them in turn. This characterization incorporates the dialectical relationship between language ideology and language practice discussed above, but it casts that relationship against its historical and institutional backdrop, which gives greater depth to their similarly dialectical relationship to language policy choices.

These policies are influenced by state traditions but are not predetermined by them, as other parts of the broader language regime are always at play as well during policymaking (Safran 2015: 256): the number of speakers of particular languages, the insistence with which different groups assert language claims, the "thickness" (i.e. penetrability) of a culture with which a language is associated, the preferences of a country's dominant ethnic group, and sometimes external pressures. In order to incorporate these other elements, Walsh (2015) distinguishes between *overt language policies* (which might be regarded as those policies that represent the long-standing official ideological stance of the state) and *covert language policies* (which might be regarded as those policies that represent newer, competing ideologies), which are often introduced by separate institutions within a single society. For example, institutions that have long upheld a one-language-one-nation ideology by pursuing "we are in Germany/the Netherlands so we speak German/Dutch here" policies could potentially find themselves at odds with a culture under pressure to make English an additional or even the main language of work in one country or the other. Seargeant's (2009: 347) concept of the *language regulation scenario* is relevant here, which he defines as "any situation in which the regulation of the language becomes the means by which social interaction take place" by relating "actual language practice to normative standards." Formulated within the context of a language regime model, a language regulation scenario can be seen as a situation in which all of the components that make up a language regime—state institutions, historical traditions of ideology, accumulated trends within the realm of policy—are expected to come into active, regulatory play simply by virtue of the nature of the situation. The teaching of a language (whether a first language or an additional one) would of course be one such example, but the establishment of official guidelines for which language or languages should be used within a workplace would be another. Different language regulation scenarios can therefore be reacting to different ideological pressures within the same language regime, and as a result different and sometimes conflicting policies can emerge.

In Germany the primary approach to most language policy was long influenced by its ideological tradition of ethnic nationalism, and the primary approach in the Netherlands was in turn influenced by that country's ideological tradition of civic nationalism combined with pillarization. For example, German authorities for a long time coped with increased immigration following the Second World War by denying that it was a country of immigration at all, to the point where Germany's first-ever official immigration law was not signed until mid-2002 (Martin 2004: 223). Early responses to an increase of Turkish immigrants in the school system saw immigrant children forced to use only German in their schooling and placed in lower-tier or even special-needs

36   2 Language Ideologies, Multilingualism, and Social Media

schools in the process (Yağğmur and Konak 2009: 274), betraying an underlying ideological notion that Turkish immigrants did not belong in German society (Beck 1999: 11–12).[1] By contrast, the Netherlands, which has never seen itself as a culturally homogeneous society, dealt with increased immigration in its early years by "pillarizing" different immigrant groups within separate educational institutions where they were encouraged to maintain their own cultures and continue using their own languages (Penninx 1996: 201, Entzinger 2006: 123–4). This in turn enabled the Dutch state to regard immigration as a temporary concern that would resolve itself naturally when the immigrant groups returned to their societies of origin, at which point there would be no longer any need for those particular pillars (Muus 2004).

However, more recently both countries, in grappling with how they might reconcile long-standing ideologies with the undeniable fact that immigrants have become a permanent part of their societies, have moved in the direction of what can be broadly construed as assimilationist language policies (Yağğmur 2009: 3–4, see also Waldinger and Fitzgerald 2004: 1179). Under these kinds of policies, immigrants are given a certain amount of agency and authority within their new society, but in return they are expected to comply fully with mainstream norms and values. In Germany this has meant a shift away from a purely ethnic conception of nationalism to new laws that allow immigrants to legally become German citizens (Geddes 2003: 79–101, Gramling 2009, Küppers and Yağğmur 2014: 10–11), as well as the advancement of other covert language policies that recognize the economic and political benefits of multilingualism (Stevenson 2015: 80). In the Netherlands, on the other hand, this has—perhaps ironically—meant an *increased* emphasis on policies promoting the Dutch language and a corresponding *decrease* in official multiculturalism (Geddes 2003: 102–25, Extra and Yağğmur 2004, Muus 2004, Bjornson 2007: 65). On the surface

---

[1] German labour market institutions did act as a competing (and sometimes mitigating) pressure to these officially entrenched ideologies, however. Even as foreign workers were excluded from participation in the formal political process in Germany into the 2000s, they were never excluded from workers' councils (the *Betriebsrat*), which always granted them some degree of power in that sphere (Geddes 2001: 13–14).

this might seem to remove the distinctiveness between the two societies, leaving Germany with an assimilationist approach to policy that is no longer based on ethnic nationalism and the Netherlands with a new assimilationism founded on the weakening of pillarization—and this could, in turn, be expected to lead to waning differences when it comes to ideologies of English as a globalizing force as well. But established language ideological traditions do not disappear overnight, and it is quite possible for a language regime to encompass a conflict between ideological pressures toward overt language policies and separate ideological pressures toward covert ones (cf. Walsh 2015). Within the context of the German language regime, the new assimilationism will therefore tend to come into conflict with each country's respective traditional ideologies that both equate a nation with its language (cf. Yağmur and van de Vijver 2012), which will likely lead to conflicting pressures, on the one hand to promote German as the sole language of education and commerce and on the other hand to accept an increasing role for English in those same domains. Conversely, while the same pressure to accept an increasing role for English also exists within the Dutch language regime, in the Netherlands it is likely to be confronted with not only the recent trend toward assimilationism on the policy front, but simultaneously with the much older traditions of civic nationalism and pillarization. As a result, we can expect continuing differences between the two countries' approaches to dealing with global English, as the tension between pressures toward overt and covert policies continues to be felt.

It could be tempting to compensate for the limited focus on state institutions to date within sociolinguistic studies of language ideology and language policy by attempting to attribute all of the ideologies that emerge within this book to state influence. But as we have seen, a single language regime is quite capable of juggling multiple ideologies that often stand in direct conflict with each other, only one of which is the official "party line." While Sonntag and Cardinal (2015: 7–8) see language regimes as encompassing all language ideologies (and thereby rendering *language ideology* obsolete as a concept separate from *language regime*), I would argue that this takes things a step too far because not all aspects of language ideology are directly traceable to state institutions. Language regimes give citizens ideological guidelines for how they

38   2 Language Ideologies, Multilingualism, and Social Media

should view their language practices, but subgroups of those citizens with common ideas and goals may well respond to these ideologies in ways that are not always predictable (or even desirable) from the perspective of the state. People can ignore official language ideologies, call them into question, or even stand in opposition to them if competing ideologies are significantly powerful. This leads to ideological pressures toward covert policies alongside longstanding overt ones, and these competing pressures can only be expected to increase in a world where the formerly occasional contact that Europeans have always had with other cultures has become a matter of daily practice. For that matter, the influence of the state on language policies is also changing. Increased globalization has led to groups promoting traditional forms of one-state-one-language nationalism in order to work out new covert strategies with which to pursue their interests, maintain positions of power, and gain access to resources (Pujolar 2007: 85). As a result, discourses and policies have emerged that may be overtly presented as pluralistic or a simple matter of pragmatism, but which ultimately serve the aims of traditional nationalisms. This increasingly globalized world has also seen the advent of language power blocs (Pujolar 2007: 86), which are international alliances of nation states that pursue linguistic and cultural agendas under the guise of "international cooperation." Native English-speaking countries, or what Kachru (1985, 1992) describes as the "inner circle" of English, constitute the strongest such power bloc. There therefore remain aspects of language ideologies that are not explainable through an analysis of state institutions alone, and while the role of those institutions is an important (and thus far neglected) influence, they are still only one among several such influences.

Beyond the State

Early conceptualizations of the phenomenon of globalization involved a strong emphasis on culturally homogenizing forces and the notion that the world is becoming more and more similar (cf. Robertson 1995: 25). Pennycook (2007: 24–5), on the other hand, argues that globalization can instead "be better understood as a compression of time and space, an intensification of social, economic, cultural and political relations, a series of global linkages that render events in one location of potential and immediate importance in other quite distant locations." Coupland (2010: 5) further argues that studies of globalization particularly "need to explore the *tensions* between sameness and difference, between centripetal and centrifugal tendencies, and between consensus and fragmentation." As the world is globalizing, then, we can see it as becoming not just more *international* (in the sense of formal agreements, conflicts, and diplomatic relations between nation states), but also more *trans-national* (cf Vertovic 1999), in the sense that "a high degree of human mobility, telecommunications, films, video and satellite TV, and the internet" (Vertovec 2009: 12) are creating "sustained linkages and ongoing exchanges among *non-state* actors based across national borders" (Vertovec 2009: 3, emphasis mine). This is not a phenomenon that is happening solely on the level of the nation state, in other words, through large structures and institutions, but also on the level of everyday life (Roudometof 2005: 118–19). One characteristic feature of this phenomenon is *superdiversity* (Vertovec 2007, Blommaert and Rampton 2011, Arnaut et al. 2015), which can be defined as a term intended to underline a level and kind of complexity surpassing anything ... previously experienced ... a dynamic interplay of variables including country of origin, ... migration channel, ... legal status, ... migrants' human capital (particularly educational background), access to employment, ... locality ... and responses by local authorities, services providers and local residents" (Vertovec 2007: 2–3). More than just a facet of transnational migration, superdiversity is a process that is having lasting effects even on those who themselves remain in one country for their entire lives.

One term that has been coined to help make sense of these phenomena is *glocalization* (Robertson 1995, Bastardas-Boada 2012, Barton and Lee 2013: 34–5). This term was coined to directly counter the idea that processes of globalization must necessarily be overriding all things local, and it can be defined as "a dynamic negotiation between the global and the local, with the local appropriating elements of the global that it finds useful, at the same time employing strategies to retain this identity" (Koutsogiannis and Mitsikopoulou 2007: 143). For example, hip-hop culture in Japan or China (Pennycook 2007, Varis and Wang 2011) or salsa dance culture in Australia or Germany (Schneider 2014) can be seen as local communities appropriating elements of global culture into something new that can be regarded as neither exclusively local nor exclusively global. Another example can be found in work such as the study that makes up this book—i.e. the fact that as the internet is becoming a globally useful tool, new specifically *local* social media spaces such as *unserekleinestadt* and *vragenuurtje* are forming within it. Barton and Lee (2013: 34–5) argue that this is "best seen as a two-way process: it is not just how the global affects the local, but how the local shapes the global. Global language practices are localized, and at the same time local practices are becoming globalized." The wider context of social media language use may therefore be transnational, but the dialectic relationship between the local and the global are what lead to the emergence of specifically national social media communities such as the ones in this book and the language practices that become commonplace in them.

With specific respect to language, Jacquemet (2005: 264) argues that the changes to language that go hand in hand with transnationalism and superdiversity lead to the need for linguists to change our instruments for analyzing language rather than try to force new deterritorialized linguistic forms and identities into the same territorialized models that we have always used. This can be understood as falling within what Pratt (1987: 59–64) termed a *linguistics of contact*, as distinct from the more conventional *linguistics of community*. As one of these new instruments, Jacquemet (2005: 264–5) proposes the term *transidiomatic practices* to refer to "the communicative practices of transnational groups that interact using different languages and communicative codes simultaneously present in a range of communicative channels, both local and distant."[2] When processes of globalization combine local and global phenomena into new, complex networks, sociolinguistic systems are being "shot through by traces and fragments of translocal ones, without becoming less local" (Blommaert 2010: 60, see also Kytölä 2016).

---

[2] In this book, the communities of *unserekleinestadt* and *vragenuurtje* are specifically national communities rather than transnational ones, but the broader context of the livejournal blogging site where they are located certainly is transnational in the sense Jacquemet (2005) means.

Given the position of English in our globalizing world, then, it is unsurprising that these practices tend to produce linguistic innovations that include a great deal of English, although other languages may be involved as well depending on the way local users come to creatively reterritorialize them (as can be seen with Spanish in salsa dancing communities in Germany and Australia (Schneider 2014)). It is important to keep this in mind as we interpret Blommaert's (2010: 18) assertion that these transidiomatic practices are not just bits of language, but simultaneously bits of culture and society, which entails the notion that they retain aspects of the languages and cultures that gave rise to them.

The original systems are still semiotically rearranged, however, which has repercussions for their *indexicality*, i.e. which specific social and cultural phenomena they refer back to. For example, Deumert (2014: 108) discusses the way the use of the spelling <da> ("the") in social media interaction might index ethnic and local belonging in the New York neighbourhood of Harlem, a lack of education and refinement up the highway at an elite university such as Harvard, or familiarity with global popular culture in many other places, all while "pointing back" at precisely the same African-American Vernacular English pronunciation of the word *the*. As a result of this sort of reorganized indexicality, Blommaert (2003: 609) has called for sociolinguists to "discover what such reorderings of repertoires actually mean, and represent, to people." In addressing how to deal with the English language in this context, Pennycook (2007: 5–6) suggests that we "need to move beyond arguments about homogeneity and heterogeneity, or imperialism and nation states, and instead focus on *translocal and transcultural flows*". We need to approach an analysis of English in this context "critically-in terms of new forms of resistance, change, appropriation and identity" and as "a translocal language [...] of fluidity and fixity that moves across, while becoming embedded in, the materiality of localities and social relations" (Pennycook 2007: 5–6). Park and Wee (2012: 129–30) therefore propose thinking of various uses of English in terms of *indexical field,* which orients our analysis away from the language's "capital" in a purely economic sense toward the language's practices and the multiple indexical meanings the language may possess within different contexts. They argue that "our analysis of the indexical meanings of English as a global

42   2 Language Ideologies, Multilingualism, and Social Media

language [. . .] should follow English as it circulates through different contexts—tracing the flow of English across social and historical contexts as it accumulates new meaning is the key to understanding its complexity in the world today" (Park and Wee 2012: 130).

In all of this talk of the subversion of old paradigms, it is tempting to ascribe a sense of freedom to these processes that is oversimplified at best and misguided at worst. In fact, the superdiversity-induced emergence of transidiomatic practices has not managed to subvert the old global indexical order to the point where notions of legitimacy in language use and ideologies about the superiority of certain communicative codes over others have disappeared or become irrelevant (Jacquemet 2010: 63, Deumert 2014). Individual creativity may be encouraged within certain groups' transidiomatic practices (more on this below), but this is not the same thing as giving licence to unsystematic "anything goes" linguistic behaviour. The resulting sociolinguistic practices are governed by community preferences for what is considered "skillful" social media communication (Deumert 2014: 144), and even local norms of use (involving multiple scales of locality and globality) that need to be attended to in order for a given type of language practice to come across as sufficiently "authentic" (Varis and Wang 2011: 81). Furthermore, these preferences do not exist entirely separately from existing language ideologies, but are instead "embedded in broader social and cultural, rather than purely individual, preferences and tastes" (Deumert 2014: 144). It will therefore be important to keep the relationship between existing ideologies and hierarchies and transidiomatic language practices in mind in an analysis of language use in social media.

Language use in Social Media

I debated for a long time how I would refer to the groups in this book, beginning with the intentionally vague concept of "online communities" and entertaining the idea of "internet communities" for a while before ultimately arriving at the notion of "social media communities." Other scholars who have done similar kinds of work have instead chosen different adjectives like "mobile" (Deumert 2014), "digital" (Baym 2015, Thurlow and Mroczek 2011, Horst and Miller 2012, Barton and Lee 2013, Georgakopoulou and Spilioti 2016a), "computer-mediated" (Herring 2001, 2007, Androutsopoulos 2011), and "networked" (Papacharissi 2011, Androutsopoulos 2015). For the title I settled on a term that emphasized the inherently *social* nature of what these two communities of young people are doing, but throughout this book I will use that term interchangeably with these other terms as well. In any case, while there are in fact distinctions between different kinds of mediated environments (see Boyd 2011: 43 for the specific characteristics of social media environments) generally it can be said that all of the above scholars are interested in language use and interaction in environments that have been termed *web 2.0*. These are digital environments that can be described as "websites built to facilitate interactivity and co-creation of content by website visitors in addition to original authors" (Walther et al. 2011: 26). These websites contrast with the World Wide Web as it was originally conceived (i.e. web 1.0), through their increased emphasis on the parts of the web that promote characteristics like "rich and interactive user interfaces," "data consumption and remixing from all sources, particularly user generated data," and an "architecture of participation that encourages user contribution" (Hinchcliffe 2006, cited in Androutsopoulos 2010: 207). More specifically when it comes to livejournal communities like *unserekleinestadt* and *vragenuurtje*, we can be seen as dealing with a smaller subset of web 2.0 experiences that Barton and Lee (2013: 36) term *writing spaces online*. These spaces encompass contexts as diverse as the photo site Flickr, Facebook, YouTube, and instant messaging services, but what they have in common is that they "provide the possibilities and constraints of what can be written, and what is likely to be written" (Barton and Lee 2013: 27). In the case of this book it is important to keep in mind that both social media communities are embedded within the wider writing space of livejournal (see Chapter 1 for more detail about this), as most community members also take part in that broader context of the site, keeping their own blogs and participating in other communities (partly or even primarily in English), and various knowledge about this context forms a backdrop for their conversations. However, the data all derives from the two communities themselves.

Before I go on to summarize the literature on characteristics of social media discourse and communication, however, I would like to repeat that this is not intended to be mainly a book about the peculiarities of social media language use. Instead, as I mentioned in Chapter 1, I envision this as a book about the transidiomatic practices of two communities of young people, one German and one Dutch, which are located (or at least began, since both communities have produced friendships and even romances that have in-person elements as well) within a social media environment. While this distinction could be regarded as merely semantic, it is nonetheless a crucial one because it has repercussions for whether this book is seen as describing *social media* language practices or simply *language practices,* and therefore the extent to which its findings can be regarded as relevant to non-mediated contexts. I do believe that relevance exists, and can be defended. First, community members mentioned again and again in the interviews that their transidiomatic practices are not limited solely to the online world (see Chapter 5 for more detail). Second, the strict dichotomy between "online" and "real life" is arguably rather tenuous in the first place (cf. Miller 2012: 147), in that many of the members of these social media communities regularly meet up face-to-face and continue their previously mediated conversations in non-mediated environments. This can in fact be regarded as one facet of superdiversity: the emergence of a world in which "many contemporary social practices seamlessly intertwine online and offline activities and they cannot be separated" (Barton and Lee 2013: 7). As a specific situational context where interaction takes place, however, social media environments do promote and develop certain kinds of practices that will be relevant to the analysis in this book. It is those practices that I will discuss in this section.

Features of Social Media Language Use

Much early research into language use in web 2.0 environments focused on what was specific and new about this brave new world of communication. This research found that such environments tend to encompass certain distinctive graphic features of page design, spacing, and the use of illustrations and colour; as well as distinctive orthographic, grammatical, lexical, and discourse features (Crystal 2006: 8). It is also clear from this research that these environments are characterized by a mixture of speech-like and text-like features, as well as some that are exclusively computer-mediated (e.g. Baron 2000, Danet 2001). In summing up these distinctions, Baym (2015: 71–2) writes:

> Online interaction is like writing in many ways. In detailed analyses of naturally occurring messages, Baron (2008) argues that, on balance, emails, instant messages, and text messages look more like writing than speech, but fall on a spectrum in between. Like writing, textual interaction online often bears an address. Messages can be edited prior to transmission. The author and reader are physically (and often temporally) separated. Messages can be read by anonymous readers who may not respond and it is not possible for interlocutors to overlap one another or to interrupt. Context must be created through the prose so that messages are often explicit and complete. There is rarely an assumption of shared physical context. Messages are replicable and can be stored. On the other hand, there are many ways in which online language resembles speech. As we saw in the discussion of immediacy above, misspellings and deletions often foreground phonetic qualities of language. Despite the challenges to conversational coordination (Herring 2001), messages are generally related to prior ones, often through turn-taking. The audience is usually able to respond and often does so quickly, resulting in reformulations of original messages. Topics change rapidly. The discourse often feels ephemeral, and often is not stored by recipients despite the capacity for storage.

Some of this research also delineates classification systems for different types of computer-mediated discourse related to different facets of the technological medium (such as synchronous or asynchronous communication, size of message buffer, and ability to quote) and different facets of the social situation (such as public vs. private, group demographics, and the purpose of the group), or addresses the ways that users compensate for the absence of visual cues. In somewhat later research along the same lines, Androutsopoulos (2010: 209) underscores the need for an analysis of the ways that web 2.0 environments are organized through hypertext and links (see also Jones and Hafner 2012: 35–48), and Barton and Lee (2013: 89) emphasize the importance of stance-taking in social media discourse. Jacquemet (2010: 53)

46   2 Language Ideologies, Multilingualism, and Social Media

further argues that the deterritorialized world of superdiversity has an impact on the indexicality of messages because the spatio-temporal contexts of an interaction cannot be taken for granted, which has repercussions for a system of deixis (Benwell and Stokoe 2006: 255).

More recently, however, there has been a move away from laying out the distinctive features of social media interaction toward understanding how these features might be used within the construction of new kinds of discourse styles and identities (Androutsopoulos 2006a: 421, Nishimura 2007, 2016) by shifting the main focus from the medium *itself* to the *user* of the medium (Georgakopoulou and Spilioti 2016b: 3). Or in other words, rather than asking "what mediation *does to* communication," we are beginning to focus more on "what people *do with* mediated communication" (Baym 2015: 67, emphasis in the original). In an attempt to give some structure to our thinking about this, Deumert (2014: 6) suggests that we can be guided by three recurring themes or topics that constantly emerge as important in various analyses of social media discourse: mobility, creativity, and inequality. Further, and moving on to a level that can be seen as one step more specific than that, Androutsopoulos (2010: 208–9) identifies four general principles of language use in social media environments: organization, interaction, self-presentation, and spectacle. Finally, diving deeper into the self-presentation and spectacle aspects of social media discourse, Deumert (2014: 110) builds on Goffman (1959) by distinguishing between three separate but related types of *performance*: performance-1 (which refers to the ordinary things people say and do with language in everyday life), performance-2 (which refers more specifically to the self-conscious and strategic use of language in everyday interactions), and performance-3 (which refers to a specifically marked and non-routine mode of speaking or writing that invokes theatricality, displays language as carefully crafted and artful, and invites aesthetic scrutiny). While aiming for different degrees of specificity regarding the particularities of digital media language use, all of these distinctions can be seen as broader characteristics of language practice within social media environments that refer to things that people do with language. As such, they are more suitable for use as analytical tools than many of the lists of features found in the previous section.

As mentioned earlier, the characteristics of computer-mediated communication that make it unique are not the specific object of study in this book. Instead, my focus is more on differences between how transidiomatic practices are used among young Germans and young Dutch. However, it is important to make mention of the distinctive features of web 2.0 spaces and what community members tend to do with them, as they will inform and guide how certain linguistic and interactional features are interpreted as they emerge as relevant in the analysis. One related concern is which languages are most common within online discourse and what implications that may have for this book. I will deal with that in the next section.

English and Beyond

While English is clearly still the dominant language of the internet, it has become increasingly less so in recent years (Berns et al. 2007: 34, Kelly-Holmes 2006, Danet and Herring 2007, Paolillo 2007, Lee 2016). Estimates from as early as 2003 report that two-thirds of internet users were not native speakers of English, and in only four of the fifteen top countries for internet use in 2004 was English even the dominant language (Danet and Herring 2007: 1–2). More recently, data suggests that English web content dropped from 80% in 1998 to 55% in 2012, and about 73% of the world's internet users have a first language other than English (Barton and Lee 2013: 43). On the other hand, the diversity of languages that can be found on the internet is not identical to the diversity of languages that can be found in the world, as the majority of the world's languages are "absent, or only minimally represented," online (Deumert 2014: 75), and the languages that dominate tend—not coincidentally—to be those languages that also tend to be regarded as those with real power and authority in the broader global social order. While it is important not to oversimplify these phenomena as being a simple result of the homogenizing trends of global capitalism (see the discussion of linguistic imperialism in the previous section), it is also crucial that we engage critically with this trend and its implications. Indeed, it is not at all certain what will happen to the smallest of small languages in such an environment (Deumert 2014: 75).

48   2 Language Ideologies, Multilingualism, and Social Media

Studies of multilingual language use in *social media* in particular have often focused on diasporic communities (e.g. McClure 2001, Fialkova 2005, Androutsopoulos 2006b, 2007, 2015). These are communities that are spread across the world either because they do not have their own nation state or because they are made up of people who have left their home countries, and social media allows them to assert ethnic identities through multilingual language practices and form transnational communities that are not bounded by geography. However, other studies focus not on digital diasporas, but on specifically local digital communities of, for example, Egyptians living in Egypt and interacting with other Egyptians (Warschauer et al. 2007) or Finns living in Finland and interacting with other Finns (Peuronen 2011) that nonetheless make copious use of the transidiomatic practices that are typical of an age of superdiversity affected by transcultural flows. It is of course common within these communities to incorporate English-derived vocabulary into their interactions both in cases where the participants are talking specifically about things of North American origin that do not have a specific term in the local language (such as certain extreme sports, as in Peuronen 2011), but even when there is a specific local term, community members may still draw on English in order to index—or align themselves with—a particular global culture. In this book, the two communities of *unserekleinestadt* and *vragenuurtje* can be situated within this niche, as in both cases they are local, even specifically *national* communities, but by virtue of being located within the wider context of livejournal in particular and digital media in general, transidiomatic practices of various types are extremely common. Furthermore, this kind of phenomenon is self-reinforcing— the fact that the global internet is giving rise to more and more of these kinds of "glocal" communities means that the transidiomatic practices that emerge within them are, in turn, becoming more and more entrenched. In analyzing these communities and their language practices, we therefore need to take an approach to the analysis of actual practices that is informed by a complex theory of language and globalization that goes beyond simplistic arguments about imperialism vs. pluralism, and which entertains the notion that both forces may be present at the same time, but in different ways and for different reasons (Barton and Lee 2013: 55).

Multilingual Language use in Interaction

Of course, a theory of language and globalization that focuses on actual practices demands a theory of multilingual language use that can actually account for those practices, even if they do not always fit conceptions sociolinguists have tended to have about how languages do and don't combine. For this reason, the concept of transidiomatic practices will be at the centre of my analysis of the multilingual language use in this book. As a reminder, these are practices used by the kinds of transnational groups that are becoming ubiquitous as the world enters a state of ever-increasing superdiversity, and can be characterized as containing "different languages and communicative codes simultaneously present in a range of communicative channels, both local and distant" (Jacquemet 2005: 264–5). Other scholars have proposed the similar terms of *translingual practice* (Barton and Lee 2013: 60–1), *polylanguaging* (Jørgensen et al. 2011), or *translanguaging* (Li 2011: 1223), but they all cover the same general types of mixing: on the one hand multilingual practices which have traditionally been described as code-switching, code-mixing, crossing, and creolization, but on the other hand types of creative and critical language-mixing not often explored in sociolinguistic research (Li 2011: 1223–4). This perspective on multiple linguistic resources within a single community works well within a theory of language and globalization that emphasizes superdiversity-induced transcultural flows and the "glocal" nature of transidiomatic practices, because it allows for the possibility of interpreting language use as influenced by the kind of diversity that becomes commonplace in an age of heightened mobility and increased digital communication. It is therefore the lens of transidiomatic practices through which I will view the multilingual language practices characterized in the sections below.

Language Alternation in Spoken Interaction

The central problem for the concept of *code-switching* amounts to the problem of how to define a linguistic system. Though intentionally somewhat vaguer than the concept of *language*, the concept of *code* still refers to

50   2 Language Ideologies, Multilingualism, and Social Media

an autonomous and bounded linguistic system that is thought to combine in particular ways with another entirely separate linguistic system (in fact, much work on code-switching has been an attempt to understand what these intersections of codes can tell us about universals of grammatical structure, e.g. Poplack 1988 and Myers-Scotton 1993). However, many such attempts to define code-switching as something essentially and entirely distinct from other concepts such as *borrowing* or *code-mixing* have been criticized as too inherently tied up with the notion of the coexistence of two linguistic systems and two bounded units of community, approaches that are inattentive to the ways that language use as socially and politically embedded practices can transcend these boundaries (Heller 2007a: 1–7). In order to bring a more sophisticated underlying social theory into our attempts to account for these phenomena, it is therefore important to approach this subject matter from a perspective that acknowledges that language is social practice, speakers are social actors, and the boundaries both language users and analysts often think of as so essential are in fact constructed products of social action. One possible alternate way of looking at these phenomena comes from Auer (1998, 2007), whose framework approaches the switching from one language to another as inherently embedded within interaction, and as best analyzed not as a kind of sociolinguistic variation, but within a form of discourse analysis inspired by conversation analysis (e.g. Clayman and Gill 2014) and interactional sociolinguistics (e.g. Jaspers 2014) that takes the inherent sequential order of conversation into account (Auer 1995). This framework is well suited to a practice-based approach to social theory because it puts the speakers rather than the linguistic system at the centre and anchors the analysis in conversation participants' own conceptualizations of their language and their world. This allows for interpretations of transidiomatic language use that see it not as the interaction of multiple autonomous linguistic systems, but as a set of practices that are inherently tied up with other kinds of social behaviour (Alvarez-Cáccamo 1998, Auer 2007). This is an approach that is better able to account for the range of linguistic practices we can witness in superdiversity, especially in environments where the performative aspects of language use are paramount, such as in hip-hop (Pennycook 2007) or social media discourse (Deumert 2014: 110).

The approach to the analysis of transidiomatic practices in this book is based on Auer's (1998, 2007) approach to analyzing language alternation in interaction. As mentioned in Chapter 1, this approach is designed to elicit those ideas and categories and relationships that are meaningful to the participants themselves, and in doing so, it focuses on the ways in which speakers switch between languages in order to alert others to the social and situational context of the conversation. Alternation between one language and another is therefore analyzed as a *contextualization cue* (cf. Gumperz 1982) that provides participants with information about how to interpret aspects of the conversation.[3] The framework further distinguishes between two types of contextualization cues: *discourse-related* cues, in which contrasts in language choice contribute to the structural organization of interactions, and *participant-related* cues, in which participants index the social meanings of different languages within the interactional context, often as a tool in identity construction. This means that while social meanings of particular languages *can* play a role within a given exchange, these meanings can only be a part of the analysis when conversation participants themselves *make them relevant*, or in other words when there is direct evidence in the local interaction that the code choice is tied to social identity in that exchange. Although original conceptualizations of this framework did presuppose the existence of two separate linguistic systems, later contributions have allowed for the possibility that individual instances of multilingual language use are not always so clear-cut. In fact, Auer (2007: 337) suggests that the starting point of such analyses should not be two languages at all, but "a collection of discursive and linguistic practices used by bilingual speakers in a community, and based on certain grammatical/lexical/phonological feature constellations." Some of these practices might involve conventional code-switching, but they could also involve the amalgamation of two codes into a single speaking style, or the creation of "mixed" or "fused" languages. The concept of

---

[3] The switch from one set of language resources to another is only one possible resource for contextualization among many, but in digital communities with multiple sets of languages in their repertoire, it increases in importance as a result of the lack of face-to-face conversational resources such as gesture or eye contact (Georgakopoulou 1997: 158).

codes (and their implied separate linguistic systems) is therefore not necessarily irrelevant within this framework, at least not in every case, but it always plays a secondary role to the meaning-making work that is being done by the practices in the context of the local interaction.

As for what sort of meaning-making work this can entail, examples are numerous. Many discourse-related functions of the use of transidiomatic practices involve a change in *footing*, a concept initially described by Goffman (1979: 5) as implying "a change in the alignment we take up to ourselves and others present as expressed in the way we manage the production or reception of an utterance," such as marking a change in topic (e.g. Alfonzetti 1998: 197–8), demarcating quotations or reported speech (e.g. Alvarez-Cáccamo 1996), marking a role shift (e.g. Zentella 1997: 94), summing up the end of a narrative (e.g. Alfonzetti 1998: 194–5), aiding in the regulation of conversational turn-taking (e.g. Auer 1995: 120), and attracting attention (e.g. Li 1998: 160–1). Discourse-related functions that do not specifically demarcate a change in footing can also involve the explication or elaboration of a previously stated idea (e.g. Zentella 1997: 95–6). A wide range of possibilities is also available when a switch is used as a participant-related tool for identity construction: for example it is possible for such a switch to enact social categories in a straightforward "when I am being an X, I speak X language, and when I am being a Y, I speak Y language" way, such as the child of German immigrant parents in Canada switching from English to German in order to indicate an affinity with Germanness and to express positive attitudes toward the language (Liebscher and Dailey-O'Cain 2013: 61–3), but it does not have to be this way. Transidiomatic practices can also draw on multiple language resources in ways that straddle both linguistic and cultural boundaries (Bailey 2007: 257). One such example is *crossing*, which is defined as "the use of language varieties associated with social or ethnic groups that the speaker doesn't normally 'belong' to" (Rampton 2005: 28); another is the kind of appropriative and creative use of the cultural and linguistic forms of global English to index a sense of connectedness between different locales (Peuronen 2011) that is common to many young Europeans' use of English in social media environments.

The aforementioned indexical nature of transidiomatic practices must therefore play a central role in our analysis and interpretation of them,

Multilingual Language use in Interaction 53

because while indexicality is a part of all language use, it plays additional, and more complex, roles in transnational communities under influence from superdiversity (Varis and Wang 2011). Evidence of the changed role for indexicality can be seen in Deumert's (2014: 108) example of how the spelling of *the* as <da> can index ethnic and local belonging, a lack of education and refinement, or familiarity with global popular culture, depending on the geographic location of the interaction and other circumstances; other work has found that different linguistic variants that all have their origins in an increased influence from global norms can nonetheless index very different things and be interpreted as differentially "exotic" despite their similar origins (Meyerhoff and Niedzelski 2003). These different indexicalities can be seen as part of language users' *heteroglossic repertoires* (Peuronen 2011: 155), which "provide speakers and writers with resources, whether multilingual or multidialectal, for expressing stances, identifications, and social personae" (Deumert 2014: 121, see also Bailey 2007: 258). Like indexicality, heteroglossia is a part of all language use, but it becomes even more essential in transnational environments such as the ones in this book, because the practices involved in multiple linguistic resources play a particularly important role in situations that call for heightened performativity and creativity (Deumert 2014: 121, Nishimura 2016). So for example, whether a particular instance of English can be interpreted as an instance of crossing must depend on whether the participants in that interaction can be shown to be constructing the situation as one in which they are "styling" a particular "other" (by using language resources interpreted as "belonging" to a particular other group), or as one where they are using language resources that are, at least in some respects, their own (perhaps by virtue of it being an international or "neutral" language that everyone has automatic permission to use). Participants can of course sometimes make such things clear by stating them overtly, but more often the way in which they do so is through *positioning* (see Chapter 1 for more detail), which is a process that is accomplished when interactants make use of grammatical and other linguistic and non-linguistic resources to make relationships to social categories relevant. It has been described as "a dynamic alternative to the more static concept of *role*" (Harré and van Langenhove 1991: 393), and as such, positionings are not fixed and enduring, but always highly

54   2 Language Ideologies, Multilingualism, and Social Media

context-dependent and changeable (cf. Liebscher and Dailey-O'Cain 2013). An analysis of positioning therefore allows us to connect particular moment-to-moment linguistic choices interactants make with larger social processes that exist beyond the here-and-now of interactions (Georgakopoulou 2007: 121).

Transidiomatic Practices in Social Media Discourse

Although it was designed for the analysis of spoken interaction, many studies have successfully adapted this sort of framework to computer-mediated contexts (e.g. Androutsopoulos and Hinnenkamp 2001, Sebba 2003, del-Teso-Craviotto 2006, Stommel 2008, Androutsopoulos 2011), because while some of the resources used for contextualization within digital environments are different, many are not, and even those resources that are different are often used in familiar ways. Indeed, Deumert (2014: 2–3) argues more generally that there is no need to reinvent the wheel when it comes to dealing with online data, although we may need to look at old ideas from a new perspective. In attempting to help fill the gap that is left by the lack of "ethnographically-based, linguistically-oriented fieldwork of digital transnational spaces" lamented by Jacquemet (2010: 61–2), then, I have situated the analysis in this book within what Androutsopoulos (2008) refers to as a *discourse-centred online ethnography*, which combines the analysis of data drawn from a social media community with in-person interviews with community members. In such an analysis, it is important to be informed by what sociolinguists already know about spoken interaction, but also to consider possible ways in which the social media context might have an influence on the transidiomatic practices we find. As already mentioned, such differences might involve inherently digital implications of heteroglossia and indexicality, but other differences can arise as well.

For example, Androutsopoulos (2015: 201) lists three parameters for transidiomatic practices in social media discourse: the constraints of digital writtenness or mediation (i.e. the ways in which the nature of the medium influences the practices that arise), access to the global mediascape of the web (i.e. making use of various recurring semiotic resources that are immediately at participants' fingertips on the global web, whether or not these involve languages participants actually have a command of), and orientation to networked audiences (i.e. the implications of public or semi-public language, of who the audience is for a given message, of issues of performance). Among the constraints of digital writtenness or mediation, one of the most crucial is multimodality (Kress 2010, Kress 2014, Jewitt 2016), which refers to the way communication takes place simultaneously across different modes or "channels." While all language use is multimodal by that definition, the analysis of multimodality becomes even more crucial in a social media environment that makes semiotic use of writing, images, moving images, and possibly even sound. In terms of access to semiotic resources, Androutsopoulos (2015: 189–90) gives the example of "copy-paste language," where participants in a social media setting such as Facebook may appropriate language bits from song lyrics or aphorisms from the web and paste them in their online writing spaces, even if these involve languages that they do not have command of. This is of interest in a digitally mediated environment because the language resources offered by such environments increase the potential for different kinds of transidiomatic practices, going beyond the codes that would be available to the same participants in a non-networked environment. Finally, the orientation to networked audiences has implications for identity construction with transidiomatic practices within specifically online spaces because of the aforementioned connection between online discourse and performance. While all identity work is to some extent less about who we essentially are and more about who we want to be to others and how others see us, the inherently performative aspect of social media interaction highlights this aspect of identity work in a way that can be more visible than in face-to-face interaction (Barton and Lee 2013: 68, see also Benwell and Stokoe 2006, Hinrichs 2006, Tsiplakou 2009, Page 2016).

While most studies of language use in digitally mediated environments have thus far been more interested in "affordances" than practices—i.e. what forms of communication are made possible by digital technologies rather than what particular groups of users do with these possibilities

(Androutsopoulos 2015: 188)—the potential for studies of social media discourse to contribute to a practice-based approach to social theory is vast. By breaking with certain essentialist restrictions such as the idea that a language is inherently a single bounded linguistic system, the notion of a certain level of competence being a prerequisite for successful multilingual practice, and the concept of the use of a language being inherently linked to its original community of speakers, approaching the use of multiple language resources as transidiomatic practices can both inform and be informed by social theories of globalization, transnationalism, and super-diversity (Androutsopoulos 2015: 186). The analysis in this book is one attempt at such a contribution, hopefully among many others to come.

Toward a Comparative Sociolinguistics of Globalization

It is important to consider all of these—at first blush seemingly unre-lated—bodies of research as parts of the same theoretical framework in this book. Any theory of global English needs to take into account the ways the language has come to be linked with *value*, not only in the economic sense (i.e. the belief that competence in English can be converted into material gain), but also moral and ethical value (i.e. the way the use of English can point to an elusive sense of good upbringing and moral integrity that are used to justify a higher social status) (Park and Wee 2012: 25–6). At the same time that the English language is being infused with value, however, it is often perceived as culturally neutral, and at the root of this is a process of layer upon layer of abstraction. As Park and Wee (2012: 173) argue, "English is first conceptualized as language-as-entity, a code with an abstract system; it is then linked with specific images of personhood, associated with circulable, recyclable person-types, which serve as figures upon which value of English can be anchored; then, finally, construction of neutral-ity detaches English from its cultural context to valorize it as a language with global convertibility. Every step of this process depends on an abstraction, delinking language from communicative context, and firing

Toward a Comparative Sociolinguistics of Globalization 57

it into isolable and identifiable categories." Once the forms of English are abstracted away from their original cultural contexts, they are free to be recontextualized differently within different local contexts, infused with new local meanings while still retaining the flavour of global culture. This can be seen as an inherent feature of superdiversity, and it is happening all over the world.

It does not happen in precisely the same ways in all local contexts, however, and the transidiomatic practices that result from these processes are not always precisely the same, either. Park and Wee (2012: 21, 86) have argued, for example, that Pennycook's (2007) findings regarding transidiomatic practices in hip-hop cannot automatically be assumed to translate directly to other fields or linguistic markets, due to the fact that the hip-hop context contains very particular ideologies of appropriation and creativity that do not necessarily apply elsewhere. Similarly, I would argue that it is just as important to understand the ways that different state traditions promote and suppress different local recontextualizations of global English, and in turn, different kinds of transidiomatic practices and different ideologies about those practices. For sociolinguists, there are therefore three key components to understanding the way this process works differently within different local contexts. The first is to situate a theory of global English within detailed analyses of actual language practices. The second is to be detailed about analyzing not just the language practices themselves, but the particular indexicalities of those practices within different local communities (a combination of an analysis of social media interaction and an analysis of interviews in which community members are invited to express their attitudes toward their language practices is crucial here). Finally, the third and final component is to root the analysis of language practices and language attitudes in an understanding of the complex and layered specifically *local* ideological contexts (consisting of longstanding influences from traditions of nationalism and other state traditions, as well as institutionalized and semi-institutionalized traditions of language policies) in which these practices and attitudes are embedded.

I hope it is apparent that one way to study the transidiomatic practices that are becoming ubiquitous in superdiversity is to study

2 Language Ideologies, Multilingualism, and Social Media

social media discourse (Varis 2016) within the context of a society's language ideologies (Park and Wee 2012). Combining an analysis of these two aspects enables sociolinguists to avoid simplistic arguments about whether globalization represents imperialism or pluralism by acknowledging that within any situation of language practice, both forces may be present at the same time, but for different reasons and in different ways (cf. Barton and Lee 2013: 55). An additional benefit of such an approach is that it can help situate a theory of global English within practices that are closer to everyday life than those practices that have been identified in arenas such as hip-hop (Park and Wee 2012: 86). While performativity is a key component of social media discourse just as it is in hip-hop, the transidiomatic practices of social media conversation are still doubtlessly closer than those of hip-hop to the linguistic and social behaviours of everyday life. This is because while both forms of language practice involve performance, the performance of social media interaction can be more easily interpreted as fitting within Deumert's (2014: 110) performances-1 and -2 as opposed to hip-hop's performance-3. Furthermore, it can even be argued that for most young people, social media interaction is such an integral part of that everyday life that "everyday life" is no longer entirely separable from it. By focusing on these kinds of ordinary day-to-day interactions, we can gain a more practice-based understanding of how the English language is appropriated and resignified across different social and cultural contexts, and of whether it comes to represent a language of global hegemony, a language of local cultural expression, or perhaps both.

This book is the first study that compares findings from two countries with separate ideological, institutional, and semi-institutionalized traditions, taking both transidiomatic practices and that ideological backdrop into account. This kind of double-barrelled analysis is the rationale for the two separate but equally important sets of research questions this book will address. The first set is microsociolinguistic, i.e. focused on questions that can only be answered by a detailed analysis of the roles the English language plays in the structures and functions of interaction, while the second set is macrosociolinguistic, i.e. focused on what young

Toward a Comparative Sociolinguistics of Globalization   59

people's use of multiple languages can tell us about the role of English in Europe and the world. These questions are as follows:

Microsociolinguistic questions
- Uses of English: How does the alternation between local languages (German or Dutch) and English structure interaction within social media discourse? How does it help construct identities among community members?
- Attitudes toward uses of English: What are individual community members' attitudes toward their use of English, and how do they describe and explain specific examples of such use?
- Differences between communities: How does the use of English differ between the German community and the Dutch one? How do the attitudes toward that usage differ?

Macrosociolinguistic questions
- Uses of English: What can the functions of language alternation (in structuring interaction in social media discourse and in identity construction) tell us about the role of English in a globalizing Europe?
- Attitudes toward uses of English: What can community members' attitudes toward particular kinds of bilingual phenomena tell us about the role of English in a globalizing Europe?
- Differences between communities: What can the two communities' differing use of English on the one hand, and the two communities' attitudes toward that usage on the other, tell us about the position of English in German society and the position of English in Dutch society?

In answering these research questions, the analysis in Chapters 3, 4, and 5 will address the issue of whether English is being transformed into a language of local cultural expression (and through that, whether it is possible to subvert the hegemonic qualities of global English). However, it does this specifically by looking at the differences between different practices as found in communities from two north-central

European countries, and considering what components of the two countries' language regimes these differences may be attributable to. In the process, I hope to contribute to a better understanding of the extent to which these practices represent either a subversion of national identities by transnational ones or the combination of the local and the global into something new that is neither wholly local nor wholly global.

3

The Who and the What: Amounts and Types of English

In the previous chapter, I outlined the theoretical foundations of this book: research on language ideologies and language policy in Germany and in the Netherlands, research on language use in social media, and research on multilingual language use in interaction. In this chapter, I will begin to put these foundational ideas to work by using them as a backdrop against which to answer the two most rudimentary questions in any comparison of the use of English in two different contexts. The first of these questions has to do with the *types* of English that are used: how can the two communities' use of English be characterized (i.e. can the use be delineated into different categories of use, and if so, how)? The second question, then, has to do with the *amounts* of English: how much English is used by each community, both overall and in terms of the identified categories, and what are the implications of those differences for the kind of comparative sociolinguistics of globalization I outlined in Chapter 2? In other words, if differences can, in fact, be found between the German and the Dutch communities in terms of how and to what extent they incorporate English into their online conversations, what can those differences tell us about the overall role

© The Author(s) 2017
J. Dailey-O'Cain, *Trans-National English in Social Media Communities*, Language and Globalization,
DOI 10.1057/978-1-137-50615-3_3

61

62   3 The Who and the What: Amounts and Types of English

of different language ideologies and different official state policies in influencing the role of English in everyday language practice? In attempting to answer these questions, I will first present the different types of alternation between local languages and English that can be found in the data (which I illustrate with a series of excerpts from conversations in both the German and Dutch communities), and then move on to a comparative quantitative analysis assessing how much English is used in the two communities. Then I will discuss the use of English vs. local languages in the usernames that the two communities' members choose for themselves, before finally coming back around to a summary of the general trends seen in the data so far and what they imply for the larger questions this book is trying to answer.

Before I get into the analysis, though, I would like to come back to the issue of how exactly to distinguish words and phrases of English origin that qualify as "English" for the purposes of this book from those words and phrases of English origin that have already become incorporated into the local languages. After all, all languages borrow words from other languages, and eventually there is always a point where those words simply become a natural part of the languages doing the borrowing. For example, "kindergarten" is a word that the English language borrowed from German, and "boss" is a word that the English language borrowed from Dutch, but it is not necessary to have any knowledge of either German or Dutch to use these words in everyday conversation, and most native English speakers are likely completely unaware of those words' foreign origins. Since this sort of borrowing is a process rather than something that happens overnight, however, the point at which a language can successfully have said to have integrated a word is anything but transparent, and many individual lexical items fall within a grey area. In fact, a great many papers have been written about how to distinguish between *borrowing* and *code-switching* for the purposes of helping to develop an adequate theory of grammatical constraints on the latter process (e.g. Poplack and Meechan 1998)—indicating that this is by no means always a simple and straightforward task.

As mentioned in Chapter 1, I have opted to code and analyze those English-origin lexical items in my data as English that were not sufficiently integrated into monolingual language use to appear in the most recent editions of the dictionaries *Duden: Das große Wörterbuch der deutschen Sprache* (for German) or *Van Dale groot woordenboek van de Nederlandse taal* (for Dutch). While it could be argued that there is a potential alternative that would be preferable from a phenomenological perspective (cf. Bailey 2007: 258)—I might have asked participants to define all of the English-origin words used in the corpus as either English or part of the local language—this would introduce several methodological difficulties that would make it impossible to put into practice. First, the unbounded and ever-changing nature of livejournal communities as discussed in Chapter 1 makes it very difficult to say who does and who does not count as a member of any community. This means that it would be just as difficult to decide who would need to be asked such a question, and who could reasonably be left out. Second, given the sheer number of English-origin lexical items in the data, even if participants *could* all be identified, asking them (or even a subset of them) to go through each one of these for the purposes of deciding whether or not they qualified as English would be an excessively tedious task that would require hours and hours of concerted effort. Third, given that some disagreement among participants would be likely in such a methodology, an arbitrary mechanism would still be necessary to distinguish the point on the scale where a word 'became' a part of the local language. Given all of these potential difficulties, using some sort of independent authority such as a dictionary seems the most reasonable option.

Such a blunt instrument is not, however, unproblematic from the perspective of a sociolinguistics of globalization that is attempting to analyze the impact of transnational and transcultural flows on language practice. If the object of analysis is the "circulation of linguistic resources and their re-embedding in new sociocultural environments" (Androutsopoulos 2010: 204, see also Blommaert 2003, Pennycook 2007), then any attempt to impose a distinction between "English" and "not English" from the perspective of an outside authority oversimplifies a very complex process. It is therefore essential that this distinction be taken simply as a way of creating a level playing field for the purpose of comparing the two communities *with each other,* not as a way of determining which kinds of English-origin language use are more "foreign" than others, and certainly not as a way of contrasting the communities with some idealized monolingual Dutch-speaking or German-speaking environment. In other words, since any method for sorting a complex process into two rather simplistic categories is less than ideal, the most important objective here is to use similar sorts of instruments to categorize the English use in each of the two communities (in this case two different mainstream dictionaries with broad appeal and widespread acceptance). In making assumptions about the *implications* of any differences that are found between the two communities with respect to English use, however, attention will need to be paid both to the inherently transnational nature of the social media setting for these conversations and to the ways in which the process of identifying one linguistic form as "English" and another as "German" or "Dutch" is not always clear.

Categories of transidiomatic practices

As already discussed in Chapter 2, sociolinguists who analyze multilingual social media discourse (e.g. Deumert 2014: 144, Varis and Wang 2011: 81) have found that being regarded as a competent or "skillful" transidiomatic conversationalist on social media requires attention to two axes of language use: creativity and normativity. These axes might seem on the surface to be competing or even contradictory, as being sufficiently creative could conceivably be interpreted as automatically failing to adhere to existing norms of use, while adhering to norms of use might imply an automatic sacrifice of creativity. What researchers have found, however, it that it is precisely at the *intersection* of the creative and the normative where social media communicators are most likely to come across as "skillful" and "authentic" to each other. This implies that knowledge about both the boundaries of individual creativity and about various relevant norms of use are an essential part of being a "skillful" transidiomatic communicator on social media.

When we are talking about norms of use in social media conversations, however, these are not precisely identical to the norms of use that

Categories of transidiomatic practices **65**

govern more formal spoken or written genres. Individual members of *unserekleinestadt* and *vragenuurtje* would undoubtedly use rather different language in a job interview or in a paper they would write for a university course than they do in interacting with each other in their communities. Instead, the norms users of social media adhere to are often specific to social media discourse, or even to individual local social media communities (cf. Varis and Wang 2011). Yet at the same time, the preferences for certain kinds of language use over others are not entirely *separate* from existing wider societal language ideologies, either, but are "embedded in broader social and cultural, rather than purely individual, preferences and tastes" (Deumert 2014: 144). This means that coming across as sufficiently skilled and sufficiently authentic in transidiomatic social media conversation tends to involve the creative appropriation of cultural and linguistic forms of global English (cf. Peuronen 2011), but in a way that is likely to be reflective of wider societal language ideologies.

Equally important to remember is the fact that neither *unserekleines-tadt* nor *vragenuurtje* exists in a vacuum. Each individual member of these communities maintains his or her own journaling blog (where they interact with some of the people from those communities, but also with people from outside of them, most of whom cannot be assumed to speak their local language), most also participate in other livejournal communities (where, as a result of the dominance of English on livejournal, there tends to be an expectation of a monolingual English-speaking norm), and all undoubtedly use other forms of (also mostly English-language) social media on the wider internet. It can therefore be assumed that the norms for what is regarded to be an appropriate and authentic use of English-origin transidiomatic practices in these communities is at least as likely to come from their contact with various Anglophone digital media (in combination with contact with other sources of informal English use as detailed in the previous chapter) as it is from their own formal English lessons in school. The implications of this influence of the broader English-dominant internet are perhaps more obvious for the normativity axis of language use, but it is no less present for the creativity one, as the models for authentic forms of creativity are also likely to have been gleaned from social media users in primarily

66   3 The Who and the What: Amounts and Types of English

Anglophone parts of the internet. The amount of creativity involved in a particular instance of English can therefore be seen as an indication of that user's general proficiency in informal English, but it can also be seen as indicative of the degree to which that user has made English a part of his or her own transnational social media repertoire. And, even more importantly for a study that aims to analyze the effects of language ideologies, it may also turn out to be indicative of the degree to which the user believes he or she has the *right* to make English a part of his or her own transnational social media repertoire.

With these influences and the importance of both creativity and normativity in mind, I was able to use the qualitative analysis software NVivo to zero in on all stretches of conversation in the data that included English. Using this software, I did an analysis of all occurrences of English in both data sets, using Auer's (1998, 2007) framework for the interactional analysis of language alternation, and was able to identify four separate categories of English language use. These ranged on a continuum from the kinds of switches that require the least amount of creativity with and knowledge of the English language, to more complex types that require advanced knowledge of not just the grammar of English, but of how the language is used informally in primarily Anglophone communities. These categories are the following, in increasing order of both creativity and knowledge of English required:

a) single-word or single-compound borrowings of terms not established as a regular part of the local language;
b) interactional language use specific to the world of Anglophone digital media;
c) larger expressions or quotes lifted in their entirety from everyday English-language interaction and used to effect in conversation;
d) phrases or sentences in English that are original to the German or Dutch interactant and not borrowed from a particular other source.

For each data set, I then coded each instance of English-origin material not found in the aforementioned German or Dutch dictionaries as falling into one of these categories. In the four subsections below, I will illustrate and clarify each category using an excerpt from conversation in each of the two communities, describing the analytical criteria I used for coding.

Single-word/single-phrase switches

The first category of single-word and single-phrase switches corresponds roughly to what Poplack et al. (1988) have referred to as *nonce borrowings,* in that these are single-word or single-phrase instances of English that are nonetheless code-switches rather than established loanwords fully integrated into the local language and used regularly by monolinguals of that language. This is the category of English language use that is most easily spontaneously borrowed into a local language, because, as these examples are single-word or single-phrase elements, they do not need to be incorporated into the local language's grammar or interactive patterns of use.

In the excerpts below (and throughout the remainder of the book), the English passages have been bolded for easier scanning. Otherwise, formatting with respect to things like line and character spacing, underlining, use of "emoticons," and punctuation and spelling has always been retained from each original post and its comments. In the interest of space and easier readability, any comments not relevant to the point of analysis have been removed, and some of the threading has been simplified. Furthermore, due to copyright restrictions, the "icons" or pictures that livejournal users use to represent themselves visually have also been removed, though wherever they are made relevant in the interaction, a description of them is provided in the analysis. The various turns in the thread are numbered with the original post (when it is a part of the excerpt) bearing the number "00," and all comments are numbered accordingly, in sequential order of posting. The usernames are italicized and appear before each turn, and correspondingly in the analysis as well. The translations follow each excerpt, divided from the original by a single line, preserving the bolding of the originally English words. Square brackets are used either to mask details that could otherwise compromise a participant's privacy such as city names or the names

68   **3 The Who and the What: Amounts and Types of English**

of landmarks that could identify a particular location (in which case the line appears as [city name] or [local landmark]), or within translations, in order to provide explanations of any unclear local-language elements.

The first example can be seen in Excerpt 3.1. It comes from a slightly longer conversation in the *vragenuurtje* community consisting of a post and a total of five comments. It is a fairly simple exchange that is mostly in Dutch, but contains a single switch to English at the end.

Excerpt 3.1: "Thanks" (Dutch community)

00: *ontplooiing:*   Goed doel voor een stel knuffels??
01: *egyptian_rose:*   Ik dacht dat edukans daar wat mee deed.
                          Moet je eens op www.edukans.nl kijken!
02: *ontplooiing:*   **Thanks**!

00: *ontplooiing:*   Charity for a couple of stuffed animals??
01: *egyptian_rose:*   I think maybe edukans would do something with them.
                          You should have a look at www.edukans.nl!
02: *ontplooiing:*   **Thanks**!

In this excerpt, user *ontplooiing* uses Dutch in her initial post to ask whether other community members know of a charity where she[1] might donate some stuffed animals that she has on hand. In the immediate response in turn 01, user *egyptian_rose* tells her that the charity Edukans might be a good solution, and tells her where to find that charity online. User *ontplooiing* then responds with the English word "thanks" in turn 02. This switch was coded as category (a), or a use of English consisting of a single-word switch into the language in an otherwise entirely Dutch exchange.

---

[1] In this excerpt as well as in all of the others throughout the book, the participants are referred to as "he" or "she" if their gender is known. If their gender is not known, the default pronoun "she" is used due to livejournal being overwhelmingly female, as discussed in Chapter 1.

Single-word/single-phrase switches **69**

Excerpt 3.2 below comes from a somewhat longer conversation in the *unserekleinestadt* community consisting of a post and a total of six comments. It is a slightly more complex excerpt that includes several single-word switches.

Excerpt 3.2: "Outdoor shoes" (German community)

00: *weltall:* ich bin auf der suche nach sogenannten **outdoor**-schuhen, in erster linie wohl für **geocaching**, spaziergänge, **'light'**-wandern, im grunde also nicht sehr anspruchsvoll – wasserfest, warmhaltend, eine ordentliche, griffige sohle. mir ist klar: ohne anprobieren geht das nicht, aber: welche marken – evt. auch modelle – könnt ihr empfehlen, womit habt ihr keine guten erfahrungen gemacht? ähnliches für (3in1)jacken.
danke im voraus!

01: *captain_lisa:* Ich hab ein paar **"Boots"** von Landrover (wird über Deichmann vertrieben).
3in1-Jacken
Da hab ich mich ja in die Columbia-Jacken verliebt, damals während meines Aupairjahres.
Sind hier aber sauteuer.

00: *weltall:* I am looking for so-called **outdoor** shoes, probably first and foremost for **geocaching**, going on walks, **'light'** hiking, in other words essentially not all that special – waterproof, heat retaining, a durable, gripping sole, it's clear to me that I won't be able to buy anything without trying it on, but: what brands – or even types of shoes – can you recommend to me, what ones have you had good experiences with? and the same thing for (hiking) jackets.
thanks in advance!

01: *captain_lisa:* I have a pair of **"boots"** from **Landrover** (they sell them at Deichmann).
Hiking jackets
I fell in love with the Columbia jackets back when I was living overseas as a nanny. They're totally expensive here, though.

In *weltall*'s post in turn 00, she specifies that she's looking for "outdoor-schuhen" (outdoor shoes) and also talks about what she wants to use them for: "geocaching" and "light-wandern" (light

70   3 The Who and the What: Amounts and Types of English

hiking), among other things (the quotation marks will be discussed in the section on flagging below). All three of these switches into English have been coded as belonging to the category of single-word switches. In the comment in turn 01, too, user *captain_lisa* talks about the "boots" she bought locally, a switch that also falls into that category.

English originating in the digital world

The second category, that of interactional language use specific to the digitally mediated world, also consists of single-word or single-compound borrowings. These are not, however everyday English words such as nouns or adjectives, but ways of representing gesture, changes in tone of voice, or facial expressions in text that are common in Anglophone social media and other digital forums. They require a somewhat more advanced knowledge of English language use than the kinds of single-word switches illustrated in the last section because using them requires knowledge of how these expressions tend to be used in social media interaction by Anglophone monolinguals.

The first digital-world excerpt is a simple one consisting only of a single post in the *vragenuurtje* community. The original conversation also included seven comments.

Excerpt 3.3: "Desperate" (Dutch community)

00: *bangkokimpact:*   [desperate]
Is er dan echt écht niemand die met me mee wil naar Paul McCartney? (woensdag 9 december a.s., [local landmark], [city name], staanplaatsen, heb niemand om mee te gaan, heb 2 kaartjes á 82,50 per stuk maar hoef dat er zeker niet voor terug)
[/desperate]

English originating in the digital world 71

> 00: *bangkokimpact:*   **[desperate]**
> Is there really really REALLY no one who wants to go to Paul McCartney with me?
> (next Wednesday December 9th, [local landmark], [city name], standing room only, don't have anyone to go with, have 2 tickets at 82.50 Euros each but certainly don't need that whole amount back)
> **[/desperate]**

User *bangkokimpact* initiates and closes her post—which is otherwise completely in Dutch—with not only the English word "desperate," but also certain syntax commonly found in digital "markup languages" to indicate that the text contained within those two tags is to appear bolded, italicized, or with some other specified visual. These kinds of square brackets indicating opening and closing tags are commonly used on message boards (such as the open-source *MyBB* software), while the use of the forward slash to indicate the the closing tag is common both to message board software and the HTML markup language from which it loosely derives. In *bangkokimpact's* post, however, these tags are not used for actual markup purposes, but in order to indicate interactionally that she is aware that the lines of text contained within the tag smack of desperation. (It is likely that the square brackets are preferred for this symbolic use to HTML-typical angle brackets because angle brackets would be read by the livejournal software as actual HTML tags.) Because of the origin of the interactional use of this kind of tag within social media discourse, this instance of English is coded as category (b), a digital-world switch.

The second excerpt in this category comes from a much longer conversation in the German community consisting of a post and 73 comments. In the post that starts the discussion, user *onlysabine* has asked for recommendations for English-language novels that she can read in order to improve her language skills. In Excerpt 3.4 below, we see one of the suggestions from the community.

72   3 The Who and the What: Amounts and Types of English

Excerpt 3.4: "LOL" (German community)

01: *ruby_red:*   die **Twilight** Bücher?;)
02: *onlysabine:*   Oh da bin ich sehr skeptisch.
    Wenn dann würde ich sie eher auf deutsch lesen, hätte sonst glaub ich Angst sie schon aufgrund meiner schlechten Englischkenntnisse doof zu finden.;)
03: *gruenpflanze:*   **LOL** lies statt **Twilight** lieber **Fanfictions**, das Sprachniveau eben-dieser Geschichten ist sicherlich höher als das, welches Stephenie Meyer an den Tag legt.

01: *ruby_red:*   the **Twilight** books?;)
02: *onlysabine:*   Oh I'm really skeptical about those.
    If I do read them I'd rather do it in German, I think otherwise I'd be afraid of finding them dumb just because of my bad knowledge of English.;)
03: *gruenpflanze:*   **LOL** instead of **Twilight** you should read **fanfiction**, the level of the language in those kinds of stories is certainly higher than what Stephenie Meyer displays.

Many suggestions result from *onlysabine*'s original post, and most of them are not included here, but one of these is the recommendation of the Twilight books by Stephenie Meyer, which comes from *ruby_red* in turn 01 of this excerpt. In response to *ruby_red*, then, the original poster expresses skepticism about that series of books in turn 02, at which point user *gruenpflanze* chimes in with agreement in turn 03. The relevant point here is that *gruenpflanze* initiates her turn with the digital-world expression "LOL," an interactive marker commonly used in Anglophone social media discourse to indicate interactional uses of laughter, whether actually occurring or hypothetical, and either at or with another parti-cipant (del-Teso-Craviotto 2006: 468). Both the expression and its common functions are simply borrowed from English-language online discourse, and incorporated into this conversation that is otherwise mostly in German. While the English-language item in *gruenpflanze*'s turn, "Fanfictions" (a German adaptation of the English term "fanfiction," i.e. a kind of amateur fiction using pre-existing characters and worlds), is coded as fitting into category (a), the "LOL" is clearly adopted from Anglophone social media language use and is therefore coded as fitting into category (b).

Larger English expressions or quotes

The third category of larger expressions or quotes requires still more creativity and knowledge of English as it tends to be used in monolingual English contexts. In part this is because these are longer stretches of English that require more advanced proficiency in order to successfully integrate them spontaneously into the local language, but this is also in part because, as with category (b) described above, their use requires an awareness of the ways that these kinds of phrases and quotes tend to work interactionally in monolingual Anglophone use of English, and this tends to be more complex with longer expressions and quotes. The first representative excerpt in this category comes from a conversation consisting of a post and 13 comments from *unserekleinestadt.*

Excerpt 3.5: "Slightly off topic" (German community)

00: *redegattung:* Gibt es hier auch Leute, die **"real"** Tagebuch führen – sprich auf Papier?
Wie regelmäßig macht ihr das?
Und weiß jemand bei der Gelegenheit, wo es solche Tagebücher gibt, wie sie in Bridget Jones oder auch Benjamin Button vorkommen? Also für jeden Tag im Jahr eine Blankoseite, die man ausfüllen kann.

01: *sadness_personified:* **Slightly off topic,** aber wenn Du Dich für Tagebücher interessierst und
mal in Berlin bist, dann empfehle ich diese Ausstellung: [url].

---

74   **3 The Who and the What: Amounts and Types of English**

00: *redegattung:*	Are there any people here who keep a **"real"** diary – in other words on paper? How regularly do you do that? And does anyone happen to know where I can find the kind of diary that appears in Bridget Jones or in Benjamin Button? I mean the kind where you have a blank page for every day in the year, that you can then fill in.
01: *sadness_personified:*	**Slightly off topic,** but if you're interested in diaries and are going to be in Berlin sometime, then I recommend this exhibit: [url].

User *redegattung* uses her post to ask a question about which community members keep paper diaries (as contrasted, presumably, with livejournal's journalling blogs, which every community member keeps), and how often they do so. She distinguishes paper diaries by referring to them as "real" diaries, using the English word, and this first switch of *redegattung*'s is of course coded as category (a)—single-word switches. The example from category (c)—larger English expressions or quotes—comes in turn 01, when user *sadness_personified* initiates her comment with the English expression "Slightly off topic." Because this is a common English phrase often found in monolingual discourse in precisely the same form that it appears here, this has been coded as category (c).

A similar example can be found in Excerpt 3.6, which is a short conversation consisting only of the post and the single comment shown here. It comes from the *vragenuurtje* community.

Excerpt 3.6: "But you get the idea" (Dutch community)

00: *12days:*	Oke, ik zoek het lied van een studentenvereniging:') Waarschijnlijk uit UTRECHT, en ik weet dat een van de zinnen "al meer dan honderd jaar. . . ." is.

Larger English expressions or quotes   75

	Het werd wat zeikerig/sloom gezongen, dus echt "al meer dan – hooooonderd jaar, la la la laaaa la la" en ja eh. **Help**?:')
01: *marina_evelyn:*	geen idee ik weet ze alleen van minerva..(leiden) ff op hyves kijken? er bestaat vast wel een utrechts studenten corps hyves ofzo:') (weet niet of die vereniging zo heet, **but you get the idea**)

00: *12days:*	Okay, I'm looking for a student association's theme song:') Probably from UTRECHT, and I know that one of the lines is "for more than a hundred years. . . .". It's sung kind of whinily/lethargically, so really "for more than a – huuuuuuuundred years, la la la laaaa la la" and yeah um. **Help**?:')
01: *marina_evelyn:*	no idea I only know the one from minerva..(leiden) maybe look on hyves? [former Dutch-specific social media site, now defunct] I'm sure there's a Utrecht student group hyves or some- thing like that:') (I don't know if that association is actually called that, **but you get the idea**)

User *12days* uses her post to ask a question about the theme song of a student association from a Dutch university, but she's not sure which association it is, and is only somewhat certain of which university. The English word "help" she uses to end her post (this sort of functional use of English as an ending of a post will be discussed further in the next chapter) was of course coded as category (a)— single-word switches—but it is the use of English by respondent *marina_evelyn* that is relevant here. After suggesting a possible place *12days* might look for an answer to her question, she finishes her turn with a parenthetical comment that begins in Dutch and ends with the English "but you get the idea." Because this is a commonly used conversational English expression that *marina_evelyn* lifted in its entirety from conventional English-language interaction, this instance of English was coded as belonging to category (c): larger English expressions or quotes.

Use of English original to the user

Finally, the fourth category of entirely original phrases and sentences not borrowed from any particular English-language source corresponds to the kinds of intersentential and intrasentential code-switching types common in bilingual communities. The use of this kind of transidiomatic practice requires a great deal of both proficiency in English (Poplack 1980) and linguistic creativity. The first such example comes from a long conversation in the *unserekleinestadt* community that originally consisted of a post and a total of 102 comments. In an earlier part of the thread that this excerpt comes from, user *couleur* (who has been adding user icons depicting the female Japanese cartoon character Hello Kitty to each of his comments) has objected to the notion that user *mistermark* is looking for male livejournal friends because their perspectives are inherently different from women's. Another objection to this then came from *couleur*, after which *mistermark* suggested that *couleur* was resisting a "natural" difference between men and women. What follows can be seen in Excerpt 3.7 below.

Excerpt 3.7: "Hello Kitty overkill" (German community)

01: *couleur:*   Ich wehre mich doch nicht gegen den Unterschied sondern dagegen, ihn als qualitatives Merkmal zu benutzen. Das ist Sexismus. Und mich persönlich würds ehrlich gesagt stören irgendwo zu sein, weil ich ein Mann bin und nicht weil ich ich bin.

02: *mistermark:*   Entschuldigung, aber das finde ich ein bisschen... sonderbar. Wenn du also mit deinen besten Freundinnen einen Trinken gehst und nicht mit deinem guten Freund von nebenan, weil du gerne einen Mädelsabend veranstalten willst, dann ist das auch Sexismus?

03: *couleur:*   Ähm... ja, das wäre es. Absolut. Eine sehr witzige Vorstellung auch.

04: *mistermark:*   Oh je. Anscheinend also keine Freundin von **"Sex and the City"**.

05: *couleur:*   Sicherlich nicht.

                         Wieso ist das eigentlich so, dass man, sobald man auch nur einen Furz Rosa im **Icon** hat, für eine Frau gehalten wird?

06: *_yvette_:*   es ist nich *nur* rosa. es ist **hello-kitty-overkill! (loving it though)**

01: *couleur:*	I'm not resisting that difference, but I am resisting using it as a qualitative characteristic. That's sexism. And personally, it would bother me to be somewhere because I'm a man and not because I'm me.
02: *mistermark:*	Pardon me, but I think that's a little bit . . . weird. If you go out drinking with your best girlfriends and not with your good male friend from next door, because you'd like to organize a girls' night out, is that sexism too?
03: *couleur:*	Um . . . yes, it would be. Absolutely. A hilarious thought, too.
04: *mistermark:*	Oh dear. I guess you're not a fan [female noun] of **"Sex and the City."**
05: *couleur:*	Of course not. Why is it always that people think you're a woman as soon as you have even the slightest fart of pink in your **icon**?
06: *_yvette_:*	It's not *just* pink, it's **hello kitty overkill! (loving it though)**

In turn 01, user *couleur* clarifies his objection to the premise of *mistermark*'s original post, during which he specifies that he too is a man. This comment is also accompanied by a Hello Kitty icon. In turn 02, however, user *mistermark* overlooks the fact that *couleur* has identified himself as a man, and formulates his assumption (whether based on *couleur*'s use of Hello Kitty icons or perhaps simply because there tend to be more female users on livejournal than male ones) that *couleur* is actually a woman. In turn 03, then, *couleur* uses the same Hello Kitty icon that he used in turn 01, and in the process mocks *mistermark*'s assumption that he must be female, but he does not directly contradict that assumption. Next, in turn 04, *mistermark* formulates his assumption again by using the female form of the German noun for "friend," i.e. "Freundin." User *couleur* responds to this in turn 05 by repeating the use of the Hello Kitty icon for the third time and proposing that *mistermark* has been making assumptions about him due to his choice of user icons, which serves to underscore his characterization of *mistermark* as being bound by gender stereotypes. In turn 06, user *_yvette_* chimes in, commenting on *couleur*'s repeated icon use with the English "hello kitty overkill. (loving it though)." Because this is not an identifiable phrase originating elsewhere and commonly used in English monolingual discourse in this form, this use of English has been coded as category (d): entirely original.

78   3 The Who and the What: Amounts and Types of English

A second example of this category of English use comes from the *vragenuurtje* community. The original conversation consisted of a post and 32 comments, a portion of which appear below.

Excerpt 3.8: "Too much of a boob fest" (Dutch community)

00: *msp:*	Gaat er hier iemand heel toevallig binnenkort iets bestellen van boohoo. com?
	Ik MOET iets hebben, maar heb geen credit card:(
01: *geraldina:*	**omg** wat is de **sale CHEAP**! OK ik lees even mee met dit **topic**, want ik wil ook wel bestellen! (en heb geen cc)
02: *tesvel:*	Ik heb een creditcard en wil meebestellen! Dus geef die bestellingen maar aan mij door, dan plaats ik de order. En dan bij thuis laten bezorgen en dat jullie het hier ophalen? Is dat handig?
03: *tesvel:*	In [city name] **that is** . . .!
04: *msp:*	:D:D:D Heldin! [web address of item] **"Poppy Cut Out Heart Dress"** 20 pond:)
05: *tesvel:*	Welke maat?
	(Deze jurk vind ik ook heel mooi, maar dat wordt echt **too much of a boob fest** met mijn borsten hierin . . . :P)
06: *msp:*	**Oh right!** Maat 16!:) Ik heb niet zo veel **boobness** dus dat zal bij mij wel loslopen.

00: *msp:*	Is there anybody here who just happens to be about to order something from boohoo.com? I HAVE to have something, but don't have a credit card:(
01: *geraldina:*	**omg** how **CHEAP** is the **sale**! OK I'm going to follow this **topic**, because I want to order too! (and don't have a cc)
02: *tesvel:*	I have a credit card and want to order too! So just pass the orders on to me, then I'll place the order. And then I'll have it delivered at home and you guys can pick it up here. Is that convenient?
03: *tesvel:*	In [city name] **that is** . . .!
04: *msp:*	:D:D:D My hero! [web address of item] **"Poppy Cut Out Heart Dress"** 20 pounds:)
05: *tesvel:*	What size?
	(I think this dress is gorgeous, too, but it would really be **too much of a boob fest** with my breasts in it . . . :P)
06: *msp:*	**Oh right!** Size 16!:) I don't have that much **boobness** so it should work out for me.

In the first comment in turn 01, user *geraldina* responds by expressing, using a mixture of Dutch and English, "omg how CHEAP is the sale," and saying that she's going to follow the "topic." The "omg" (oh my God) falls into category (b), i.e. interactional language use specific to digitally mediated spaces, while "cheap," "sale," and "topic" all fall into category (a), i.e. single-word switches. Then *tesvel* responds to *msp* in turn 02, saying that she will place the order, and adding as an after-thought in turn 03 that the others can then pick them up from her place "in [city name] that is" (with the "that is" switch into English being coded as belonging to category (c), i.e. of English language use that is a larger-than-one-word expression spontaneously borrowed into the local language). User *msp* responds in turn 04 by giving the web address of the item she wants, and *tesvel* then asks her what size she wants. To this question, *tesvel* tacks on the parenthetical comment in turn 05 that she loves the dress too, but that it would be "too much of a boob fest" on her. This switch into English is coded as category (d), i.e. original English use not borrowed from any particular other source. User *msp* then responds in turn 06 with an "oh right" (category (c)) and gives her size. In terms of coding, the "boobness" in the following sentence (signifying the size of her bosom in the specification that the dress in question should work for her) deserves further consideration. It is, of course, a single word, but instead of being a word common to English use, it is one created spontaneously by *msp* herself by using the rules of English noun suffixing. Therefore, it was coded as category (d), i.e. as original to *msp*.

Quantitative analysis

Already from the excerpts above—and particularly from the contrast between the last two—it is apparent that there are important differences between the two communities. While at least some examples of all four of the types of English use can be found in both communities, the excerpts presented here seem to suggest that there might be more English use in most of the categories in *vragenuurtje* than in *unserekleinestadt*. Excerpt 3.7, from the German community *unserekleinestadt*, comes from a long and involved conversation with many participants, only one of whom uses a notable amount of English (apart from the two turns that include the English-language name of an American television show and the livejournal-specific term "icon"). Excerpt 3.8, on the other hand, from the Dutch community *vragenuurtje*—which also comes from a longer and involved conversation with many participants—contains a great deal more switches back and forth between English and Dutch, including all four identified types of English use and casual, interactional use of English from three separate participants. If this contrast is indicative of the broader data set, then there are widespread differences between the two communities that are worthy of further investigation and analysis.

It is impossible to come to this conclusion simply based on this one pair of examples, however. For that matter, even if I were to present a large number of additional contrasting examples, it is important to be cautious about making any broad, generalized statements about the *amount* of English use in the two communities based on a qualitative analysis alone. A supplemental *quantitative* analysis is therefore required in order to give these impressionistic conclusions weight—one that looks first at the overall amount of English in each community, and second at the amount of English falling into each of the four identified categories. This is helpful because a difference in the overall amount of English would suggest a difference in the degree to which casual, interactional English use has become commonplace in the two communities, while more English in one community of the types requiring more knowledge of and creativity with English would suggest a greater degree of comfort with the idea of making English a part of the interactional repertoire in that community. Finally, it seems that it would also be useful to understand how many of these occurrences of English in the data are flagged (which would mark an instance of language alternation as unusual in some way), since consistent flagging could be indicative of a lower degree of comfort with language alternation in general.

To get a clearer picture of the overall use of English in the two communities, I counted the total number of words for each data set and compared it to a count of the number of *English* words for each data set. As we can see in Figure 3.1, the German data set contains a total of

Quantitative analysis 81

Fig. 3.1 Percentages of English use in the two communities

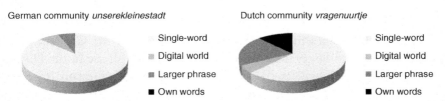

Fig. 3.2 Percentages of use of the four identified categories of switching

459,782 words, of which 5051 (1.1%) are coded as English. The Dutch data set, on the other hand, contains a total of 495,208 words, of which 183,829 (37.1%) are coded as English.

The difference is striking: the Dutch young people not only use more English in their online interactions than their German counterparts, they use *massively* more of it. I also calculated a second statistic for the relative frequency of individual *instances of English use* in the two communities (this time disregarding the number of words and looking only at the number of instances in which English was used), and in this alternate calculation *vragenuurtje* also came out on top, with 2617 instances of English use in the German community and 4242 in the Dutch community.

In order to look at potential differences between the two communities in terms of the different *kinds* of switching, I further calculated for each community the amount of English use falling into the four identified categories. As we can see in Figure 3.2, there were 2277 (87.01%) single-word switches in the German community *unserekleinestadt* (category (a)), 186 (7.11%) instances of interactional use of English specific to the digitally mediated world (category (b)),

82   3   The Who and the What: Amounts and Types of English

152 (5.81%) switches involving longer English-language phrases or quotes (category (c)), and 2 (just over 0%) switches involving longer stretches of English that are entirely original to the interactant (category (d)). The Dutch community *vragenuurtje*, on the other hand, contains 2643 (62.3%) single-word switches, 222 instances of interactional use of English specific to the digitally mediated world, 855 switches involving longer English-language phrases or quotes, and 522 switches involving longer stretches of English that are entirely original to the interactant.

Interestingly, this means that there are only a few hundred more single-word switches in the Dutch community than the German one, despite the much larger number of instances of English use in the Dutch community. One look at the percentages explains the reason for this: single-word switches are a much larger percentage of the total occurrences of English use in the German community than in the Dutch community. Both the number and percentage of all other types of English use are higher in the Dutch community, and the fourth category, which requires the most knowledge of and creativity with English, is rarely found at all in the German community, with only two instances in total (one of which can be seen in Excerpt 3.7 above).

As briefly mentioned earlier, it is also relevant to note any differences between the practice of "flagging" switches to English as unusual in some way, as this could be indicative of a lower degree of comfort with transidiomatic practices in general. In spoken conversation, for example, the flagging of an instance of language alternation often consists of conversational elements that are unique to spoken language, such as false starts, hesitations, or lengthy pauses (Poplack 1988). In written conversations such as the ones that can be found in *unserekleinestadt* and *vragenuurtje*, however, flagging takes somewhat different forms. Two examples of written-language flagging can be seen in Excerpt 3.2 above: in the post in turn 00, user *weltall* marks her first switch to English by talking about "so-called outdoor shoes" (using "so-called" as a sort of metalinguistic comment to flag the switch), and one of her later switches by putting single quotes around the "light" in "'light' hiking" (using the quotes to serve a similar purpose). In the comment in turn 01, *captain_lisa* also marks her switch to English by putting double

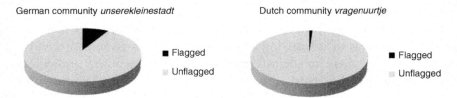

Fig. 3.3 Percentages of flagged vs. unflagged switches in the two communities

quotes around her own "Boots." Other possible ways of flagging a switch found in the data include the use of *italics*.

To ascertain the relative amounts of flagging in the two communities, each coded switch was further tagged as being either flagged or unflagged, and the percentages of each were computed for each community. The results can be seen in Figure 3.3 below.

As we can see, the flagging of instances of language alternation is relatively unusual in both communities, indicating a reasonable degree of comfort with transidiomatic practices in general. There are only 220 instances of it in the German community (8.39%) and 44 instances of it in the Dutch community (1.04%). However, despite its rarity, it is still interesting that a much greater percentage of flagged switches can be found in the German community. In fact, despite the greater overall number of switches in the Dutch community, there is even a larger number of flagged switches in the German community in terms of raw numbers. This difference is especially relevant given the much higher percentage of greater than single-word switches in the Dutch community, which one might expect to be more likely to be considered exceptional (and therefore worthy of flagging) due to an often greater length and complexity.

Transidiomatic practices in username choice

An additional indication of community members' degree of comfort with transidiomatic practices can be gleaned from the use of different languages in their livejournal usernames. When looking at this issue, it is

84   3 The Who and the What: Amounts and Types of English

important to remember that in the livejournal setting these usernames are not chosen simply for use in any particular communities. While they do play the role of identifying a particular user in a given community, users also use them to identify each community member's individual journalling blog, to participate in any other livejournal communities they frequent (most of which are statistically likely to be Anglophone-dominant and English-only), to make comments in discussions on other people's journals, to send private messages, and so on. Community members are therefore aware that the usernames they choose need to fit into that wider livejournal context, not just into specific norms they are familiar with from the communities of *unserekleinestadt* and *vragen-uurtje*. I would argue, however, that this only makes usernames more interesting as a potential way of gauging comfort with transidiomatic practices. Given that members of both communities experience similar combinations of local and transnational pressures (such as the presence of networks of other users consisting of both other German and Dutch nationals and people from other places, in additional to any more general norms for username creation on livejournal), any differences between the two communities in terms of the amount of English used in usernames seems to point to a difference between how German and Dutch livejournal users react to that same combination of pressures in making decisions about how to present themselves through their usernames.

In any case, usernames are certainly an essential part of the creation and maintenance of any livejournal presence. They are always completely lowercase, and always one word (which means that multiple words in a phrase used as a username need to either be run together or separated by dashes or underscores). Each username is also unique, which means that if someone has already created an account using the word or word you most want, you need to either choose a different username or modify your chosen username with extra characters like underscores (leading to usernames with this format: *_username_)* or sometimes single or multiple iterations of the character "x" (leading to usernames with this format: *xxusernamexx*). Like the icons that accompany users' posts and comments, usernames are displayed every time one makes a post or a comment, either in one's own journal or in a community. However, unlike

Transidiomatic practices in username choice

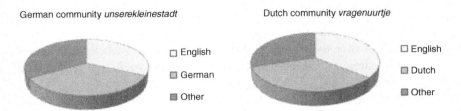

Fig. 3.4 Percentages of different languages in usernames

icons, which each user can have many of, there is only one username per account. Users do of course vary with respect to how much thought goes into choosing their usernames, and it is always possible to change one's username later (for a small fee). At the very least, however, all livejournal users are confronted with the question of which username they want to choose at the point of signup, which entails at least a couple of moments of thinking about how they want that username to represent them.

This brings us to the question of which languages the members of *unserekleinestadt* and *vragenuurtje* tend to use in their usernames, given the transnational backdrop of the livejournal social media setting. A total of 336 unique users were found in the *unserekleinestadt* data set, while a total of 432 unique users were found in the *vragenuurtje* data set. The overall patterns for the use of English, the local language, or the catch-all category "other" (including other known languages as well as gibberish, strings of numbers, or unidentifiable languages) in the two communities can be seen in Figure 3.4 below.

Username choice was divided across the "English," local language, and "Other" categories fairly consistently for both communities, though there were still small differences. In the German community *unserekleinestadt*, the largest category consisted of those users who chose German-language usernames, with a total of 116 users. A few example usernames from this category that I have permission to refer to are *gerdimaus* (presumably a nickname consisting of the common girls' name "Gerda" and the German word *Maus*, or "mouse"), *tinchen* (a shortened version of the common girls' name "Christina," plus the German diminutive suffix *-chen*), and *holunder* (a German word referring to the elderflower/elderberry plant). The "Other" category was not far behind, though, with a total of 112 users. Example usernames from this category include *isa_guiny* and *_jolinor_*. Finally, the English category is the smallest, though still very close to the other two, with a total of 108 users. Example usernames from this category include *killanangel, misery_chick, try_to_fly,* and *xtra_ordinary*.

In the Dutch community *vragenuurtje,* the largest of the three categories consisted of those who chose English usernames, with a total of 156 users. Example usernames from this category are *falsesmile, dustgalaxy, carpoolaccident, _intrinsic, bangkokimpact,* and *cereous* (an English word meaning "waxlike," but given that it's pronounced the same as 'serious', it seems likely to be an intentional play on words). Not at all far behind, however, was the group of users who chose Dutch-language usernames, with a total of 147 users. Example usernames from this category are *aspirientje* (a Dutch word meaning "aspirin tablet"), *liefsvanmij* (a Dutch phrase meaning "with love from me"), *momentopname* (a Dutch word meaning "snapshot" or "moment in time"), and *oktobergoud* (a Dutch word meaning "October gold"). Finally, the "Other" category trailed for the Dutch community, with a total of 129 users. Example usernames from this category are *drynwyn, luna_puella, martyne_,* and *72639.* These differences suggest that the German users of *unserekleinestadt* have a slightly greater tendency to choose German usernames and the Dutch users of *vragenuurtje* have a slightly greater tendency to choose English usernames, though it should be noted that it is not particularly marked in either community to choose usernames with English, local-language, or some other language in them. The small differences between the two communities were not found to be statistically significant.

Summary of trends

The overall trends in the analysis thus far point to both a great deal more English in the Dutch community *vragenuurtje* in general than in the German community *unserekleinestadt,* and a great deal more of the kinds of English that require more knowledge and creativity in the former. This suggests that there is a difference between the two communities both in terms of the extent to which transidiomatic practices have become a common part of these users' normal social media discourse, and the extent to which users are comfortable with this. Furthermore, the greater tendency in the German community to flag their switches to English as being somehow unusual is also an indication of less comfort with transidiomatic practices, and the slightly lower tendency in the German community to choose English-language usernames might also be seen as indicative of this.

What, then, can these differences tell us about the overall role that different language regimes and different language ideological traditions have played in influencing the role of English in everyday language practice? Not much that can be seen as conclusive—at least not yet. The analysis in this chapter tells us both that German users use less English than their Dutch counterparts and that they do so with less ease than their Dutch counterparts do; what it does not tell us, however, is why this is the case and what this implies about their language ideologies. A more complete understanding of the picture will therefore require going further than just the types of switching that occur in the data and the amount of English used in each community, to an investigation of the interactional functions of transidiomatic practices (whether they serve conversation-structuring purposes, or identity-related ones, or perhaps a combination of the two, for example) and of the attitudes toward transidiomatic practices that can be found among members of both communities.

An examination of the types and amounts of English as employed by users of *unserekleinestadt* and *vragenuurtje* therefore raises more questions than it answers. It is clear that the Dutch community is generally more comfortable mixing English with their Dutch than the German community is with mixing English with their German; what is not yet clear is why this is the case. Is it a simple matter of the greater proficiency among the Dutch than among the Germans that Berns et al. (2007: 111–19) discuss, or are there perhaps separate language ideologies at play as well, resulting from the rather different language regimes in Germany and the Netherlands as discussed in Chapter 2? This question and the issues that arise from it will be addressed in the two chapters that follow. For example, though the more creative of these four categories of English use could be seen as instances of

88   3 The Who and the What: Amounts and Types of English

crossing (Rampton 2005), i.e. the "use of a linguistic feature or variety that is usually associated with a social group that the speaker doesn't obviously or 'naturally' belong to," whether or not it can be regarded as a clear-cut example of this depends on whether they are styling a particular Other social group, or viewing English as a culturally neutral language that they can use—in a thoroughly glocalized, semiotically rearranged way (cf. Blommaert 2010: 18)—to style their own local cultural identities. The larger question I will therefore attempt to answer in the next two chapters is this: if English is indeed seen as "a necessary professional qualification which has to be learned like other formal qualifications" by German youth, and as "one means to express themselves and their cultural orientation" by Dutch youth, as Hasebrink et al. (2007: 115) hypothesize, how are these differences reflected in these two online communities' language use, and what can this tell us about the differential reach of global English in different European countries?

4

The How: Interactional Functions of English

The previous chapter dealt with the most rudimentary questions dealing with the comparison of the German community and the Dutch one: those having to do with the *types* of English and the *amounts* of English used by each community. Through this analysis, it became clear that the Dutch community is generally more comfortable mixing English with their Dutch than the German community is with mixing English with their German, but it was impossible to determine why this is the case simply through an analysis of the types and amounts of English used. In this chapter I will therefore approach the same data from a different angle, and in the process analyze the interactional functions of transidiomatic practices in light of the foundational ideas regarding language ideologies and language policy, language use in social media, and multilingual language use in interaction discussed in Chapter 2. In other words, the main questions here are as follows: how is the act of switching to English commonly used either to structure the interaction or to construct identities; are there differences between the two communities in terms of these functions; and if

© The Author(s) 2017
J. Dailey-O'Cain, *Trans-National English in Social Media Communities*, Language and Globalization,
DOI 10.1057/978-1-137-50615-3_4

90   4 The How: Interactional Functions of English

there *are* differences, then what can they tell us about the overall role of different language ideologies and different official state policies in influencing the role of English in everyday language practice? In answering these questions, I will first discuss the most common discourse-related functions of language alternation in the form of a series of analyses of representative excerpts, and then move on to do the same with the most common participant-related functions. At the end of the chapter, I will summarize the trends in the data and discuss how this analysis brings us one step closer to understanding the book's broader concerns.

In Chapter 2 I briefly discussed the public discourses regarding the influence from English on the local languages of both Germany and the Netherlands. I outlined the fact that in Germany, that public discourse has been overwhelmingly characterized by purism (Spitzmüller 2005, Barbour 2005, Onysko 2009, Dodd 2015), and has been particularly concerned with the effects of individual lexical items or *anglicisms*. In the Netherlands, on the other hand, while the effect of particular lexical items has indeed been a small part of the public discourse about this topic (Edwards 2014: 203–4), there the main focus has been about the increasing use of English in previously Dutch-only domains such as higher education and business (de Bot 1994: 11–12, de Swaan 2000, Van Hoorde 2013: 15). In fact—again as discussed in Chapter 2 —in the Netherlands, there is considerable ambivalence about whether this changing situation should be resisted or simply accepted.

Further evidence of these differences between the two countries' public discourses can also be found in online discussions. Such online discussions are of course simply one small part of the public discourse in question, but they are a particularly interesting part of it for a book such as this one, due to the fact that they promote a back-and-forth exchange between people that is more interactive and more informal than journalistic pieces about the subject. As a result, people will often use these online discussions to talk about not just the *existence* of influence from English, but to try and sort through possible *reasons why* mixing English-origin words and phrases with the local languages has become increasingly common. Both gutefrage.net, based in Germany, and goeievraag.nl, based in the Netherlands, are popular websites for asking

The How: Interactional Functions of English 91

questions and receiving answers from fellow citizens, and both sites do in fact contain threads initiated by questions that amount to "why are people using so many English words lately?"[1]

Given what we already know about the different stances that tend to be taken on this topic in Germany and the Netherlands, it is perhaps unsurprising that the responses to this question in the German thread are much more overtly critical of the use of English: explanations come up a number of times along the lines of people wanting to create the impression that the contributor is highly educated or trying to sound more important than they are, with several commenters make angry-sounding comments about these practices in general in between the attempts to explain them, and with more neutral explanations—such as the idea that this is a matter of normal language change or the notion that an English form is often shorter than a German one—being met with skepticism. By contrast, the analogous Dutch thread is much less emotional, the notion that certain English phrases simply "sound better" meets with no argument or critical engagement, and even the few more overtly critical comments (such as the notion that the Dutch don't have sufficient imagination to speak their own language or the idea that they're just blindly following Americans' lead) assume an air of fatalism rather than one of outrage.

What is perhaps most interesting of all, however, are not the differences between these two threads, but what they have in common. Despite these overall differences in tone, the most common explanation offered is more or less identical in both threads: the idea that the main reason why people incorporate English words and phrases into their local-language interactions has to do with wanting to seem "worldly," "trendy," and/or "cool." Such a characterization comes up again and again, and in neither thread is it ever met with any argument. Indeed, this particular explanation for the use of English is typical of the wider

---

[1]. On the German gutefrage.net site, the thread I refer to was found at http://www.gutefrage.net/frage/warum-benutzt-man-heutzutage-so-viele-anglizismen. On the Dutch goeievraag.nl site, the equivalent thread was found at

   http://www.goeievraag.nl/wetenschap/taal/vraag/63557/engelse-woorden-gebruikt-goede-nederlandse. Both threads were retrieved on June 29, 2016.

public discourse on this topic in both countries, despite ideological differences between the two about whether or not such practices are to be tolerated. This kind of widespread agreement should make us sit up and take notice, since at the very least it is an indication of an explanation that is widely accepted in both societies. However, we should be hesitant about taking these kinds of arguments at face value without delving deeper, i.e. without any sort of empirical analysis.

In an attempt to offer up such an analysis, this chapter will examine the interactional functions of transidiomatic practices within this book's two social media communities. As already discussed in Chapters 1 and 2, the conversation analysis-based approach to the analysis of language alternation that was proposed by Auer (1998) has demonstrated that it can be fruitful to divide such switches into two functional categories: those that are used for *discourse-related* purposes that serve to structure conversation, and those that are used as a *participant-related* tool that results from the preferences of one or more of the conversation participants. This is a distinction that can help us better understand what is going on with the transidiomatic practices in these two social media communities: analyzing discourse-related switching can reveal whether the language alternation in these social media communities structures conversation similarly or differently to the ways it does so in face-to-face bilingual communities, while analyzing participant-related language alternation can point us toward the way that switching from one language to another can serve as a tool in positioning. Both of these types of language alternation, but especially the latter of the two, can further tell us more about the relationship between the transidiomatic practices of the two communities and the wider societies in which these communities exist.

The categories identified below emerged within an initial NVivo-guided qualitative analysis, in which I first identified all instances of language alternation in both data sets and then drew conclusions about the recurring patterns in those instances. Whenever possible, I identified the main function of each switch, and then sorted them into categories based first on whether they could be described as cases of discourse-related or participant-related language alternation, and secondarily on subcategories consisting of more precise and specific functions within those main groupings. Guided by this set of secondary categories, I then chose excerpts that best represented the patterns in the wider datasets for a more detailed analysis. The qualitative analysis presented in this chapter is therefore not intended to provide an exhaustive list of all of the functions of English in my data—in fact, it is arguably impossible to do so because there is a seemingly never-ending set of functions that contextualization cues can perform, and in practice they are often multifunctional—but to provide more insight into the set of functions that appear in the data most often, and which are therefore potentially most useful and most salient to the members of the two communities.

Discourse-Related Language Alternation

As I discussed in Chapter 2, the alternation between one language and another is always analyzed within Auer's framework as one of two types of contextualization cue that provide participants with information about how to interpret aspects of the conversation. This means that when a switch from one language to another is a *discourse-related* cue, the contrast between one language and another serves to help organize a discourse by marking a particular stretch of interaction as different from another in some way, such as by summing up the end of a narrative (e.g. Alfonzetti 1998: 194–5), aiding in the regulation of conversational turn-taking (e.g. Auer 1995: 120), or attracting attention (e.g. Li 1998: 160–1). It is possible for these discourse-related functions to index bilingual norms within the wider world, such as when bilingual German-Italian children switch into German as "the in-group of language of peer interaction" from Italian as "the out-group language of their parents" in Auer's (1998: 5) work, but this is not always the case. For example, Alfonzetti (1998: 207) found in one case that the same conversational function could be carried out by switching in either direction, which indicates that the discourse-structuring functionality of the switch depended not on any particular social meaning of either code, but on the juxtaposition between them. This implies that any analysis of

94   4 The How: Interactional Functions of English

discourse-related language alternation needs to consider the existence of possible implications of the wider societal context and existing language norms, but that it should not be surprising not to find them upon looking for them, and it also suggests that the difference between when these do and do not exist might in and of itself tell us something about the particular societies in question. Either way, however, if similar kinds of discourse-related functions can be shown to appear in the social media communities of *vragenuurtje* and *unserekleinestadt* as are typically found in long-standing bilingual communities, this tells us two things. For one, it will tell us that it is too simplistic to explain away all English-origin material in people's interactions as attempts to come across as "worldly," "trendy," or "cool." For another, it will tell us that the kinds of discourse-structuring transidiomatic practices that are common in face-to-face bilingual communities like the Spanish-speaking community in New York City or German-Italian bilinguals in Germany are just as ever-present in the social media interaction of young Dutch and German people when interacting with their own fellow citizens.

Switching to English to Mark an Off-topic Aside

One type of discourse-related switch commonly found in spoken conversation is the use of a switch from one code to another to set an off-topic conversational aside apart from the rest of the interaction (e.g. Zentella 1997: 94). An example of this sort of switch in one of the communities discussed in this book has already been mentioned in the previous chapter: in Excerpt 3.5, from the *unserekleinestadt* community, user *redegattung* made a mostly German post inquiring how common it was for community members to keep diaries, and user *sadness_personified* initiated the response in her comment by writing "slightly off-topic:" in English before switching back to German for the actual content of her comment. It might be tempting to explain this by suggesting that an English expression was only used here because there is no adequate German equivalent, but this is not in fact the case: a quick Google

Switching to English to Mark an Off-topic Aside   95

search suggests that phrasings such as "um mal ein bisschen vom Thema abzulenken:" ("to go off-topic for a bit:") or "mal ein bisschen vom Thema weg:" ("just a bit off-topic:") are not at all uncommon in German online conversations. Instead, the use of English as a contextualization cue to set the marker as separate from the rest of the comment serves to strengthen the transition-marking function that is already contained in the semantic content of the phrase "slightly off-topic." In a community where everyone can be presumed to be able to understand not just German, but also English, it is not at all unusual for language alternation to take on this sort of additional conversation-structuring function.

Further examples along similar lines can be seen in the two excerpts below, both taken from the Dutch community *vragenuurtje*. The first of these, Excerpt 4.1, comes from a larger conversation consisting of a post and 69 comments about the transportation impacts—or lack thereof—of an overnight snowfall.

Excerpt 4.1 "Offtopic" (Dutch community)

00:*liefsvanmij*:   Wie kan ook niet naar werk/school/studie door de sneeuw?
In [province name] rijden geen bussen meer, dus ik heb lekker een extra dagje vrij.;)

01: *ohnonotme*:   HIHIHI IK KON OVERAL MAKKELIJK TUSSEN DOOR FIETSEN:D

02: *roosje_mij*:   Handig, zo'n fiets:D
Alleen vanavond ik moet naar school in [city name].. Over binnendoor wegen. Dus ik weet nog niet wat ik ga doen, k kijk het even aan. (aangezien ik geen eigen auto heb, en liever niet de auto vd zaak in de prak rijd....)

03: *arbre*:   ***offtopic***
je gaat naar school **in my hometown**:P (ja heel boeiend haha).

00: *liefsvanmij*:   Who else can't go to work/school/university because of the snow?
In [province name] all bus service is cancelled, so I'm enjoying an extra day off.;)

01: *ohnonotme*:   HEEHEEHEE I COULD EASILY RIDE MY BIKE THROUGH EVERYTHING:D

02: *roosje_mij*:   A bike sure is useful for that:D

96   **4 The How: Interactional Functions of English**

> The only problem is tonight I have to get to school in [city name].. On backstreets. So I don't know yet what I'm going to do, I guess I'll see. (considering that I don't have my own car, and I'd rather not smash up the company car...)
>
> 03: *arbre:*   ***offtopic***
> you're going to school **in my hometown**:P (yeah really exciting haha).

Both the initial post in turn 00 and each of the first two comments in turns 01 and turns 02 are all in Dutch. It is only in turn 03, where the first off-topic comment is made, that English is used. In initiating this turn, user *arbre* sets her comment off from the rest of the conversation with a set of contextualization cues that go hand in hand with the semantic content of the word "offtopic": asterisks, a switch to English, and a carriage return that resulted in the remainder of her comment being on a separate line. It is in fact common for contextualization cues to bundle together in this way, with multiple cues serving the same function (Auer 1995: 194), in this case the function of marking the observation that *roosje_mij* is going to school in *arbre*'s hometown as a conversational aside that does not have to do with the main topic of the recent snowfall and its effects on community members' transportation needs.

Excerpt 4.2 below, which also contains the use of English to mark a conversational aside, comes from a larger conversation consisting of a post and seven comments. The post by user *onderduiker* in turn 00 is about possible places to celebrate New Year's Eve and the cost.

Excerpt 4.2 "I love your sheldon icon" (Dutch community)

00: *onderduiker:*   Met oud & niew organiseren [name of music club] & [name of outdoor location] in [city name] samen een oud & niew iets. Feestje in [name of music club] kost 25 eurie, een **combi-ticket** (zodat je naar beide feesten kan en een guitig armbandje krijgt om wachtrijen te omzeilen) kost 40 eurie. Er staat dat deze er maar beperkt zijn. Maar het is me niet duidelijk of ik met 't kaartje van 25 eurie ook naar beide feesten mag, zonder dat guitige armbandje, zegmaar? ik heb er

Switching to English to Mark an Off-topic Aside   97

	namelijk echt geen behoefte aan 40 eurie neer te tellen voor iets waarvan ik niet eens weet of 't wel leuk is. Oh, en wie gaat het nog meer in 't [name of music club]/[name of outdoor location] vieren?
01: *lisa:*	Volgens mij mag je dan niet naar beide feesten. Dus [name of music club] is 25 euro, en [name of music club]+[initials for outdoor location]=40 euro. Als je alleen 25 euro betaald mag je dus ook alleen in [name of music club] blijven. Ik weet niet precies hoe ze dat gaan doen, de gm afsluiten, maar ik heb iets gehoord over een tent ofzo.. Ik ga het daar niet vieren omdat ik geen zin heb om 25 neer te tellen voor iets waarvan ik niet weet of ik het wel leuk vind.:) Ik heb er wel veel mensen over gehoord, maar die wisten het ook niet zeker vanwege die 25 euro.
02: *lisa:*	PS **i love your sheldon icon** <3
00: *onderduiker:*	For New Year's, [name of music club] & [name of outdoor location] in [city name] are organizing a New Year's something or other together. The party in [name of music club] costs 25 euros, a combination ticket (so you can go to both parties and so you can get an awesome little wristband in order to avoid the lineups) costs 40 euros. They say that there's only a few of those. But it's not clear to me if I can go to both parties with the 25-euro ticket, without the awesome little wristband, you know? i really don't feel like forking out 40 euros for something if I don't even know if it's fun. Oh, and who else is going to celebrate in [name of music club]/[name of central outdoor location]?
01: *lisa:*	I don't think you can then go to both parties. So [name of music club] is 25 euros, and [name of music club]+[initials for outdoor location] =40 euros. If you only pay 25 euros, you can only stay in [name of music club]. I don't know how exactly they're going to do that, fencing it off, but I heard something about a tent or something like that.. I'm not going to be celebrating there because I don't feel like forking out 25 euros for something if I don't even know if it's going to be fun.:) Of course, I've heard a lot of people talking about it, but they weren't sure either because of the 25 euros.
02: *lisa:*	PS **i love your sheldon icon** <3

Both the original post (turn 00), and the first comment (turn 01), are completely in Dutch. However, as an addendum to her on-topic comment in turn 01, user *lisa* adds a second comment in turn 02, completely in

98   **4 The How: Interactional Functions of English**

English, about her feelings about *onderduiker's* user icon containing the character Sheldon from the American television show *The Big Bang Theory*. As in the two excerpts already discussed, this switch has the effect of marking the comment in turn 02 as an aside that is not directly relevant to the flow of the conversation—a function that is further reinforced by *lisa* using not only a carriage return, as in Excerpt 4.1, but an actual completely new comment, to set it off from her on-topic comment in turn 01. However, it also differs from those in the previous two excerpts discussed above because it is not only the actual marker of the aside (in this case the term "PS," short for "postscript"—an English-origin term that has been incorporated into Dutch letter-writing for so long that it could easily be used by Dutch monolinguals without any difficulty) that is in English, but also the content of the aside itself ("I love your sheldon icon"). There is insufficient context to do anything but speculate about what might account for this additional use of English, though it seems quite possible that *lisa* is using English to index the wider (often English-language) livejournal world beyond the *vragenuurtje* community where it is more common to discuss American television shows than it is to discuss Dutch places to celebrate New Year's Eve. Regardless of the specific explanation for this particular example, however, it is interesting to observe that both approaches to marking an aside are common: approaches where only the marker of the aside is in English (as in Excerpts 3.5 and 4.1) and approaches where the entire turn is in English following the use of the English marker (as in Excerpt 4.2).

Switching to English to Mark a Transition

A related but somewhat different function—that of using English to mark a conversational transition—can be seen in the three excerpts in this next section, all taken from the Dutch community *vragenuurtje*. In the first of these, Excerpt 4.3 (which comes from a larger conversation of this post and seven comments), user *flowergirl* makes a post that is nearly all in Dutch except for two uses of the English word "anyhow."

Switching to English to Mark a Transition   99

Excerpt 4.3 "Anyhow" (Dutch community)

00: *flowergirl*: Ik snap de NS echt niet hoor, een paar sneeuwvlokken en niks doet het meer blijkbaar?!
Anyhow ik dacht even leuk mijn broertje op te zoeken in [city 1] terwijl ik morgenochtend vroeg in [city 2] moet werken en NU hoor ik dat er een aangepaste dienstregeling is.
Wat blijkbaar inhoud dat ik vast zit in [city 1] tot het zomer wordt?!:D Wat een grap.
Anyhow, ik krijg de pagina met aangepaste dienstregelingen niet geopend vanwege een storing (ironisch)
Ik wil graag weten of ik morgen wel weg kan, aangezien ik het vanavond blijkbaar kan vergeten.
Krijgen jullie hem wel geopend of ook een **error**?
Op de **homepage** van www.ns.nl–> aangepaste dienstregelingen –> vertrektijden vanaf uw station (als je hem wel geopend krijgt kan je dan even [station name] invullen en kijken hoe laat de eerste paar treinen gaan morgen ochtend? of niet gaan..)

00: *flowergirl*: I don't understand the national train service, a few snowflakes and nothing works anymore apparently?! **Anyhow** I thought I'd go and look my brother up in [City 1] while I have to work tomorrow morning in [City 2] and NOW I hear that they've cancelled a bunch of trains. Which apparently implies that I'm stuck in [City 1] until the summer?!: D What a joke.
Anyhow, I can't open the page that tells me which trains are cancelled because there's a problem (ironic)
I'd like to know if I actually can leave tomorrow, because apparently I'm not going to have any luck tonight.
Can you guys manage to get it open, or do you get an **error** too?
On the **homepage** of www.ns.nl –> cancelled trains –> departure times from your station (if you do get it to open can you maybe put in [station name] and look what time the first couple of trains are leaving tomorrow morning? or aren't leaving..)

Making this post seems to serve two simultaneous purposes for *flowergirl*, and understanding her two uses of "anyhow" requires an understanding of how she has organized her post as an interplay between these two purposes. The first purpose is to vent her frustration at the fact

100 4 The How: Interactional Functions of English

that the snowfall-induced cancelled trains mean that she is stuck overnight in City 1 when she has to work in City 2 the following morning, and the second purpose is to find out whether any other community members have more information than she has about which specific trains have been cancelled. The initial sentence of the post—"I don't understand the national train service, a few snowflakes and nothing works anymore apparently?!"—fits squarely within her first purpose of complaining, but by the second sentence she is ready to transition from that to explaining the background for her question. This transition is initiated by the first "anyhow." This background is followed by two more sentences aimed primarily at venting frustration, and then ultimately by another transition to explaining why she needs other community members' help, which is initiated by the second "anyhow." In both cases, the English adverb "anyhow" serves to transition from more generic complaining to the more specific purpose of giving background necessary for understanding her ultimate question ("I'd like to know if I can actually leave tomorrow") toward the end. As with the "slightly off-topic" example discussed earlier, there are certainly numerous Dutch adverbs that could have provided similar semantic content to "anyhow," but the use of the English word serves to further strengthen the transitional function already suggested by its semantic content.

Excerpt 4.4, which comes from a conversation consisting of a post plus nine comments, also contains an example of the transitional nature of an adverb being strengthened through the contextualization cue provided by a switch to English. In it, user *lookingback* is asking about how to get Dutch subtitles for a film that she is watching on her computer.

Excerpt 4.4 "Anyhoe" (Dutch community)

00: *lookingback*:   Hoe kan je ondertiteling in een film krijgen? is daar een speciaal programmaatje voor?

01: *guido*:   in **VLC** zit dat automatisch. &ondertiteling kan je downloaden, enige punt is dat je wel de goede ondertiteling bij de juiste versie van de film moet hebben, anders loopt je ondertiteling achter of voor. andere programma's dan **VLC** weet ik niet of ze 't automatisch doen, **Media Player** iig niet.

Switching to English to Mark a Transition   101

02: *lookingback*:	ik klink misschien als een dikke **noob** nu maar...**VLC**? wasda:P
03: *guido*:	GHA, **NOOB**! lala ik ben flauw.
	anyhoe, **vlc** is een programma waarmee je films afspeelt (www.video lan.org).
	en www.nlondertitels.com is wel een goede **site** om ondertitels te downloaden **btw**.
04: *lookingback*:	**thnx mate**:P

00: *lookingback*:	How can I get subtitles in a film? is there a special program for that?
01: *guido*:	it's an automatic part of **VLC**. &you can download subtitles, the only issue is you do need the right subtitles to go with the right version of the film, otherwise your subtitles will be behind or ahead. other programs than **VLC** I don't know if they do it automatically, in any case **Media Player** doesn't.
02: *lookingback*:	maybe I sound like a big fat **noob** now but...**VLC**?whatis?:P
03: *guido*:	ha ha, **NOOB**! lala I'm lame.
	anyhow, **vlc** is a program you can play films on [url to download program].
	and www.nlondertitels.com is a good **site** where you can download subtitles **btw**.
04: *lookingback*:	**thnx mate**:P

At first glance, this excerpt appears somewhat more complicated than 4.3, due to the presence of a number of switches other than the one marking the transition. However, the function of the English-Dutch hybrid word "anyhoe" in turn 03 of this excerpt is essentially identical to that of the two uses of "anyhow" in Excerpt 4.3. User *guido* creates the adverb "anyhoe" (consisting of the English word "any" and the Dutch word "hoe," which translates as "how") to mark the transition from his amusement over *lookingback*'s use of the word "noob" (short for "newbie," or someone who is new at something) to actually answering her questions about what VLC is and about where she can find subtitles for her non-Dutch-language film. What is in fact different here is the conglomerate word consisting of elements from both languages, but just as in Excerpt 4.3, the transition in question uses a switch to English to contextualize a move from a less informational mode to a more informational one.

102   **4 The How: Interactional Functions of English**

Excerpt 4.5 is a short exchange on the weekly "vraagvrije vrijdag" (question-free Friday) post that is made in the *vragenuurtje* community every Friday. These posts—which specifically stand in contrast to the *vragenuurtje* community's stated rule of only permitting posts in which a question is asked—are made each week in order to specifically give users a space in which they can make comments they want about anything at all without having to turn what they want to say into a question. As such, the resulting post and its comments cannot be regarded as a single conversation, but as a series of smaller conversations that are occurring simultaneously. The practice of making these posts in the *vragenuurtje* community can be traced back to the weekly "Free for All Friday" (or "FFAF") posts in the popular English-language celebrity gossip-related livejournal community Oh No They Didn't (ontd.livejournal.com, or ONTD), which create a recurring weekly space for members of that community to post off-topic comments. Likely as a result of the weekly post's ONTD origins, the "vraagvrije vrijdag" conversations in the *vragenuurtje* community are often characterized by a much higher level of performed enthusiasm and other kinds of strong affect than are normally found elsewhere in that community. This sort of atmosphere is encouraged by the initial post, which is itself always very over-the-top enthusiastic in affect (see Excerpts 4.16 and 4.17 below for more detail about this). Excerpt 4.5 is one conversational offshoot within the context provided by one weekly "vraagvrije vrijdag" post, in this case one consisting of a post and 173 comments. In this excerpt, user *geraldina* has responded to the initial post (which, using language common to all of the "vraagvrije vrijdag" posts, has encouraged users to post whatever they felt like posting), with the following conversation-initiating comment.

Excerpt 4.5 "But in good news" (Dutch community)

01:    *geraldina*: IS HET AL 2010 **OMG**. Laat dit jaar aub snel voorbij gaan verdomme. **But in good news**, ik heb net betaald gekregen voor mijn eerste **freelance writing/ translating job**. **YAY.**

02:	*onderduiker:* **Oe**, gefeliciteerd!:D Dat voelt vast goed!	
01: *geraldina*:		IS IT 2010 YET **OMG**. Please let this year be over fast, dammit. **But in good news**, I just got paid for my first **freelance writing/ translating job**. **YAY**.
02: *onderduiker:*		**Ooh**, congratulations! I'm sure that feels good.

There are several switches here that are not specifically transitional, such as user *geraldina*'s first switch to English in turn 01, "OMG" (oh my God), her use of English to express "freelance writing/translating job" and the subsequent "YAY," as well as user *onderduiker*'s Dutch spelling of the English exclamation "ooh" in turn 03. User *geraldina*'s switch to English in "but in good news," however, can be seen as having the function of marking a transition, both in terms of a shift from one topic to another and in terms of one mood to another, as she moves from a critical and negative formulation about her distaste for what has happened in the year 2009 and a positive formulation of her professional success. This is similar to Excerpt 4.3 in that both excerpts are simultaneously a transition from one topic to another and a shift in footing.

Switching to English to Mark a Closing

The final common type of discourse-related switch that I was able to identify in the data is that of using English-origin transidiomatic practices to mark a closing to a post. This function can be seen in the four excerpts in this next section, all taken from the Dutch community *vragenuurtje*. Because these are used to contextualize the structure of posts rather than interjectionally between users, each excerpt consists only of the post, not its comments. The first of these, Excerpt 4.6 (a post that did not receive any comments), is a simple example in which user *rncaesaria*, a hairdresser, makes a post requesting volunteer models to receive haircuts by trainees in one of her classes.

104   **4 The How: Interactional Functions of English**

Excerpt 4.6 "Let me know" (Dutch community)

00: *rncaesaria*: gezocht modellen voor korte creatiefe kapsels, boblijns! op woensdag middag in [city name]! **let me know!**

00: *rncaesaria*: Looking for models for short creative haircuts, bobs! on wednesday afternoon in [city name]! **let me know!**

User *rncaesaria*'s post is all in Dutch apart from the closing line, "let me know," which is in English. Similarly to the way this sort of switch is used in spoken-language conversation to mark the end of a narrative (e.g. Alfonzetti, 1998: 194–5, Zentella, 1997: 94), *rncaesaria*'s switch to English serves the function of contextualizing this line as the closing or punchline to the post. In this case this closer is not set off from the rest of the post with a carriage return, which allows the switch to English to take on the full weight of that contextualization.

Excerpt 4.7 below is a complex post with a question about dealing with the privilege of riding the train for free as a student when one is no longer technically a student. The original conversation consisted of this post and 18 comments.

Excerpt 4.7 "Discuss" (Dutch community)

00: *niceaa:*   vraagje voor de afgestudeerden /studie-afkappers:
als je uitgestudeerd bent, en je gaat je "papieren" OV inleveren, dan wordt je verteld dat je je OV-chipkaart mag houden.
wat je er vervolgens mee moet doen weet niemand precies en wordt nergens duidelijk aangegeven (ik ben nu zo ver dat ik na uitgebreid speuren en bellen erachter ben dat je hem moet laten "omzetten" (dus aangeven dat je geen student meer bent en er dus niet meer gratis mee mag reizen) bij één of ander "punt", ergens.)
maar gisteren stapte ik in de metro en ik dacht, eens kijken of dat ding nog werkt, of dattie er geld afhaalt of wat dan ook, en je kan er dus gewoon nog steeds gratis mee reizen zolang je dit dus niet laat "verwijderen" of "omzetten" ofzo.

> mijn vraag is:
> 1. wisten jullie dat al?
> en
> 2. doen jullie dit ook? of zijn jullie heel braaf;)
> volgens mij valt het ook niet echt te controleren nml en krijg je er verder ook geen boete voor? (behalve als er gecontroleerd word en ze vragen of je je papieren kaart ook kunt laten zien)
> **discuss!**

> 00: *niceaa:* question for people who just graduated /are about to graduate from university:
> when you're done with university, and you turn in your "paper" bus pass, then you're told that you can keep your electronic bus pass.
> nobody knows exactly what you have to do with it after that and I can't find any clear explanation anywhere (I've gotten to the point where after extensive sleuthing and phoning about it I found out that you have to get it "converted" (in other words indicate that you're not a student anymore and that you therefore aren't allowed to ride for free anymore) at some vague "spot", somewhere.)
> but yesterday I got on the subway and I thought, let's see if the thing still works, or if it takes money off or whatever, and turns out you can just keep riding for free as long as you don't get it "erased" or "removed" or whatever.
> my question is:
> 1. did you guys know about this already?
> and
> 2. do you do this too? or are you good little boys and girls;)
> as far as I know there's no real way of checking it and you don't seem to get any sort of penalty for it?
> (except if the ticket checker comes by and they ask you to show your paper ticket too)
> **discuss!**

This example is similar to the example in Excerpt 4.7 in that it is also all in Dutch apart from the final line (in this case a single word). This is a much longer post, however, and in fact, it is rather unusual in the *vragenuurtje* community for such a long post to contain only one instance of English-origin transidiomatic practices. It uses carriage returns as a structuring device that divides the posts into clear sections. These begin with a line contextualizing who the post is for ("question for

106   4 The How: Interactional Functions of English

people…"); followed by a sentence giving general background to the problem ("when you're done with university…"); then by a paragraph elaborating why she hasn't done anything about the problem yet ("nobody knows exactly what you have to do with it after that…"); then by a personal event that affected how she thought about the issue ("but yesterday I got on the subway…"); then by a marker of the immediately upcoming question ("my question is…"); then by the two questions in numbered order and set apart by carriage returns and the word "and"; then by a summary of her understanding of the situation ("as far as I know there's no real way of checking it"); and then as the very last section, the English word "discuss." The final "discuss" therefore is set apart by the same carriage returns that divide the rest of the long post's sections from each other, but also by the switch to English, which serves to contextualize that section not simply as one more section analogous to all of the others, but as the final one. It is possible that the English in this final line may also simultaneously serve a participant-related function by indexing essay questions in school English classes in which a long description of a situation can be followed by a command to "discuss!," but if so, this function is an additional one to the primary discourse-related function of marking a closing.

An additional example of this function of marking a closing can be seen in Excerpt 4.8 below. It is a request for a certain kind of video remix of popular songs, and it is a post that received no responses.

Excerpt 4.8 "Inspire me" (Dutch community)

00: *ellenn_:*   **Hi** iedereen! Ik ben op zoek naar **remixes**, maar wel te verstaan een bepaald soort. Ik zoek **remixes** die ook de tekst helemaal opnieuw **mixen**, mag tot andere betekenis of onverstaanbaar – een soort **jelly language**. Hier twee **remixes** die zijn zoals ik bedoel:
[two youtube videos]
Zulk soort spul dus,…**So: Inspire me!**

00: *ellenn_:*   **Hi** everyone! I'm looking for **remixes**, but specifically of a certain kind. I'm looking for **remixes** that also mix up the text, maybe into another meaning

> or in to something unintelligible – a sort of **jelly language**. Here are two
> **remixes** that are the sort of thing I mean:
> [two youtube videos]
> That kind of stuff then...**So: Inspire me!**

There are several single-word or single-phrase switches in this excerpt (the greeting "hi," the word "remixes," and the description "jelly language," which appears to be the poster's own personal characterization of the sort of remix she is looking for), but it is the final "so: Inspire me!" in the last line that serves to contextualize the closing. Like Excerpt 4.6 but unlike Excerpt 4.7, the contextualized closing does not appear following a carriage return on its own line, which means that the switch to English again carries the weight of contextualizing the closing all on its own, without any additional bundled contextualization cues.

A final example of a switch to English to mark a closing can be seen in Excerpt 4.9 below, which comes from a conversation consisting of a post with 12 comments. Here, user *mfpim* makes a short post to ask for help in finding a place to stay in London for herself and her boyfriend.

Excerpt 4.9 "Thanks" (Dutch community)

00: *mfpim*: **yo,** ik ga met nieuwjaar naar london **(again)** 29-dec tot 3 jan. maar nu met ze 2tjes ik en me vriend, maar ik moet nu nog een hotelletje/hostel hebben **anyone** een idee?
thanks

00: *mfpim*: **yo,** I'm going to london for new year's **(again)** Dec 29 to Jan 3. but there's only going to be two of us me and my boyfriend, but I still have to find a hotel/hostel **anyone** got an idea?
thanks

108 4 The How: Interactional Functions of English

As with the previous excerpt, there are several switches here in addition to the one that contextualizes the closing: the post begins with the greeting "yo" (which originally comes from African-American Vernacular English, but which has entered into the transidiomatic practices of young people around the world through hip-hop music, cf. Pennycook 2007, Peuronen 2011: 162), switches to Dutch, and then uses a switch to English alongside the parentheses to mark the aside "(again)" (a further example of the function of switching to English to mark an off-topic aside, as discussed earlier in this chapter). However, the final English-origin "thanks"—which is simultaneously contextualized by setting it apart from the previous line with a carriage return—clearly serves to mark the closing or end of the post. It should be said that this sort of post-closing English-origin "Thanks" is found extremely frequently in both communities, but particularly in the Dutch community *vragenuurtje*.

In this section, three main discourse-related functions of switches to English were identified: that of marking an off-topic aside, marking a transition within a longer stretch of text, and marking a closing to a post. These are related in that they all serve to structure the sort of online conversation that is common within social media communities, demarcating one sort of section of a post or type of discourse from another. Because the discourse-related function of these cues has no specific semantic content, the different components that make up these posts and comments would all presumably be able to exist in these conversations without switching to English (or for that matter without any other sort of contextualization cue) to alert readers to their existence. However, as with the types of spoken language found commonly within bilingual communities, these kinds of transidiomatic practices serve the purpose of structuring the interaction and making the mechanisms of conversation run more smoothly. Sometimes these switches to English are bundled together with other contextualization cues such as carriage returns, individual comments, or asterisks, which further serve to strengthen the contextualization function, but the fact that the switch to English often performs the function on its own indicates that these are not a requirement. Furthermore, it is possible for these discourse-related switches to have the additional function of evoking a shift in footing (as in Excerpts 4.3 and 4.5, where the switch to English simultaneously contextualizes a transition from one topic to another and a shift in mood), or of performatively indexing the wider world of English beyond these communities and the specific identities it is associated with there (as in Excerpt 4.2, where the switch to English evokes an English-language environment where it is more common to discuss specifically English-language things than it is to discuss specifically local ones), but in all cases, the main function of the switch is discourse-structuring. This is common to both face-to-face multilingual communities and other computer-mediated ones (Androutsopoulos 2006b: 533), but it is markedly different from participant-related language alternation, where the identity-related aspects of interaction are foregrounded, and switches into or out of English serve to position oneself or others.

Participant-Related Language Alternation

Auer (1998: 8) explains the basic difference between discourse-related and participant-related switching from the perspective of the participants, by stating that in discourse-related switching, participants search for an explanation for the question of "why use that language now?" within the structures of the conversation, while in participant-related switching, they search for explanations within the individual who performs this switch, or perhaps that person's co-participants. For example, in a setting where participants are known to be struggling to use a language other than their native one, such as in certain types of language classrooms (e.g. Liebscher and Dailey-O'Cain 2004), participant-related switching can result from something as basic as one participant's lack of knowledge of how to express something in his or her second language, or another participant's known comprehension-related preference to be addressed in his or her first language (and certainly switching is often understood in these ways in such a context, even when it is not intended that way, as can be seen in Dailey-O'Cain and Liebscher 2009). However, participant-related switching is not limited to situations where there is a competence-related deficit in one or more participants, but can also be related to participants' *preferences* for one language or another.

110   4 The How: Interactional Functions of English

And while participant-related switching associated with preference is sometimes interpreted as simply an idiosyncratic matter specific to a given individual (e.g. Chanseawrassamee and Shin 2009: 61–3), Guerini (2006: 105) argues that switching that can be traced back to participants' preferences can be revealing of "the code choice that speakers consider suitable within a certain communicative context—disclosing the conversational moves that speakers carry out in order to select a language variety which might be accepted by all the participants."

As such, participant-related language alternation can tell us two things. First, it can be used by participants as a tool in positioning themselves and others, and this can in turn reveal information about individuals' identity construction. However, it can also tell us about the kinds of transidiomatic practices that are more or less acceptable in different communicative contexts within a community. This can be done in a straightforward way, as in the previously mentioned example of when a child of German immigrant parents in Canada switches from English to German in order to indicate an affinity with Germanness and express positive attitudes toward the language (Liebscher and Dailey-O'Cain 2013: 61–63), but transidiomatic practices can also draw on multiple language resources in ways that straddle both linguistic and cultural boundaries (Bailey 2007: 257). Some of these kinds of practices can be analyzed as crossing, or "the use of language varieties associated with social or ethnic groups that the speaker doesn't normally 'belong' to" (Rampton 2005: 28), but as discussed in Chapter 2, whether a particular instance of language alternation can be interpreted as crossing must depend on whether the participants in that interaction can be shown to be constructing the situation as one in which they are "styling" a particular "other" (by using language resources interpreted as "belonging" to a particular other group), or whether they are constructing the situation as one where they are using language resources that are, at least in some respects, their own (perhaps by virtue of that language being an international or "neutral" language that everyone has automatic permission to use). This latter type of use is better understood not as a type of crossing, but as a way of switching to a non-native language to index a general sense of connectedness between different locales (e.g. Peuronen 2011). Analyzing these kinds of participant-related switches in the *unserekleinestadt* and *vragenuurtje* communities can therefore tell us a great deal about which kinds of linguistic resources community members choose to appropriate and what purposes that appropriation serves, as well as how the indexicalities of particular kinds of Anglophone and transnational identities can become semiotically rearranged differently in different national contexts.

Switching to English to Provide Information about Gesture, Facial Expression, or Tone of Voice

One type of participant-related switch commonly found in both communities is a switch to English in order to provide information about gesture, facial expression, or tone of voice. Writing out these kinds of cues in some way is a common strategy used in social media for compensating for social cues that are normally conveyed by these channels in ordinary face-to-face interaction (Herring 2001), and in both the *unserekleinestadt* and *vragenuurtje* communities, these cues are often—though not exclusively—in English. One example of this sort of switch has already been mentioned in the previous chapter: in Excerpt 3.3, from the *vragenuurtje* community, user *bangkokimpact* wrote a post that was entirely in Dutch apart from being preceded and followed by the English word "desperate" in a way that was framed to make it look like markup language. The effect of these "tags" in such a post is to make the language in her post "sound" or "look" desperate, as if it were accompanied in a face-to-face conversation by a desperate tone of voice, a desperate-appearing facial expression, or desperate-looking gestures. The switch to English, then, serves to evoke the wider social media context in which *bangkokimpact* presumably first encountered the use of a "markup language" type of syntax to indicate a tone of voice, facial expression, or gesture.

Two additional examples of this function can be seen in Excerpts 4.10 and 4.11 below, which come from the German and Dutch communities, respectively. The first of these comes from a larger conversation of a post and 15 comments, and the conversation deals

112   4 The How: Interactional Functions of English

with a concern of *begeistert*'s about how to deal politely with gifts of money. While *begeistert* does not specify that she is talking about receiving gifts in the context of a party rather than a situation of the gift-giver and the gift-receiver sitting alone in a room, *anappleaday* makes it clear in her turn (by using language like "every envelope," "guests," "in front of everybody") that she is assuming that is what *begeistert* means.

Excerpt 4.10 "Shrug" (German community)

00: *begeistert*:   Ich hatte gestern Geburtstag und bin auf ein bekanntes Problem gestoßen: Einige meiner Verwandten haben mir Geld geschenkt, was natürlich an sich sehr praktisch ist und meine Oma macht auch immer ganz niedliche Geldgeschenke, in dem sie irgendwas dekoriert, aber einige schenken das Geld ja einfach in einen Umschlag – Ohne Karte. Jedesmal frage ich mich, ob ich reingucken darf.
Wenn eine Karte drinnen wäre, könnte man ja die Karte lesen und sehen, wie viel Geld es ist, aber es gibt immer wieder Situationen in denen ich mich frage: Darf ich nachgucken, wie viel Geld es ist? Auch bei Gutscheinen. Ich habe einen Gutschein von Thalia bekommen und vorne stand nur Gutschein drauf und ich wusste, dass drinnen der Betrag steht und habe mich nicht getraut nach zu gucken.
Das Schlimmste sind eigentlich die Karten auf denen vorne so ein winzig kleiner Umschlag ist, wo man weiß, der Schenker hat die Karte genommen, um vorne Geld rein zu tun und man liest dann die Karte und fragt sich wieder: Darf ich nachgucken?

01: *anappleaday*:   Das sagt der Knigge dazu. [link to url]
Ich persönlich würde allerdings in jeden Umschlag schauen - ich fänd es unhöflich das nicht zu tun, so als würde mich der Inhalt überhaupt nicht interessieren. Ich denke es kommt auch immer auf die Gäste drauf an. Meine Verwandschaft ist da relativ cool und so lange man den Umschlag nicht total zefleddert und das Geld laut vor allen zählt ist bei meinen Leuten alles gut. *shrug*

00: begeistert: Yesterday was my birthday and I was confronted with a familiar problem: Some of my relatives gave me money, which of course in and of itself is very practical and my grandma also always makes really cute little money presents where she decorates something, but some people just give the money in a simple envelope – Without a card. Every time I ask myself if I'm allowed to look inside.

> If there were a card inside, you could read the card and see how much money it is, but there keep being situations where I ask myself: Am I allowed to check and see how much money it is? With gift cards too. I got a gift card from Thalia [German bookstore] and on the front it just said gift card and I knew that inside it would say the amount but I didn't dare look.
>
> The worst example are the cards where in the front there's such a teeny tiny envelope, where you know that the giver just grabbed the card in order to put money inside and you read the card and then ask yourself again: Am I allowed to look?
>
> 01: *anappleaday*: This is what Knigge has to say about that. [link to url] I personally would absolutely look in every envelope – I would think it was impolite not to do that, as if the contents didn't even interest me. I think it always also depends on the guests. My relatives are pretty cool and as long as you don't crumple up the envelope or count the money out loud in front of everybody, my people think everything is just fine. ***shrug***

In response to *begeistert*'s question, which is all in German, *anappleaday* first links to the online version of the Knigge, which is a German "everyday politeness" authority similar to the Miss Manners guides common in the United States. Then, on a new line, she talks about her personal approach and why she handles these situations that way, then talks about how the approach could differ depending on whether the guests are more or less laid-back about such matters. This paragraph ends with the English word "shrug," which is used to represent a gesture. As in the previously discussed Excerpt 3.3, this gesture is indicated by a sort of stylized "markup language," but in this case it is simplified to a simple one-word term for the gesture in the place where it would occur in *anappleaday*'s turn if this were a face-to-face conversation, surrounded by asterisks in order to set it off as a gesture that accompanies her turn rather than a word she "says." Also as in Excerpt 3.3, the switch to English serves to index the wider English-language internet, where such ways of expressing gesture are common, and to position *anappleaday* as a part of that wider internet.

114   4 The How: Interactional Functions of English

Excerpt 4.11 comes from a larger conversation of a post plus 23 comments. In it, user *littleliar* is asking the rest of the *vragenuurtje* community what sort of hair colour might look good on her.

Excerpt 4.11 "Roll eyes" (Dutch community)

00: *littleliar*:   Inmiddels heb ik mijn haar al een lange tijd de kleur "wit" en alle kleuren daaromheen gehad en ik word het ondertussen een beetje zat. Dus ik ben op zoek naar een nieuwe leuke kleur. Iemand enig idee wat leuk kan staan bij mij?
Zo ziet het er momenteel uit (met uitgroei)
[photo of a young blonde woman]
Help mij!

01: *classicism*:   rood!

02: *diertje*:   ik denk dat inderdaad, roodbruin/kastanje wel heel mooi is. en er moet gezegd worden dat jij heel erg mooi bent.

03: *littleliar*:   Hmm ik ben niet zo'n fan van rood. Maar misschien is het het proberen waard *roll eyes*
En bedankt:)

00: *littleliar*:   By now I've had my hair in a "white" colour for a long time and all the similar colours too and at this point I'm getting a bit sick of it. So I'm looking for a nice new colour. Does anyone have an idea what would look good on me?
This is how it looks right now (with roots)
[photo of a young blonde woman]
Help me!

01: *classicism*:   red!

02: *diertje*:   yeah, I also think reddish brown/chestnut is really pretty. and I have to say that you are really beautiful.

03: *littleliar*:   Hmm I'm not such a fan of red. But maybe it's worth trying *roll eyes*
And thanks:)

In her initial post in turn 00, *littleliar* explains why she's looking for a new hair colour, asks what colour might look good on her, and provides a recent picture of herself for context. In response, user *classicism* suggests that she might want to try red in turn 01, and user *diertje* provides her agreement along with a compliment on *littleliar*'s appearance in turn 02.

Finally, in turn 03, *littleliar* expresses her reluctance about the colour red, followed quickly by the comment that maybe it's worth trying anyway. This sentence is accompanied by the English term "roll eyes," surrounded by asterisks, and the lack of a period at the end of the word "trying" has the effect of contextualizing the eye-rolling as "occurring" at the same time as she is "saying" "maybe it's worth trying." She then switches back to Dutch to thank *diertje* for the compliment. As in the previous two examples in this category, both the asterisks indicating a sort of markup language and the switch to English serve to contextualize the phrase "roll eyes" as a facial expression, with the English specifically indexing the wider, largely English-language, internet context, and to position *littleliar* as a part of it. It is important to note, however, that in the wider data set the use of these kinds of conversational functions is not *required* to be accompanied by a switch to English (as the Dutch-language tone-of-voice markup language "*hysterisch*" in msp's turn 01 in Excerpt 4.15 below attests), but English-origin transidiomatic practices do in fact seem to be used much more commonly for these purposes than either German in *unserekleinestadt* or Dutch in *vragenuurtje*. This suggests that the preference for using English is not simply an individual one, but a community-wide one, and the fact that it holds true for both communities suggests that it may be indicative of what is seen as most accepted in young German and Dutch speakers' social media interaction in general.

Switching to English to Lighten or Mitigate an Evaluative Comment

The second category of participant-related switches that I was able to identify in the data is the use of English to lighten or mitigate an evaluative comment. This type of switch is found in the following three excerpts, which come from both the German and Dutch communities. The first of these is in Excerpt 4.12 below, which comes from a longer conversation consisting of a post and 54 comments in the *unserekleinestadt* community, and involves a discussion about students and their exams.

116   **4 The How: Interactional Functions of English**

Excerpt 4.12 "I like" (German community)

00: *xtra_ordinary:* Hallo zusammen,
ich habe mal eine Frage an die Studenten unter euch: Wie läuft das
bei euch, wenn ihr wissen müsst, was ein Dozent in einer Vorlesung
behandelt hat, den ihr selbst nicht hattet? Beispiel: Ihr schreibt eure
Bachelor-Arbeit und als Zweitkorrektor habt ihr einen Dozenten,
den ihr nicht kennt und der euch nun sagt, was ihm in seinem
Fachgebiet wichtig ist? – Oder ihr müsst eine Klausur noch mal
schreiben und der Dozent, der die Klausur stellt, ist euch unbekannt,
weil ihr einen anderen hattet?
Her mit euren Meinungen, bitte keine "Du bist ein Arsch, wenn du
es nicht tust"-Bemerkungen. Ich möchte einfach nur wissen, was ihr
tun würdet.

01: *marronglace:* bei uns läufts so ab. wer mitschreibt verteilt oft und gerne seine
mitschriften (wenn sie gut und komplett sind) gegen geld oder eine
andere mitschrift. also reines tauschgeschäft. unter freunden
bekommt man gelegentlich auch so was ausgetauscht, ohne dafür
was geben zu müssen (außer vl mal einen cafe oder so spendieren).

02: *mistermark:* Totales **Business, I like**:)

00: *xtra_ordinary:* Hello everyone,
I have a question for the students among you: How is it where you
are when you want to know what a professor dealt with in a class that
you didn't have yourself? Example: You're writing your bachelor's
thesis and one of the committee members is a professor that you
don't know and who tells you now what's important to him in his
research area? – Or you have to take an exam over again and the
professor who's giving it is unknown to you because you had a
different one?
Give me your opinions, just please no "you're an ass if you don't do
it" kinds of comments. I just want to know what you guys would do.

01: *marronglace:* here it's like this. the people who take classes pass around their notes
(if they're good and complete) happily and frequently in exchange
for money or other notes. so it's a pure barter thing. among friends
you occasionally find stuff like that being passed around without any
money changing hands (except they might buy you a coffee or
something at some point).

02: *mistermark:* Total **business, I like**:)

Switching to English to Lighten or Mitigate an Evaluative Comment   **117**

In the initial post in turn 00, user *xtra_ordinary* asks a question that she specifically aims at the other German post-secondary students in the *unserekleinestadt* community: how they deal with the task of learning the information that is taught in courses she is not taking and will not be taking, but which she will nonetheless be expected to know when it comes time to take her exams. In turn 01, user *marronglace* responds to *xtra_ordinary*'s question by saying that at her university, people handle this by exchanging a good set of notes for a given class for either money or a different set of notes (with the exception that people will sometimes give their friends notes without expecting anything in return). Then, in turn 02, user *mistermark* makes a short comment characterizing the way they do things at *marronglace*'s university as "Total business," a phrase in which the English word is used for "business." The use of the English term (albeit as a capitalized noun, which is the prescribed norm for written German) as opposed to any possible German equivalent has the effect of making it clear that the attitude surrounding these practices is a businesslike one, not that making money from notes is any particular student's actual business, which it could otherwise sound like if German were used. Then, finally, *mistermark* adds an approving evaluative comment to his characterization of how they do things at *marronglace*'s university: "I like," and this comment is also in English. However, the comment is not only in English, the ordinarily transitive verb "like" is also used without an object, which is a common playful alternate way of expressing approval of something on the wider, largely English-language internet (this is sometimes realized as "me like" or "me likey"). It is also followed immediately by a smiley face. The cumulative effect of these three cues—the switch to English, the playful syntax, and the smiley face—is to add a certain lightness or playfulness to *mistermark*'s approval of the practices at *marronglace*'s university, which could otherwise run the risk of sounding more formal and serious than he likely intends. In addition to this, the switch to English specifically indexes the wider internet where expressions like this are common.

The next example of this type of cue comes from the *vragenuurtje* community, and it can be seen in Excerpt 4.13. The excerpt comes from a short conversation consisting of a post and six comments, and it deals with a discussion about how user *_anch_* should ask out someone she's interested in dating.

118   4 The How: Interactional Functions of English

> **Excerpt 4.13 "His loss" (Dutch community)**
>
> 00: _anch_: Hoe vráág je iemand op date?
> Ik voel me echt zo'n nerd.
> Enige mogelijkheid is eigenlijk **facebook**/email, of ik moet via mijn vrienden zijn telefoonnummer krijgen.
> Maar ik durf echt niet, ik ben zo'n schijterd. Ik weet gewoon niet wat ik moet zeggen!
>
> 01: onderduiker: Hm..ik zou persoonlijk gaan voor **facebook**/email. Iemand uit het niets smsen/bellen vind ik vaak zo opdringerig overkomen.
> En gewoon doen joh. Ik bedoel, ook al zegt hij nee, wat dan nog? **His loss.**
>
> 00: _anch_: How do you even ASK someone on a date?
> I really feel like such a nerd.
> The only possibility I can think of is **facebook**/email, or else I have to get his phone number from my friends.
> But I don't dare do it, anyway, I'm such a scaredy-cat. I just don't know what to say!
>
> 01: onderduiker: Hmm..personally I would go for **facebook**/email. Texting or phoning somebody out of the blue can often come across as so pushy.
> And just do it already. I mean, even if he says no, so what? **His loss.**

In the initial post in turn 00, _anch_ expresses that she would like to ask out a guy, but she's not sure what medium to use, and that she's just generally afraid to do it in the first place. User *onderduiker* responds in turn 01, in a comment that she divides into two parts by using a carriage return. In the first part she suggests Facebook or email as a way of getting in touch with the guy, and then explains this by saying that unsolicited phone calls or text messages can come across as pushy. This part is all in Dutch. In the second part of her comment, then, she tries to persuade _anch_ to just get up her courage and ask him out, saying that even if he says no, it's "his loss" (the last two words of which are in English). Similarly to the previous excerpt, the switch to English in this excerpt has the effect of indexing the wider internet where English expressions like this are common, and both positioning *onderduiker* as a part of that

Switching to English to Lighten or Mitigate an Evaluative Comment   **119**

wider internet and adding a certain sort of carefree attitude to the message that she seems to be hoping _anch_ will be able to adopt.

The final example of this type of cue also comes from the *vragenuurtje* community, and it can be seen in Excerpt 4.14. The excerpt comes from a much longer conversation consisting of a post and 72 comments, in which the original poster, _echinacea_, asks a question that a number of other community members perceive as ridiculous.

Excerpt 4.14 "Is she for real" (Dutch community)

00: _echinacea_:	Wat vinden jullie van de naam "fin" ?
	Als in inwoner van finland? Ik vind het erg raar, je noemt je kind toch ook niet duitser?
01: *weregonnamakeit*:	God, jij moet echt een **award** krijgen voor je vragen.
02: *dyrnwyn*:	was dat sarcasme? ik vind namelijk wel dat ze iets toevoegt aan mn leven;)
03: *weregonnamakeit*:	Punt. Iedere keer als ik iets van haar lees, denk ik, **is she for real**?
00: _echinacea_:	What do you guys think of the name "fin" ?
	As in inhabitant of finland? I think it's really weird, you don't call your kid germany, right?
01: *weregonnamakeit*:	God, you really should get an **award** for your questions.
02: *dyrnwyn*:	was that sarcasm? because I actually do find that she adds some value to my life;)
03: *weregonnamakeit*:	Point. Whenever I read something by her, I think, **is she for real**?

In the original post in turn 00, user _echinacea_ asks what people think of the Irish name "Finn," which is pronounced the same as the Dutch word for "inhabitant of Finland" (and which she has interpreted as the same word). She then adds that she thinks it's weird, because one doesn't name a child after other countries. In response, user *weregonnamakeit* sarcastically says that _echinacea_ (who has already made a number of posts on the same day that other community members have regarded as silly) should "get an award" for her questions, with "award" being used in English. As a response to *weregonnamakeit*'s comment,

120   4 The How: Interactional Functions of English

user *dyrnwyn* asks in turn 02 whether *weregonnamakeit's* comment was intended as sarcasm, and adding that she finds that *_echinacea_* actually adds value to her life (a "winky face" smiley is tacked on to the end of this comment to contextualize it as said in a teasing or joking way). Finally, *weregonnamakeit* responds again in turn 03 to express the reaction she has whenever she reads a post by *_echinacea_*: "is she for real"? This final evaluative comment is accompanied by a switch to English, which has the effect of contextualizing the comment as light-hearted and playful,[2] when in Dutch it could easily come across as overly serious or judgmental. In this case, the expression could have been gleaned from either the wider internet or from English-language films and media, as the expression "is [person] for real?" is common in both.

Of course, not all evaluative comments in the data are in English. However, when English *is* used to express an evaluative expression— whether positive or negative—the use of these transidiomatic practices has the effect of softening or mitigating an evaluation that could other-wise be interpreted as more serious than the user intends it to be. This is accomplished by indexing a world of unserious-seeming English expressions that community members have picked up from the wider, largely English-language internet, as well as from English-language television and films, and positioning the user performing the switch as a legitimate user of these English expressions. The evaluative comments in question can serve to evaluate either something that one's said oneself, or something that someone else said. It is also interesting to note that the evaluative expression is never set apart on a separate line, which suggests that despite the contextualizing effects of the switches involved, it is meant to be seen as firmly embedded in the conversation rather than at a junction between one part of the conversation and another.

---

[2] . In this particular case, the "is she for real" switch may also have a possible additional discourse-related function of marking a quoted internal thought—especially given that the use of a discourse-related switch to mark a quotation is a common use of switching in spoken conversation (e.g., Alfonzetti 1998: 198–207). There are not enough examples of a switch to English being used in this way to call this a main function of language alternation in either of my two data sets, but it does appear to be a secondary function of the switch in this particular excerpt.

Switching to English to Indicate Lightheartedness among Strong Affect

The fifth and final main function of switches to English is that of adding a certain lightheartedness or trivial nature to strong affect, thereby mediating what could otherwise be read as much more intense than it is intended to come across. This function of the use of English to communicate a certain playfulness is related to the previous function of communicating gesture, facial expression, or tone of voice, and has also been found in other single-nationality social media communities (e.g. Peuronen 2011: 162). All of the excerpts I was able to identify with this function come from the *vragenuurtje* community, and the following two excerpts therefore both come from there. The first of these comes from a conversation of a post plus 46 comments, in which user *annabanana* posts a picture of Dutch folk singer Jan Smit—who is now a grown man, but many community members would have strong memories of him dating from when he had several hit songs in his pre-pubescent and barely-pubescent years—in a rather revealing underwear ad on a bus shelter of a busy city street.

Excerpt 4.15 "I don't wanna see" (Dutch community)

00: *annabanana*: **Yay** of **Nay**?
[picture of Jan Smit in an underwear ad on a bus shelter]
En waarom?
Er Staat er bij mij eentje op de hoek van de straat en ik hoor veel voorbij fietsende vrouwen er kritiek op geven, dat ik er stiekem wel om moest lachen dat het zo "leeft" bij de mensen. Veel reacties zijn dan ook een **Nay**.

01: *msp*: NEEEE IEWW sorry maar die bobbel, JANTJE HEEFT GEEN PENIS JA.
hysterisch.
oke ik vind hem niet shockerend, maar **I don't wanna see**!!@##

02: *geraldina*: **LOL THISSS.**

00: *annabanana*: **Yay** or **Nay**?
[picture of Jan Smit in an underwear ad on a bus shelter]
And why?

122   4 The How: Interactional Functions of English

> One of these has been put up on the corner of my street and I hear a lot of women riding by on their bikes criticizing it, and I secretly find myself laughing about how much of a "thing" it is with people. So I view all these reactions as a **Nay**.
>
> 01: *msp*:   NOOOOO EEEEW sorry but the little bump, LITTLE JAN DOESN'T HAVE A PENIS NO.
> *hysterical*
> okay I don't think it's shocking, but **I don't wanna see**!!@##
>
> 02: *geraldina*:   **LOL THISSS.**

User *annabanana*'s post in turn 00 begins with a single line setting the frame for the post: "Yay or Nay?" While the term "yea or nay" is familiar to English speakers from official oral voting in government settings, this phrase has entered into the informal public internet context spelled instead as "yay or nay,"[3] and this phrase is frequently found in online discussions where people are asked to express their spontaneous positive or negative reactions to something. By using this phrase, which would be familiar to community members from the wider English-speaking internet, *annabanana* establishes that the frame for this conversation is a request for the same sort of playful, spontaneous, from-the-gut reactions. She then provides a picture of the ad she is asking for that sort of snap judgment about, and then, on another separate line, asks community members to give a reason for their reaction. Finally, in an additional paragraph, she gives information about why she is asking: the ad is on a bus shelter on the corner of her street, and *annabanana* has been amused to observe lots of women spontaneously making negative remarks about it (which she has interpreted as those women "voting" "nay").

User *msp* then provides her requested reaction in turn 01: a strongly phrased negative response that is all in capital letters (indicating a loud tone of voice), prosodic spelling in "NOOOOO" and "EEEEW" (indicating vowel lengthening), and a "markup language" type of tag indicating how

---

[3] . A Google search reveals published pieces with the titles "3D Printing Yay or Nay? Tell Us How You Really Feel During Tomorrow's Twitter Chat," "Body Hacking, Yay or Nay?," and "Period Panties, Yay or Nay?," among many others.

her tone of voice is to be read ("*hysterical*"). Toward the end of this turn, *msp* also provides an explanation for her extreme negative reaction: she doesn't want to be confronted with images that portray the celebrity who she still thinks of as "little Jan" as a sexual being. Then, on a separate line, she backtracks a bit, saying that she "doesn't think it's shocking," but switches to English for her gut reaction of "I don't wanna see." Several things characterize this reaction as highly emotional, such as the use of multiple exclamation marks and the fact that these exclamation marks are followed by other characters that can be found near the exclamation mark on the keyboard ("@##"), as if to suggest that *msp* has become so emotional that she's having trouble hitting the right keys. However, the switch to English contextualizes this as a playful use of language familiar to community members from the wider internet world, thereby making her response read as playfully self-mocking rather than literally hysterical. Finally, *geraldina* responds to *msp* in turn 02, with an affirming (and English) "LOL THISSSS." Similarly to *msp*'s turn, *geraldina*'s response uses all capital letters and lengthened letters, but her switch to English helps contextualize this as a lighthearted playfulness rather than literal shock.

Another example of this function for a switch to English can be seen in Excerpt 4.16, which, like Excerpt 4.3 above, occurs as a comment on the weekly *vraagvrije vrijdag* (question-free Friday) post that gets made in the *vragenuurtje* community every Friday. This excerpt is a single conversational offshoot within the context provided by a particular weekly "vraagvrije vrijdag" post, in this case one consisting of a post and 173 comments. In the first comment on the post, user *dhr_waaromniet* uses the dedicated question-free space to point out to the other participants that popular child video blogger Tabby Ridiman has returned to video blogging.

Excerpt 4.16 "Tabby is back" (Dutch community)

01: *dhr_waaromniet:*   **tabby is back!!!!**
02: *ohnonotme:*   **JEEEEEEEEEEEEEEJ**:D
03: *rainbow_:*   **I LOVE TABBBBBYYYYYYYYYYYYYYY**
                           ben alleen wel benieuwd hoe ze op school is
04: *_seventeen_:*   **you make me day haha**

05: *rainbow_:*	SHE's HOMESCHOOLED	
	this explains...so much.	

01: *dhr_waaromniet:*	tabby is back!!!!	
02: *ohnonotme:*	YAAAAAAAAAAAAAY:D	
03: *rainbow_:*	I LOVE TABBBBBYYYYYYYYYYYYYY	
	I'm just curious how she is at school	
04: *_seventeen_:*	you make me day haha	
05: *rainbow_:*	SHE's HOMESCHOOLED	
	this explains...so much.	

This exchange is unusual, even in the Dutch community, for being nearly entirely in English. Turn 02 is an adaptation to Dutch phonology of the English exclamation "yay" (a sort of English-local-language phonetic spelling that is common in multilingual social media interaction, e.g. Peuronen 2011: 162), but apart from that, the only Dutch here is in user *rainbow_*'s line "I'm just curious how she is at school" in the second half of turn 03. It is no accident that that line also stands out from the rest of the excerpt by being of a somewhat more serious nature than the expressed excitement over being able to watch Tabby's videos again. In each of the other turns, the use of English functions as a way of mediating the four exclamation points in turn 01 and the use of all capital letters in turns 02, 03, and 05, adding a certain lightheartedness to the expressed affect and contextualizing it as playful rather than literally so excited that they are all screaming. As in Excerpt 4.15, the switch to English helps contextualize what might otherwise come across as serious emotional investment as a certain lighthearted playfulness.

Language Mixing to Index a General Sense of Transnationalism

If—as seems likely—the very presence of transidiomatic practices tends to index a sense of transnationalism and interconnectedness among locales (cf. Peuronen 2011: 156–7), then all of the above examples can

Language Mixing to Index a General Sense of Transnationalism 125

likely be said to have this effect alongside their other functions. Furthermore, this effect is probably known among all participants and therefore anything but accidental—in fact, it is notable that these kinds of transidiomatic practices never meet with any criticism or even comment, suggesting that they are in fact viewed as "authentic" and "appropriate" ways to interact in such a community. However, there are a few excerpts in the data—all of them in the *vragenuurtje* community, and all of them in the context of the *vraagvrije vrijdag* posts—in which indexing this sense of transnationalism can be shown through an interactional analysis to be the *main* effect of the transidiomatic practices rather than an additional effect alongside a separate main function. One example of this can be seen in Excerpt 4.17 below, which is a longer stretch of conversation stemming from the same *vraagvrije vrijdag* post as Excerpts 4.3 and 4.16.

Excerpt 4.17 Question-free Friday (Dutch community)

00: *laviefantasque:* **Post** hier je **shit** die je wel wil delen maar niet in je eigen **LJ** wil posten, je **drama**, je anonieme vragen, je verzoekjes om nieuwe vriendjes, je **spam**, je leukste/stomste/grappigste **YouTube** filmpjes, je **omegle-convo's**, je **lolcats**, je anonieme gezeik op hoe gaar deze **community** wel niet geworden is, je frustraties over dat het vrijdag is, je jubilaties over dat het bijna weekend is (of toch al weekend voor de meesten), ennnn al het andere dat je maar kunt bedenken. **We welcome sparkly fonts, gifs, big font, rage, anonymous, joy, squee, Chuck Bass, ANYTHING!**

01: *laviefantasque:* **let's start early**, het is ten minste ~vrijdag~ en ik ben overdag vast heel druk
en **ONTD is bringing me so much lolz right nowbrb have to rehost pics.**

02: *laviefantasque:* [four pictures of celebrities in amusing poses, including Ellen Page and Taylor Swift]
ELLEN > TAYLOR man tswift can go away already plz ugh. ef rehosting, tinypic won't mind right. ahhh the lolz. they kill. now I sleep.

03: *isolde:* **Twitter is down:(**

04: *oktobergoud:* **YAY FIRST PAGE!**

126   4 The How: Interactional Functions of English

	en **wooow** jij bent vroeg O_OIK HEB ME VERSLAPEN want ik moet naar een bruiloft en kon gisteravond niet meer met de treinnn want er waren zoveel vertragingen **lol**
05: *geraldina*:	YAY IK STA OP DE **WAITING LIST** OM MEE TE DOEN AAN HET [university name] WINTERSCHOOL **PROGRAMME**!!!!! Duim allemaal dat ik uiteindelijk mee mag doen **please**?:D En en. Ik voel me nog steeds dodelijk gaar, maar **fuck** die **shit**, vitamines slikken dan maar want ik heb genoeg te doen. En vandaag ga ik lekker veel verven, want ik heb praaachtige **aqua**/turquiose verf: DEn supergoedkoop mooie dingetjes bij [name of local shop] gescoord, zoals n Lundia kast die ik ga ombouwen tot lage kledingkast, en van die mooie ouderwetse blikken en een hoedendoos:D
06: *geraldina*:	Oooh en lilirossol, luna_puella, sappho en wie dan ook – ik heb eindelijk gister maar een **feminist icon** gemaakt vanwege de **fuckery articles** op **ONTD**:D
07: *lilirossol*:	Ohh heb ik **ontd** drama gemist? wat was er wat was er? en **yayyyy** haha. en **yayyy** ik heb zin in woensdag! ben heeeeel benieuwd:) en ik ga duimen!
08: *geraldina*:	**Naah** dat gelul dat de film **Avatar** zo feministisch is en al, **lololol**. En ja ik ook!

00: *laviefantasque:*	**Post** here your **shit** that you want to share but don't want to **post** in your own **LJ**, your **drama**, your anonymous questions, your requests for more readers, your **spam**, your most awesome/dumbest/funniest **YouTube** videos, your **omegle-convo's**, your **lolcats**, your anonymous complaining about how tired and boring this **community** has or hasn't gotten, your frustrations about it being Friday, your jubilation about it being almost the weekend (or actually already is for most of you), annnnnnd everything else that you can think of. **We welcome sparkly fonts, gifs, big font, rage, anonymous, joy, squee, Chuck Bass, ANYTHING!**
01: *laviefantasque*:	**let's start early**, at least it's –Friday– now and I think I'm going to be really busy during the day and **ONTD is bringing me so much lolz right now** **brb have to rehost pics.**
02: *laviefantasque*:	[four pictures of celebrities in amusing poses, including Ellen Page and Taylor Swift] ELLEN > TAYLOR **man tswift can go away already plz ugh.** **ef rehosting, tinypic won't mind right.ahhh the lolz. they kill. now I sleep.**
03: *isolde*:	**Twitter is down:(**
04: *oktobergoud*:	**YAY FIRST PAGE!**

Language Mixing to Index a General Sense of Transnationalism   127

	and **wooow** are you ever early O_OI OVERSLEPT because I have to go to a wedding and yesterday evening I couldn't catch a traaaaaain because everything was late **lol**
05: *geraldina*:	**YAY** I AM ON THE **WAITING LIST** TO PARTICIPATE IN THE [university name] WINTER SCHOOL **PROGRAMME!!!!!** Everybody cross your fingers that I finally get to participate **please**?:D And and. I still feel totally dead, but **fuck** that **shit**, I'll just take some vitamins because I have enough to do. And I'm going to spend today painting a lot, because I have a beauuuutiful **aqua**/turquiose paint:D And I scored super cheap gorgeous things at [name of local shop], like a Lundia cupboard that I'm going to turn into a little closet, and a couple of old-fashioned tins and a hat box:D
06: *geraldina*:	Oooh and lilirossol, luna_puella, sappho and whoever else – I finally made a **feminist icon** because of the **fuckery articles** on **ONTD**:D
07: *lilirossol*:	Ohh did I miss **ontd** drama? what was it what was it? and **yayyyy** haha. and **yayyy** I'm looking forward to wednesday! I'm reeeeeally curious:) and I'll cross my fingers!
08: *geraldina*:	**Naah** the bullshit that the film **Avatar** is so feminist and everything, **lololol.** And yeah me too!

It is important to remember that unlike other posts in both communities, the *vraagvrije vrijdag* posts do not serve as the start of a single conversation, but instead offer a space where people can make any comments they feel like making, about anything they feel moved to talk about. Therefore, the responses are not contributions to one single conversation, but a collection of conversations all happening simultaneously, one per thread. The previously mentioned origin of these posts as this community's analogue to the ONTD "Free For All Friday" posts is also important here, not only because many community members also read and participate in the ONTD community, but because the deliberate homage to ONTD that is apparent to most community members specifically gives *vragenuurtje* participants license to play with language in a way that is common to and established within the ONTD community (in terms of the use of English, but also in terms of certain acronyms, certain common expressions, a performatively over-the-top affect, and even particular kinds of subject matter) but is not nearly as common elsewhere in the *vragenuurtje* community.

128   4   The How: Interactional Functions of English

The language for the post providing the space for *vraagvrije vrijdag* is always the same, and this is shown in *laviefantasque*'s turn 00. It is a very specific mix of Dutch and English that indexes the weekly "Free For All Friday" posts in ONTD through a number of similar phrasings, as well as through the general style of run-on-sentences. The post consists of two sections divided by a carriage return, where the first section is mostly in Dutch with a large number of single-word switches to English ("shit," "drama," "lolcats," "community," etc.), and the second section consists of a single line, all in English: "We welcome sparkly fonts, gifs, big font, rage, anonymous, joy, squee, Chuck Bass, ANYTHING!" The cumulative effect of these cues is strongly evocative not just of the wider English-language internet, but of the ONTD community in particular—and in the responses that follow, the *vragenuurtje* members respond in kind.

Even in the *vragenuurtje* community, where the use of English is extremely common, it can usually still be said that the base or default language is Dutch, and all switching for the purposes of discourse-related or participant-related contextualization is usually done *into* English. In the comments in response to the weekly post that form individual *vraagvrije vrijdag* conversations, though, efforts to pinpoint any single base language are futile, because the transidiomatic practices that occur in these conversations are more indicative of a mixed code than they are of code-switching. The first two comments in turns 01 and 02, which are also made by *laviefantasque,* are indicative of the mixture of a playful use of English, wider-internet-specific phrasing, performatively over-the-top affect, and celebrity-related subject matter that is typical here. "Let's start early," she begins in English in turn 01, and then to communicate why she's commenting immediately after making the original post instead of waiting for the following morning, she uses a few words of Dutch to talk about her upcoming busy day and then an internet-language-inspired English again to talk about the particular things that are prompting her to comment now ("ONTD is bringing me so much lolz right now"). She ends this comment on a new line by again using an internet-language-laden English to communicate that she's going to leave and be back again in a subsequent comment, in which she will post pictures ("brb have to rehost pics"). She then returns in the immediately following comment in turn 02, where she posts four pictures of celebrities followed by commentary about those pictures, again entirely in that particular internet-world English that is common on ONTD.

By this point it could be easy to assume that this sort of ONTD-inspired style is unique to *laviefantasque,* but the language used in turns 03–08, all of which are comments made by other participants, is similar. In turn 03, user *isolde* chimes in to observe that "Twitter is down," a comment that is entirely in English. Then user *oktobergoud* responds directly to *laviefantasque*'s second comment in turn 04 by communicating in English ("YAY FIRST PAGE!") that she is excited to have begun contributing to this week's *vraagvrije vrijdag* post quickly enough for her comments to show up on the first page. Apart from two single-word switches ("woooooow" and "lol"), most of the rest of her comment is in Dutch, but even there the ONTD influence is visible: lengthened vowels, all caps, a Japanese-style smiley to indicate surprise ("O_O"), and lots of carriage returns that give the effect of short, excited sentences. User *geraldina*'s three subsequent comments in turns 05, 06, and 08, as well as *lillirossol*'s in turn 07, show a similar sort of style: more Dutch than English, but only barely, as well as an over-the-top affect indicated by a high degree of exclamation mark and "smiley" usage, capital letters, a higher degree of internet-inspired language use than is typical in other conversations (e.g. "lol") and the repetition of letters to indicate vowel or consonant length.

While all conversational contextualization relies on a certain degree of performativity in order to cue participants as to a given message's meaning, the kinds of contextualization that we see in the non-*vraagvrije vrijdag* excerpts above fall clearly into Deumert's (2014: 110) performance-2 (the self-conscious and strategic use of language in everyday interactions), while the *vraagvrije vrijdag* excerpts 4.5, 4.16, and particularly 4.17 above cross the line into what could more adequately described as Deumert's performance-3 (a specifically marked and non-routine mode of speaking or writing that invokes theatricality). The style reserved for the *vraagvrije vrijdag* conversations is also the style that can most clearly be analyzed as crossing (e.g. Rampton 2005), because rather than simply choosing among the linguistic resources in their own repertoires in a strategic way, and thereby claiming that entire set of language resources as, at least in some respects, their own, in the *vraagvrije vrijdag* conversations community members are actually "styling" a particular "other" by using language resources interpreted as "belonging" to the ONTD community. This very stylized use of transidiomatic practices to index a general sense of transnationalism therefore comes closest to having the suggested "wanting to sound cool" or "wanting to sound trendy" as its primary function, but even here that characterization is too simplistic, as it only occurs within the limited, specified context of the *vraagvrije vrijdag* conversations and references another limited, specified context, namely the "Free For All Friday" conversations in the ONTD community.

As with the discourse-related functions, several general observations can be made about the different participant-related functions. Three categories of participant-related functions of English-origin transidiomatic practices were identified in this section: switching to English to lighten or mitigate or an evaluative comment, switching to English to indicate lightheartedness among strong affect, and language mixing to index a general sense of transnationalism. In all cases, the two communities' use of these kinds of participant-related switches were found not to be related to linguistic competence, but always preference-related, and revealing of the types of transidiomatic practices that participants consider to be both appropriate and authentic within the context of their community's interaction. In particular, it can be said that both participants' ordinary switches to English and the type of mixed code heavily laden with English that is typical of the *vraagvrije vrijdag* conversations generally have the function of indexing the wider English-speaking world, particularly the internet world, and positioning community members as people who have the right to use that world's language.

Summary of Trends

The above analysis and the conclusions drawn from it provokes two separate but related issues that expand on issues that I was not able to address thoroughly in Chapter 3. The first of these can be summarized as the question "why switch?"—or, more specifically, if in fact it would indeed be possible to find sufficient linguistic resources within

Summary of Trends   131

participants' own languages of German and Dutch to perform the discourse-related and participant-related contextualization tasks described above, what do they need English for at all? The clear response to this is that English is so ubiquitous in the societies where these young people live that it is already present whenever they are conversing with each other due to the common frame of reference of English-language popular culture and the wider English-language internet culture, so we should not be surprised that it has taken on the kinds of functions of conversational contextualization that are so common in face-to-face bilingual communities. Indeed, it would be surprising for it not to be used in such ways. Which brings me, then, to the second issue, which can be summarized as the question "why English?"—or, more specifically, what is it specifically about the *English* language (as opposed to simply any other language that community members might tend to know and use) that is specifically suited to performing the kinds of contextualization functions described in this chapter? Peuronen (2011: 156) suggests that this sort of practice can be attributed to the fact that participants are often referring to things of North American origin, but I actually found it difficult to make a case based on the data that community members frequently switched to English specifically in order to index and align with a particularly Anglophone culture or subculture, as has also been attested elsewhere (Heller 2007b). Instead, all indications suggest that English is used so often in these communities because it is uniquely suited to allow participants to index and align with a wider transnational world of communication—particularly internet-based communication—where English is common because it is viewed as a culturally neutral international language that belongs to everyone.

This, in turn, brings us to the question of differences between the two communities. Unfortunately, it is impossible to provide a quantitative analysis of the three discourse-related and the three participant-related functions of language alternation that I was able to identify in the two communities, as they are not a closed set of options, one and only one of which can be assigned to each instance of language alternation. Therefore, it is impossible to say definitively that these types of

132   4 The How: Interactional Functions of English

English usage are more common in the Dutch community than the German one. However, it should be apparent simply based on the excerpts in this chapter that the use of English as a contextualization cue is overwhelmingly more common in the *vragenuurtje* community than in *unserekleinestadt*. Indeed, this should not be surprising, since most of the uses of English as contextualization cues fall into the categories of interactional language use specific to the world of Anglophone digital media, such as larger expressions or quotes lifted in their entirety from everyday English-language interaction and used to effect in conversation, or phrases or sentences in English that are original to the German or Dutch interactant and not borrowed from a particular other source; and as we know from the analysis, the vast majority of switches found in the German community are of a single-word nature. In any case, this overwhelming impressionistic evidence is certainly an indication that the young people in the Dutch community are using language alternation in ways that more readily resemble the full spectrum of uses found in spoken language in bilingual communities than the young people in the German community seem to be doing. Additionally, it can be said that the types of participant-related language alternation most clearly associated with evoking and aligning with the aforementioned wider transnational world of communication—switching to English to indicate lightheartedness among strong affect and language mixing to index a general sense of transnationalism—are limited exclusively to the Dutch community.

This chapter therefore adds another piece to the puzzle of the questions left dangling at the end of Chapter 3, without yet quite answering them. First, it is abundantly clear that the "people only use English to sound cool" types of arguments widely found in the popular media are too simplistic, and do not actually explain the full range of functions found in the language alternation in these two communities. Second, there is an indication that members of the Dutch community are using English in ways more closely resembling the spoken language of face-to-face bilingual communities than those used by members of the German community, and this again raises the question of whether the reason for this is simply proficiency-related, or whether there are ideologies contributing to the differing patterns on both sides. To definitively answer these questions, an analysis of the language attitudes in the two communities is necessary in order to show the ways in which these attitudes are revealing of differences in larger and more widespread ideologies. This will be the subject of Chapter 5.

5

The Why: Ideology, Positioning, and Attitudes toward English

The previous two chapters were concerned with the types and amounts of English used by each community on the one hand, and the interactional functions of language alternation on the other. Based on the findings in these chapters, it is clear that not only can *more* English be found in the Dutch community than in the German one, but that members of the Dutch community are also much more likely to make use of the full range of interactional functions similar to those found in face-to-face bilingual communities such as the Spanish-speaking community in New York City or German-Italian bilinguals in Germany. However, while it is also clear that there are differences between the ideologies behind the two communities' conceptualizations of the role of English (see Chapter 2), an argument cannot be made based on the analysis thus far that the differences in language use can be attributed to these differences in language ideologies. In order to address this issue, this chapter will therefore leave the social media data behind and move on to investigate the language attitudes as expressed in the interviews that I carried out with a subset of participants in each community. The analysis of these attitudes will focus on interactants' positioning in a

© The Author(s) 2017   **135**
J. Dailey-O'Cain, *Trans-National English in Social Media Communities*, Language and Globalization,
DOI 10.1057/978-1-137-50615-3_5

136   5 The Why: Ideology, Positioning, and Attitudes toward English

series of representative interactional excerpts, as well as on the different ways in which that positioning is often revealing of wider societal ideologies in the two communities.

The study of attitudes towards different languages or varieties of language has occupied social scientists at least since the middle of the twentieth century. At the same time, however, attitudes cannot be directly observed. An attitude, after all, is "a hypothetical construct" that is "latent, inferred from the direction and persistence of external behaviour" (Baker 1992: 10–11). Attitudes are internal, in other words—they are thoughts and ideas in people's minds that are largely hidden away unless externalized in some way—and sometimes they are not externalized at all. In order to observe and analyze these attitudes, therefore, social scientists have found different ways to externalize those internal manifestations. These approaches include experimental methods, such as the direct methods that explicitly inquire about perceptions of languages or dialects as for example in perceptual dialectology (e.g. Preston 1999; Garrett 2005; Anders et al. 2010) or indirect methods such as the matched-guise technique (e.g. Lambert et al. 1960, Giles and Ryan 1982), in which stereotyped attitudes are traditionally accessed by rating speech samples on a Likert scale with respect to a series of adjective pairs such as "educated"/"not educated" or 'short"/"tall." More recently, these approaches have also expanded to include different kinds of non-experimental qualitative methods that address the ways that language serves not just to *convey* people's perceptions, but also to more actively *construct* those perceptions (e.g. Potter and Wetherell 1987, Liebscher and Dailey-O'Cain 2009, Cuonz and Studler 2014). In all cases, however, the objects of analysis are always external *expressions* of attitudes, believed to represent those "underlying" internal thoughts and ideas to a greater or lesser extent. This, again, is because it is impossible to study attitudes at all without studying their expression, whether that expression is carried out in a questionnaire or an interview designed to elicit language attitudes, or unelicited, as in a newspaper article or a naturally occurring conversation. This expression of attitudes also always occurs within some kind of context: both in the sense of the immediate local context (e.g. did the expression happen within a written editorial, a talk show, a political speech, a questionnaire, an interview, or

The Why: Ideology, Positioning, and Attitudes toward English 137

an informal conversation, and how was it influenced by the place of that expression in the surrounding interactional context, such as the sequential order of interactional elements) and the wider societal context (e.g. demographic characteristics of the participants in the expression that might have an influence on it).

It is this latter sort of context that is key to understanding the relationship between language attitudes and language ideologies. As discussed in Chapter 2, language ideologies are "a mediating link between social structures and forms of talk" (Woolard 1992: 235), and this implies that individual attitudes both shape and are shaped by wider ideologies. While attitudes are sometimes viewed simply as the product of a given individual's psychology and/or life experience, Pan and Block (2011: 393) argue that like language itself, language attitudes are fundamentally heteroglossic, because "individually expressed beliefs draw on the voices of many as opposed to being a purely individual matter." Language ideologies that are expressed through attitudes-in-interaction commonly emerge as *stances,* a concept that DuBois (2007: 163) defines as "a public act by a social actor, achieved dialogically through overt communicative means (language, gesture, and other symbolic forms), through which social actors simultaneously evaluate objects, position subjects (themselves and others), and align with other subjects, with respect to any salient dimension of the sociocultural field." In other words, people express their language-ideological stances as language attitudes, whether explicitly, i.e. through metalanguage (Jaworski et al. 2004), or implicitly, i.e. by implicature (cf. Grice 1975) and by invoking the rules of the sequential order of interaction.

While there is no single agreed-upon methodology for studying language ideologies (Coupland and Jaworski 2004: 37), Gal and Irvine (1995) have suggested that any such study should include at least in part a discussion of three semiotic processes through which they may work. The first of these processes is *iconicity,* which "involves a transformation of the sign relationship between linguistic practices, features, or varieties and the social images with which they are linked" (Gal and Irvine 1995: 973). Central here is the previously mentioned concept of indexicality; however, linguistic practices that have been iconized do not merely index social groups, but are also understood as being representative of those groups' inherent nature or

138   **5 The Why: Ideology, Positioning, and Attitudes toward English**

essence. The second process is *recursiveness*, in which a contrast between groups that is actually meaningful at one level of the relationship between language and social organization is projected onto other levels. This can have the effect of creating subcategories or supercategories on either side of this actually meaningful contrast in an attempt to "create shifting 'communities,' identities, and selves [...] within a cultural field" (Gal and Irvine 1995: 974). The third process is *erasure*, in which the push to stereotype a set of linguistic practices leads to the ignoring or discounting of kinds of people or practices that do not fit within that stereotype. This process has the effect of essentializing groups and conceptualizing them as homogeneous, which can serve to either "generate linguistic differences or exaggerate and increase already existing differentiation" (Gal and Irvine 1995: 975). In wider societal discourses, these three processes are most visible as collective phenomena that frequently recur as "sets of beliefs articulated by users as a rationalization or justification of perceived structure and use" (Silverstein 1979: 173) which then come to be regarded as being universally true (Seargeant 2009: 348–9). But they are also visible within individual expressions of language attitudes, as the means by which participants construct those attitudes as ideological stances within an interaction. Methods of analysis that allow researchers to identify these three processes at work in such local interactions are the ones that best allow us to understand the relationship between language attitudes and language ideologies in any given community or society.

The method I use to analyze the interview data in this chapter is therefore the conversation analysis-based approach to language attitudes previously outlined in Chapter 2. As previously stated, this approach involves the analysis of expressed language attitudes within their interactional context as forms of *positioning*. Because positioning is a process by which interactants make their orientations toward social categories relevant (Harré and van Langenhove 1991), interpreting language attitudes in light of it can reveal both the ways in which social categories are evoked in the expression of attitudes and the ways in which the conversational context affects their expression. This sort of analysis must of course take the directly expressed surface meanings of interview participants' expressions of attitudes into account, but it is simultaneously also able to take other kinds

The Why: Ideology, Positioning, and Attitudes toward English 139

of indirectly expressed messages into account that are only accessible through an analysis of semantic and pragmatic aspects of interaction and a sequential analysis of communication between participants.

The connection between interactants' positionings and any social categories that emerge as relevant in the interaction is then made through an analysis of their *membership categorization*, which is a way of analyzing the "situated and reflexive use of categories in everyday and institutional interaction, as well as in interview, media and other textual data" (Benwell and Stokoe 2006: 38). These membership categorizations are inherently tied not just to group identities, but also to wider societal discourses, because these discourses are what provide the context within which the category is to be interpreted. After all, when one interactant positions someone by connecting that person to a membership category, other members of this community must rely on their societal knowledge of what it means to be labelled with such a category in order to understand what is meant (cf. Maheux-Pelletier and Golato 2008: 692). Approaching the analysis of the language attitudes in this chapter through the lens of positioning therefore makes it possible to observe and analyze the processes of iconicity, recursiveness, and erasure as they may sometimes occur within the positioning in the expressed language attitudes in the interviews. This not only helps make the general relationship between language attitudes and wider societal ideologies in the *unserekleinestadt* and *vragenuurtje* communities apparent, but it also allows us to gain access to the differences between the two communities in terms of the way different ideologies may be at work within them.

I again used NVivo as a tool to help identify the common categories within the interviews of language attitudes regarding transidiomatic practices, perceptions of reasons for their use, and ideological stances regarding the position of English in the world, after which I was able to sort excerpts into these categories (and further, into subcategories that emerged through this analysis). As with my analysis of the interactional functions of the use of English in chapter 4, I then chose excerpts for a more detailed analysis that best typified the range of diversity of stances within each category. This means that in cases where the attitudes expressed and ideological stances taken were largely similar between participants and across communities, only one representative excerpt

140   5 The Why: Ideology, Positioning, and Attitudes toward English

could be analyzed for that category, while in cases where there was a greater range of variation either within or between communities, I made sure to choose excerpts that provided each piece of that puzzle, while still making sure to focus on stances and attitudes that were expressed many separate times in the data. However, the overarching focus that connects the different parts of the analysis is on identifying the similarities and differences between the attitudes and ideologies that are in play within the German and Dutch communities. The sections and subsections that follow present this analysis, followed at the end of the chapter by a summary of the trends that the analysis reveals.

Attitudes Toward Transidiomatic Practices

In this section, I will present and analyze a series of representative excerpts that reveal each community's attitudes toward their own transidiomatic practices. Within these excerpts, I will focus on the different stances participants take as they are expressed in terms of individual attitudes. In this analysis, I will also be on the lookout for the ways that ideological processes may occur within the stances taken in the excerpts. The data has been categorized into types of stance rather than by groups of individuals, because it was found that the same people often expressed somewhat different—or even completely different—stances within different contexts. The subsections below represent the most common types of stance within the larger category of attitudes toward transidiomatic practices, namely "mixing is common," "mixing is neutral," "mixing is good," "mixing is bad," and "mixing is rule-governed."

Mixing is Common

I began each interview by asking whether the participants had noticed the more general phenomenon I was studying—the fact that people sometimes use English-origin transidiomatic practices within their otherwise local-language conversations. The first excerpt in 5.1 below is the response to that question from the 24-year-old German participant *sonnenkind*.

Attitudes Toward Transidiomatic Practices   **141**

Transcription conventions are as follows: each turn is numbered for ease of description in the analysis. I as the interviewer am always listed as "JD," while the interview participants are listed with two-letter abbreviations for their actual or pseudonymous usernames. All words of recent English origin are bolded in the original transcripts, and this bolding is preserved in the English translations so that any mixing within the interviews is evident. The transcript also differs from usual orthographic spelling in several respects, e. g. CAPITALIZATION in the transcript is used to mark intensity, rising intonation is indicated with a question mark (?) and falling intonation is indicated with a period. Vowel or consonant length is indicated by repeating the letter representing the sound in question, and false starts are marked with a single dash following the word. Unclear passages are marked with (single brackets) and commentary with ((double brackets)), while conversational overlap is indicated with either [single square brackets] or [[double square brackets]], a change in pitch with *asterisks*, a smiling voice with $dollar signs$, a laughing voice with @at signs@, and standalone laughter with standalone at signs like this: @@@. Pauses lasting a beat (.), two (..), or three (. . .) are indicated as shown; longer pauses are indicated in seconds. The English translations appear separately below each original excerpt, as in Chapters 3 and 4. While no translation is ever a perfect representation of the original, every attempt has been made to preserve all relevant pragmatic detail in the English translations—both in terms of word meanings and in terms of other interactional detail—so that as little of that detail as possible is lost to readers who find it easier reading to focus primarily on the translations. Wherever the translations are lacking in any important detail, additional explanations are provided ((in double-bracketed comments)).

Excerpt 5.1 "Advertising" (German community)

01 SK: also es fällt mir im alltäglichen gespräch NICHT auf?
02 JD: nein?
03 SK: aber es fällt mir in der WERbung sehr sehr stark auf also (.) oder in- so wenn mans irgendwo liest oder wenn man zeitschriften kauft (.) da fällt mirs sehr sehr stark auf. (.) aber im gespräch mit ner person eins zu eins fällts mir nicht auf.
04 JD: zum- zum beispiel was- was fällt dir auf in der werbung.

142   5 The Why: Ideology, Positioning, and Attitudes toward English

05 SK: es gibt ganz viele englische **slogans**. also auch parfümkette **come in and find out** oder so was (.) das kann man auf deutsch sagen. oder auch ganze werbungen die nur auf englisch gestaltet sind wo ich mich frage in deutschland es gibt ja auch menschen die kein englisch SPRECHen WArum macht man das nur auf englisch. also

06 JD: m-hm. m-hm.

07 SK: ähm oder auch so einfach bestimmte SCHLAGwörter die daneben auf englisch einfach nur sind man erzählt es auf deutsch und dann plötzlich ein englisches wort dass komisch herausguckt weil man es für **cool** oder für **hip** hält und dann als würde (.) es ein jüngeres publikum ansprechen oder jünger erscheinen lassen.

08 JD: ähm und kannst- kannst (.) du mir ein beispiel geben? von- von etwas was ein jüngeres publikum ansprechen würde?

09 SK: ähm (.) was fällt mir jetzt gerade ein (.) es gibt zum beispiel immer autowerbungen wo's auch immer also um **MOTion** geht und nicht um bewegung zum beispiel oder so was ähm (.) daa

10 JD: wie klingt- also du BIST doch ein teil von diesem jüngeren publikum

11 SK: ja ICH finds lächerlich. @@@@

12 JD: du findest es lächerlich.

13 SK: ich finds lächerlich @@

14 JD: ähh (.) also gibt's einen- so ein bisschen einen geFÜHLSsunterschied? zwischen **MOtion** in einem deutschen gespräch und bewegung [im deutschen

15 SK: [JAAA na-natürlich es KLINGT natürlich (.) ahm (.) jaaaa es klingt GRÖSSer und freier und so (.) **MOOOtion** es ist (.) also beWEGung ist so KLEIN und DEUTSCH und verPACKT und **MOtion** ist gross und frei und hat so auch ein bisschen etwas von die freiheit von den grossen weiten strassen die man in deutschland eben nicht hat die man im auto ja haben will- transportieren will- das macht schon sinn das in der werbung zu tun aber (.) ich mags trotzdem nicht.

16 JD: ok ok GUT (.) ähm (..) un- un- und findest du das im allgeMEINen nicht gut? oder gibt es- gibt es bestimmte sachen die du besser findest als- als andere. oder vielleicht

17 SK: ähm jaaaa (.) also ich mag- also ich mag (.) ich MAG unsere sprache (.) und ich mag auch das englische sehr aber ich finde es schade wenn man das so verMISCHT und keine deutschen worte mehr nimmt. (.) weil (.) es sind eigenständige sprachen und ich finde so sollten sie bleiben. @

01 SK: well i DON'T notice it in daily conversation?

02 JD: no?

03 SK: but i notice it really really strongly in ADvertising so (.) or in- like when you read it somewhere or when you buy magazines (.) then i notice it really really strongly. (.) but in conversation with a person one-on-one i don't notice it.

04 JD:	for- for example what- what do you notice in advertising.	
05 SK:	there are lots of english **slogans**. so like a perfume chain **come in and find out** or something like that (.) you can say that in german. or even whole ads that are only in english where i ask myself in germany there are people who don't SPEAK english WHY do they only do that in english. so	
06 JD:	m-hm. m-hm.	
07 SK:	um or also just certain KEYwords that are in english alongside that you're talking in german and then suddenly an english word that sticks out in a funny way because people think it's **cool** or **hip** and then as if it would (.) appeal to a younger audience or make someone seem younger.	
08 JD:	um and can- can (.) you give me an example? of- of something that would appeal to a younger audience?	
09 SK:	um (.) what pops into my head right now (.) for example there are always car ads where it's always about **MOTion** and not about motion ((the German term)) for example or something like that (.) theeere	
10 JD:	how does it sound- i mean you yourSELF are a part of this younger audience	
11 SK:	yeah I think it's ridiculous. @@@@	
12 JD:	you think it's ridiculous.	
13 SK:	i think it's ridiculous @@	
14 JD:	uhh (.) i mean is there a- like a little bit of a difference in FEELing? between **MOtion** in a german conversation and motion ((the German term)) [in a german	
15 SK:	[YEEEAH of- of course it SOUNDS of course (.) um (.) yeeeeah it sounds BIGGer and FREEr and stuff like that (.) **MOOOtion** (.) it's (.) i mean MOtion ((the German term)) is so SMALL and GERMAN and packed UP and **MOtion** is big and free and it also has a little bit to do with the freedom of the big wide streets that we just don't have that you want to have in a car- want to transport- it does make sense to do that in an ad but (.) i still don't like it.	
16 JD:	ok ok GOOD (.) um (..) an- an- and- do you dislike it in GENeral? or are there- are there certain things that you like better than- than others? or maybe	
17 SK:	um yeaaaaah (.) um i like- i mean i like (.) i LIKE our language (.) and i like english a lot too but i think it's too bad when people MIX everything and don't use german words anymore. (.) because (.) they're independent languages and i think they should stay that way. @	

Over the course of the first four turns, it becomes clear that user *sonnenkind* hasn't particularly noticed the use of English in German everyday conversations, and instead that the practice is something that she associates with advertising. In the fifth turn, however, *sonnenkind*'s first ideological

144   5 The Why: Ideology, Positioning, and Attitudes toward English

stance emerges. She juxtaposes her first example of a German perfume chain using the English slogan "come in and find out" with the statement "you can say that in German." This immediate juxtaposition has the effect of simultaneously implying that it would be better to communicate such slogans in German and providing a reason for this implication: whenever it is *possible* to say things in German, people *should* do so. She then reinforces this stance with an additional but related stance expanding on why this is the case: there are people who don't speak English in Germany, and they are excluded from advertisements that use English. In turn 7, she then mentions a reason that she believes could be behind why advertisers might want to make use of transidiomatic practices: "people think it's cool or hip" and therefore it could "appeal to a younger audience or make someone seem younger." However, her use of "suddenly" and "sticks out in a funny way" to describe the appearance of words of English origin in German sentences turns what could have been a way to excuse the practice into a way of further denouncing it. In fact, in turns 11 and 13, she confirms that she finds this practice "ridiculous," and punctuates her stance with laughter.

Then, after I ask her in turn 14 whether she perceives "a little bit of a difference in feeling" between the use of the German word and the English word for "motion" in a car advertisement, she expands on this stance. Two things are particularly telling here: *sonnenkind*'s stance that English provides an automatic mental association with largeness and with freedom, specifically because of the "freedom of the big wide streets" that supposedly exists in new-world countries like the United States but not in old-world countries like Germany, and her stance that Germanness is inherently associated with being "small" and "packed up." She finishes this turn by acknowledging that "it does make sense to do that in an ad" but reiterating that knowing that doesn't make her like the practice any more. Finally, after I invite her to expand on what exactly she doesn't like, *sonnenkind* says in turn 17 that while she has a fondness for both languages, there are two specific things she dislikes: she doesn't like it "when people mix everything," and she doesn't like it when people "don"t use German words anymore." She finishes by saying that "they're independent languages"—a stance that is simply stated as a fact without any hedging that would mark it as a personal opinion—and that she thinks they should stay that way.

Attitudes Toward Transidiomatic Practices 145

By contrast, Excerpt 5.2 is a response to the same question by 26-year-old Dutch community member *bucket*:

Excerpt 5.2 "Pure brain" (Dutch community)

01 BK: ja heellll veelll zelfs.
02 JD: ja?
03 BK: ja (..) en (..) dat is wel grappig want op de m- gaan we meteen terug
04 JD: mm-hm
05 BK: op de middelbare school gebeurde het heel VEEL en toen was het een soort STATussymbool zo van (.) kijk s hoe goed ik engels kan oh supervet ik ben werelds ennuh
06 JD: en nu is dat ANders.
07 BK: nou nu (.) omdat (.) in mijn omgeving iedereen engels spreekt hoef je niet meer te laten zien dat je zo goed engels spreekt? duss (.) kan je gewoon nederlands (.) praten want je hoeft niet meer te bewijzen of zo? um maar ik zie in mijn- in mijn vriendenkring (.) WEL dat (.) um (.) soms dekt het gewoon de LAding beter. of (.) ben je zoveel met engelstaligen in aanraking geweest dat dat gewoon
08 JD: in je hoofd zit
09 BK: [ja
10 JD: [ja
11 BK: dat dat gewoon eerder uitkomt dan (..) iets nederlands. (..) en dat is gewoon puur (.) um (.) BREIN. volgens mij wat dan het meest geactiveerd is (.) dat komt er dan het eerste uiiiit? of tenminste dat heb ik zelf heel erg gemerkt? dus dat is wel (.) ja we doen het. ja we DOEN HET.

01 BK: yeah an awwwful looot even.
02 JD: yeah?
03 BK: yeah (..) and (..) that's funny because in m- let's go right back
04 JD: mm-hm
05 BK: in high school it happened a whole LOT and back then it was a kind of STATus symbol like (.) look how good my english is oh awesome i'm worldly and uh
06 JD: and now it's DIFFerent.
07 BK: well now (.) because (.) in the circles i travel in everybody just speaks english you don't have to show off that you speak such good english anymore? sooo (.) you can just (.) speak dutch because you don't have to prove it or anything anymore? um but i see in my- in my group of friends (.) i DO see that (.) sometimes it just fits the MEANing better. or (.) you've been hanging around with english speakers so much that it just
08 JD: is in your head
09 BK: [yeah

146   5 The Why: Ideology, Positioning, and Attitudes toward English

> 10 JD: [yeah
> 11 BK: that it just comes out more quickly than (..) something dutch (..) and that's just pure (.) um (.) BRAIN. i think what you have activated most strongly is (.) that just comes ooooout first then? or at least that's what i've noticed a whole lot myself? so it really is (.) yes we do it. yes we DO IT.

Participant *bucket* starts by saying that she has actually noticed the use of transidiomatic practices "an awful lot," and in turn 5, she talks about how back in high school, people used English as "a kind of status symbol" in order to convey proficiency in English (and along with that, an implied worldliness). Her use of the past tense throughout this turn and her immediately previous one cause me to note in turn 6 that she seems to be implying that this is no longer the case, and she responds to this by saying in turn 7 that because everybody she knows is now proficient in English, this has caused English to be less useful as a tool for demonstrating worldliness. But although she says this means they can now "just speak Dutch," she also says that she and her friends have continued to use transidiomatic practices anyway, specifically when English "fits the meaning better" (turn 7) or when English is "activated most strongly" in her "brain" (turn 11).

A comparison of these two excerpts reveals that both participants identify the same general trend of using English to sound hip and cool and worldly (more on this later in the chapter), though the German participant iconizes this practice as typical only of the advertising world, while the Dutch participant personalizes it by positioning it as something she and her friends used to do back when they were high-school students. In doing so, the German participant positions this use of transidiomatic practices for deliberate effect as limited to an arena where she is an audience member rather than a practitioner, which in turn makes it easier for her to stand in judgment over these practices without having to stand in judgment over her own community. Through these critical stances, she presents an ideology—one that is remarkably consistent with the rather purist wider German public discourse that trivializes any influence from English as "anglicisms"—that languages are and should be kept separate. By contrast, the Dutch participant characterizes this sort of deliberate strategic use of transidiomatic practices as something that all Dutch young people do when they are teenagers, and although the original strategy behind these practices to make them look cool is no longer necessary now that they are older and more proficient in English, to her it is neither good nor bad but simply self-evident that the transidiomatic practices have remained in their repertoire anyway.

While these two excerpts do deal primarily with the *commonness* of transidiomatic practices, I have chosen to begin with them because they also contain a lot of the contrasting themes that will appear again and again throughout the rest of this chapter. I will show, for example, that while many German participants are far less critical of transidiomatic practices than *sonnenkind* is here, her tendency to characterize English as a foreign element in German interactions is characteristic of both much of the rest of the German data and what we already know of the kinds of purist ideologies toward English that are common in the wider German society. Similarly, the self-evidentness of English in Dutch interaction as exemplified here by the Dutch participant *bucket* is a stance that weaves itself throughout practically every line of every excerpt of data from the *vragenuurtje* community, and while Dutch participants tend to present this stance as ideologically neutral, it is in fact representative of the ideology of English that is typically found in wider Dutch society: one that is mostly unconcerned with the increased use of specific English lexical items and occasionally even uncertain how concerned it should be about the loss of previously Dutch-only domains (see Chapter 2). Over the course of the rest of the chapter, I will analyze a number of different types of excerpts that often include conflicting ideas, but these two more general stances will prove to be remarkably consistent throughout.

Mixing is Neutral

In this next section, I will analyze excerpts that exemplify a stance that mixing is neither positive nor negative, but simply neutral. Identified subcategories within that consist of the stance that mixing is understandable, and that mixing triggers more mixing.

148   5 The Why: Ideology, Positioning, and Attitudes toward English

Mixing is Understandable

The stance that mixing is understandable is found in both the *unserekleinestadt* and the *vragenuurtje* communities, but there are enormous differences in the specific positionings that make up this stance in each community. I begin with Excerpt 5.3, which also comes from the same German participant *sonnenkind* who we already know from Excerpt 5.1. It emerged within my discussion with *sonnenkind* of the conversation in the *unserekleinestadt* community that is seen in part in Excerpt 3.2, about "outdoor shoes" and "geocaching."

Excerpt 5.3 "Everybody knows what is meant" (German community)

01 SK: also **outdoor** schuhe (.) ja **outdoor** schuhe würde mir nicht auffallen weil es GIBT kein adequates deutsches wort in meinem wor- also ich würde es AUCH sagen das- **outdoor** schuhe tatsächlich uhmm ich würde das auch (.) so nennen?
02 JD: und- und findest du dass auch ok?
03 SK: ähm (.) ich fänd es schön wenn es ein deutsches wort gäbe was ähm (..) was halt genausogut- also bei **outdoor** schuhe weiss jeder was man meint.
04 JD: mm
05 SK: und ich fänd es toll wenns ein adequates deutsches wort dafür gäbe was- (.) man benützen würde aber das gibt es halt [nicht
04 JD: [ja (.) ja ja
05 SK: insofern (..) ähm (.) benutz ich das AUCH? genauso wie bei **geocaching**? (.) da fällt es nicht so auf (.) also das ist halt einfach so ähm das GIBT es nur auf englisch. (.) also es gibt ja kein deutsches ich bin da mal einfach darüber gestolpert mal vor einer weile? hab es angeguckt von der seite finde es auch toll und es gibt keine deutsche bezeichnung es hat nie jemand eine erfunden (.) es ist weiss nicht ob es-
06 JD: wie kann mans bezeichnen
07 SK: ähm
08 JD: @@@
09 SK: jaa es ist [wie könnte man das bezeichnen
10 JD: [ja ich- mir fällt auch überhaupt nichts ein
11 SK: jaa mir auch nicht
12 JD: @@@@@@
13 SK: aber da müsste man mal überlegen
14 JD: ist auch schwierig zu beschreiben [was es überhaupt ist
15 SK: [ja ja schatzsuche

Attitudes Toward Transidiomatic Practices   149

```
16 JD:   ja schatzsuche
17 SK:   vielleicht
18 JD:   vielleicht
19 SK:   ja


01 SK:   so outdoor shoes (.) yeah outdoor shoes wouldn't be something i'd notice
         because there ISn't an adequate german word in my voca- i mean i would say it
         TOO the- outdoor shoes actually uhmm i would also (.) call it by that term?
02 JD:   and- and do you think that's okay?
03 SK:   um (.) i would appreciate it if there were a german word that um (..) that fit just-
         i mean everybody knows what's meant by outdoor shoes.
04 JD:   mm
05 SK:   and it'd be great if there were an adequate german word for that which- (.)
         people would use but that doesn't [exist
06 JD:                                     [okay. (.) okay okay
07 SK:   and so (..) um (.) i use it TOO? just like with geocaching? (.) so i don't tend to
         notice it (.) that's just what it's called um it only EXISTS in english. (.) i mean
         there's no german i stumbled onto it once a while back? had a sideways look at it
         i think it's great and there's no german term nobody ever invented one (.) it's i
         don't know if it-
08 JD:   what might you call it
09 SK:   um
10 JD:   @@@
11 SK:   yeah it's [what could you call it
12 JD:             [yeah i- nothing's occurring to me at all
13 SK:   yeeah me neither
14 JD:   @@@@@@
15 SK:   but you'd have to come up with something
16 JD:   it's even hard to describe [what that is in the first place
17 SK:                             [yeah yeah treasure hunt
18 JD:   yeah treasure hunt
19 SK:   maybe
20 JD:   maybe
21 SK:   yeah
```

User *sonnenkind* begins by asserting in turn one that there isn't an "adequate german word" for "outdoor shoes" in her vocabulary. This has the effect of positioning "outdoor shoes" (or *Outdoorschuhe*, as it is used in German) as a term that is still foreign, i.e. not actually part of the German language yet, by virtue of its (partial) English origin. However,

150   **5 The Why: Ideology, Positioning, and Attitudes toward English**

what follows is a series of justifications for why it is acceptable to use this term anyway: she would also use it (turn 1), it's a term everyone would understand (turn 3), and the German term that would make things 100% acceptable simply doesn't exist (turns 3 and 5). She then compares the use of "outdoor shoes" with the use of the term "geocaching" from the same discussed excerpt, saying that it's a similar situation where "nobody even invented" a German term for this hobby of Anglophone origin. Turns 6 through 19 then consist of the two of us negotiating a possible German-origin term for the concept of geocaching, the difficulty of which (as per the hesitations and the length of time it takes her to come up with something) only serves to underscore *sonnenkind's* point that this represents an acceptable exception to her view that mixing is generally an unacceptable practice.

Excerpt 5.4 comes from the same Dutch participant *bucket* who we also already know from Excerpt 5.2. It came about toward the end of that interview, when I was asking her general questions that attempted to discern whether there were any hard limits for her on the acceptability of the use of English.

Excerpt 5.4 "Really old people" (Dutch community)

01 JD: maar iedere nederlander leert engels op school nu. (.) hè? en (..) je komt op- op andere manieren met het engels in contact. dat heb je ook [ZELF gezegd.

02 BK: [ja.

03 JD: toch zijn er nederlanders die niet zo goed engels [[spreken.

04 BK: [[ja (..)
dat vind ik echt ONbegrijpelijk

05 JD: ah (..) en (..) zij- zijn er mensen die dit soort gebruik- het taalgebruik- het engels door het nederlands heen- die dat- dat helemaal niet zouden beGRIJpen
((3-second pause))

06 BK: of die er überHAUPT zijn. die dat

07 JD: ja.
((2-second pause))

08 JD: ZIJN er (.) [mensen die

08 BK: [ja dan denk ik wel meteen aan HEle ouwe mensen?

09 JD: mm je Oma of [[zo.

10 BK:	[[ja. (.) bijvoorbeeld (.) ik was vandaag bij een client en die was drieennegentig. en die werd geBELD. en dat was een italiaan die zei *ik bel uit italië?* (.) in het engels? (.) en toen zei zij ja neem JIJ het maar wantuh jij kan engels (..) en ik niet. dus mensen die drieennegentig zijn die kunnen geen [engels
11 JD:	[mm mm ((4-second pause))
12 BK:	en- [EN dan denk ik
13 JD:	[moet je- moet je daar REkening mee houden
14 BK:	ja maar dat is (..) umm (..) ja maar (..) daar MOET je wel rekening mee houden maar ik denk dat dat (..) automatisch gebeurt gewoon aan gewoon door degene die tegenOVER je zit. (..) dus (..) dat (..) meer de ROLverdeling al wel bepaalt wat voor taal je gebruikt dan dat je HEEL nadrukkelijk denkt van (.) ik moet nu dit of dit zeggen? (..) want die begrijpt dan niet het engels. en het taalgebruik bij ouderen is sowieso anders dan met vriendinnen.
15 JD:	klopt.
16 BK:	spreek ik over het algemeen veel netter? (.) @@@ veel beSCHAAFDer

01 JD:	but every dutch person learns english in school now. (.) right? and (..) you come in- in contact with english in other ways. you said that [yourSELF.
02 BK:	[yeah.
03 JD:	but there are still dutch people whose english isn't so [[good.
04 BK:	[[yeah (..) i find that compLETEly incomprehensible.
05 JD:	uh (..) and (..) are- are there people who this kind of use- language use- english mixed into dutch- who would- who wouldn't understand that at ALL. ((3-second pause))
06 BK:	you're asking whether they exIST at all. whether there
07 JD:	yeah. ((2-second pause))
08 JD:	ARE there (.) [people who
08 BK:	[yeah okay the first thing that comes to mind is REALLy old people?
09 JD:	mm your GRANDma or [[someone like that.
10 BK:	[[yeah. (.) for example (.) today i was at a client's and she was ninety-three. and someone CALLED her. and it was an italian who said *i'm calling from italy?* (.) in english? (.) and she said yeah YOU take it because uh you speak english (..) and i don't. so people who are ninety-three don't speak [english
11 JD:	[mm mm ((4-second pause))
12 BK:	and- [AND then i think

152 **5 The Why: Ideology, Positioning, and Attitudes toward English**

13 JD:	[do you- have to take that into accOUNT
14 BK:	sure but that's (..) um (..) yeah but (..) you DO have to take that into account but i think that that just (..) happens automatically just um just because of the person who's sitting aCROSS from you. (..) so (..) that (..) it has more to do with the ROLES we play that already determine what kind of language you use then that you then think REALLy emphatically like (.) i have to say this or this? (..) because she doesn't understand english. and with old people language use is different anyway than it is with your friends.
15 JD:	true.
16 BK:	just generally i speak more properly? (.) @@@ more CULTivated

The beginning of this excerpt represents an attempt by me to assert a premise that Dutch people exist whose English isn't especially good, so that I can then go on to ask whether it is important to keep those people in mind when you're using transidiomatic practices. Participant *bucket* rejects that premise outright by saying that she finds the idea that such Dutch people exist "completely incomprehensible." I then ask whether there are Dutch people who might not understand the kind of mixing we have been discussing in the interview at all, and what follows is an uncharacteristically long pause of three seconds, a request for clarification (turn 6), another uncharacteristically long pause, and ultimately the start of a rephrasing of the question by me (turn 8). Together, these hesitations and requests for clarification suggest still more difficulty on *bucket*'s part with the very premise of the question: the notion that there are Dutch people who might not understand the kinds of transidiomatic practices that are typical in the *vragenuurtje* community. Finally, however, she does come up in turn 8 with a category of people who might in fact have such difficulties: "really old people," which she clarifies in turn ten as referring to the category of old people typified by a 93-year-old who she met through her job. This further serves to underscore how rare *bucket* considers a lack of English knowledge to be in the Netherlands by positioning a lack of English in a Dutch person as something you need to go several generations into the past in order to find. Then, when I ask her in turn 13 whether you would need to take such a person's lack of English into account when talking to her, she explains that that "just happens automatically" when you're talking to such a person, and that there are already plenty of other ways in which language use is different with this category of "really old people" than it would be with her friends, so this doesn't require any special effort.

From the perspective of the German participant, there is simply no legitimately German way to express certain concepts, which in turn means that everyone understands the terminology for these concepts in English, and that makes it okay to use that terminology in German interactions. It is interesting to note that she could have decided to go another way by positioning the words for which there are no German-origin equivalents as fully integrated and therefore fully "German" words in their own right, but instead, she opted to position the situation of words like "outdoor shoes" and "geocaching" as an exception to her overall stance: while she admits that it would be *better* for there to be German-origin terms for people to use, the fact that these do not exist makes it acceptable to use English-origin terms instead. This stance weakens the rigidity of her "no mixing is best" ideology (see the discussion of Excerpt 5.1 above), but it preserves the ideology of the German language as one that can be kept entirely separate from outside influences, as foreign terms still cannot become German simply by virtue of being the only options. The Dutch participant, on the other hand, positions it as entirely obvious that there is no reason not to use transidiomatic practices except in very specific and fairly uncommon situations, situations that are marked by other conventions of formality in language and interaction anyway. Her stated reasoning for this is actually quite similar to what underpins the reason for the acceptability of the use of certain kinds of English words for the German participant: apart from people so old that they stand out as "really old," everyone would understand it. However, there are two crucial differences between the Dutch participant's stance and the German participant's. First, the Dutch participant does not position the understandability of transidiomatic practices as limited to specific areas of vocabulary for which no Dutch-origin equivalent exists, but instead extends it to the entire repertoire of transidiomatic practices that is typical for the *vragenuurtje* community. Second, the Dutch participant positions the act of refraining from using transidiomatic practices as nothing but an ordinary part of a more formal register, and the use of a formal register in the appropriate

154   **5 The Why: Ideology, Positioning, and Attitudes toward English**

situations as a natural part of language use that doesn't require any special effort.

Mixing Triggers More Mixing

The stance that some mixing triggers more immediately following mixing is found only in the *unserekleinestadt*—i.e the German—community, a fact that is interesting in and of itself. It is actually brought up quite frequently in that community as an explanation for why mixing occurs in a particular excerpt of community conversation, but Excerpt 5.5 emerged within my discussion with the 23-year-old participant *urlaubssommer* of the conversation in the *unserekleinestadt* community that is seen in part in Excerpt 3.7, about "hello kitty overkill."

Excerpt 5.5 "I suddenly just stay in the language" (German community)

01 JD: es ist (.) es ist (.) **hello kitty overkill**
02 US: ja?
03 JD: und dann? (.) **loving it though.**
         ((8-second pause))
04 US: ok (. . .) hmm (.) **hello kitty overkill**. ja (.) also ((3-second pause)) s find ich is son typischer? (.) gebrauch dann für die englischen wörter um sich einfach selber mehr (.) halt so expressiviTÄT zu- zu- zu verleihen? ähm (.) halt weil das so **overkill** (.) kenn ich jetzt gar keinen deutschen begriff [dafür
05 JD: [mhm
06 US: das erscheint mir auch wieder wie so ein typischer (.) populärer ähm ENGlisch (.) terminus (.) und dann (.) **hello kitty overkill** (. . .) und dann hab ich das gefühl dass sie einfach auf englisch weitergemacht hat weil sie jetzt einmal den englischen begriff da drin hatte (.) dass sie das da jetzt einfach [fortgesetzt hat
07 JD: [also
08 US: [[dann macht sie das
09 JD: [[also fängt sie mit **mit hello kitty OVerkill** an? und dann- dann macht sie einfach weiter auf ENGlisch
10 US: ja. ja
11 JD: ok
12 US: also das passiert mir teilweise auch wenn ich dann einmal einen englischen begriff benutze=
13 JD: mhm

14 US: =dass ich dann auf einmal DRIN bleibe in der sprache.

01 JD: it's (.) it's (.) **hello kitty overkill**
02 US: yeah?
03 JD: and then? (.) **loving it though.**
          ((8-second pause))
04 US: okay (. . .) hmm (.) **hello kitty overkill.** ja (.) so ((3-second pause)) i think of
          this as kind of a typical? (.) use of english words to give oneself more (.) uh a
          kind of exPRESSiveness? um (.) i mean because that **overkill** (.) at the moment
          i can't think of a german word for [that
05 JD: [mhm
06 US: and again to me that seems like a (.) popular um ENGlish (.) term (.) and then
          (.) **hello kitty overkill** (. . .) and then i have the feeling that she just continued
          in english because she already had the english term in there (.) that she just
          [went on with that
07 JD: [so
08 US: [[then she does that
09 JD: [[so she starts **with hello kitty OVerkill**? and then- then she just keeps going in
          ENGlish
10 US: yeah. yeah
11 JD: okay
12 US: i mean that happens to me sometimes too when i use an english term=
13 JD: mhm
14 US: =that i suddenly STAY in the language.

User *urlaubssommer* is attempting here to explain two uses of transidiomatic practices by another user: first the words "hello kitty overkill," and next the immediately following words "loving it though." She explains the first of these as "a typical use of english words to give oneself more uh a kind of expressiveness" (turn 4), but positions the latter as a result of the first use of English triggering an immediately following use of English (turns 6 and 9). She then supports this positioning by stating that this is something that sometimes happens to her as well (turns 12 and 14).

Interestingly, a similar sort of "triggering hypothesis" has been used by linguists in an attempt to explain similar phenomena (e.g. Clyne 1967, Broersma and de Bot 2006), though as this is a study of attitudes and ideologies rather than a study of the accuracy of non-linguists being asked

156   5 The Why: Ideology, Positioning, and Attitudes toward English

to do amateur linguistic analysis, my interest here is of course limited to the stances within participants' explanations as social phenomena. As such, what is most intriguing here is the fact that the triggering hypothesis comes up with reasonable frequency in the German community and not at all in the Dutch one, even though there are of course many more excerpts in the Dutch data than in the German data in which one stretch of English immediately follows another stretch of English. It is difficult to make an argument concerning the *absence* of something in one's data, but judging from the kinds of explanations that were provided by my Dutch participants, I would argue that this is a result of the use of English feeling so normal and natural to them that it simply does not occur to them to explain it as something that might have been triggered by a previous use of English-origin material. I will discuss this general tendency further in the following section.

Mixing is Good

In the following section, I will analyze excerpts that exemplify a stance that mixing is good. Identified subcategories consist of stances that some things just "sound better" in English, that some things can be said more quickly or simply in English, that mixing is useful for distinguishing a youth subculture, and that mixing is useful for making distinctions in meaning that would be more difficult without English.

Some Things "Sound Better" in English

The stance that there are certain kinds of things that simply "sound better" in English comes up in both communities, though it is noticeably more common in the Dutch one. This section will consist of four excerpts, two from the Dutch community and two from the German one, that represent an increasing degree of social complexity in terms of the reasoning for why these particular transidiomatic practices are positioned as "sounding better." The first of these, in Excerpt 5.6, comes from the 24-year-old Dutch participant *laviefantasque*, and it concerns the conversation in the *vragenuurtje* community that is seen in part in Excerpt 4.7, about the use of "discuss" at the end of a long post that's primarily in Dutch.

Attitudes Toward Transidiomatic Practices 157

Excerpt 5.6 "Discuss" (Dutch community)

01 JD: wa- waarom staat daar (.) di**SCUSS**? en niet- ah- waarom zou JIJ dat doen. als jij dat was.
02 LV: omdat *discussier* @klinkt echt heel [stom@. @@@@
03 JD: [oké.
((3-second pause))
04 LV: ja (.) het is gewoon- het is sim- het is een simpel- het is natuurlijk een ACTiewoord en het betekent meerdere dingen van- in plaats van- ja. (.) ik heb twee VRAgen (.) geef antwoord maar ook MEER (.) een mening (.) en dat is dat lekker in één woord en ik denk dat het daarom daar zo staat.
05 JD: en als je dat in het NEderlands zou zeggen dan (.) zou je MEER WOORden voor-
06 LV: OOK en ik denk dat het woord *discussie*? in het nederlands? een LA[ding heeft?
07 JD: [ja (.) maar je kunt wel zeggen (.) heb het erover (.) [of zo.
08 LV: [heb het erover. @@@ dat is echt anders.
09 JD: @@@ hoe KLINKT dat. (.) hoe komt dat echt ANders op jou Over.
10 LV: als je zegt (.) HEB het erover?
11 JD: hmhm. ((2-second pause)) of ZOIETS.
((3-second pause))
12 LV: ja. ((4-second pause)) ja. dan zou ik wel denken van *waarom gebruik je @@ DIE woorden nou weer?* (.) heb het erover (.) ja. beSPREEK [het (.) zoiets (.) ja.
13 JD: [hm. hm.
((3-second pause))
14 LV: nee.
15 JD: nee?
16 LV: @@@

01 JD: why- why is it (.) di**SCUSS**? and not- uh- why would YOU do that. if this were you.
02 LV: because *discussier* @sounds completely [stupid@. @@@@
03 JD: [okay.
((3-second pause))
04 LV: yeah (.) it's just- it's a sim- it's a simple- of course it's an ACTion word and it means multiple things ins- instead of- yeah. (.) i have two QUEStions (.) give me an answer but also MORE a (.) an opinion (.) and you can put that in one word and i think that's why she put it like that.
05 JD: so if you were to say that in DUTCH then (.) you would need MORE WORDS for-

158   5 The Why: Ideology, Positioning, and Attitudes toward English

```
06 LV:   that TOO and i think that the word *discussion*? in dutch? has a particular
         conno[TAtion?
07 JD:            [sure (.) but you can say (.) talk about it (.) [or something.
08 LV:                                                            [talk about it. @@@ that's
         really different.
09 JD:   @@@ how does that SOUND. (.) how does that really come acROSS to you
         DIFFerently.
10 LV:   if you say (.) TALK about it?
11 JD:   hmhm. ((2-second pause)) or SOMEthing like that.
         ((3-second pause))
12 LV:   yeah. ((4-second pause)) yeah. then i'd think something like *why are you using
         @@ THOSE kinds of words?* (.) talk about it (.) yeah. disCUSS [it (.) some-
         thing like that (.) yeah.
13 JD:                                                                 [hm. hm.
         ((3-second pause))
14 LV:   no.
15 JD:   no?
16 LV:   @@@
```

This excerpt begins with a question from me in turn 1 about why *laviefantasque* might end a long, primarily Dutch post with the English-origin word "discuss" if this were her. Her response positions the literal Dutch equivalent "discussier" (which has connotations of debate as opposed to the much more conversational-sounding ones in the English term "discuss") as the only possible alternative while at the same time rejecting that alternative as unacceptable because it is "stupid" (turn 1), because it doesn't fully encompass the desired connotation of opinion (turn 4), and because the Dutch equivalent has unintended connotations (turn 6). In turn 7 I then propose a possible alternative: instead of translating literally, the user could have said "talk about it" or some other possible way of expressing the meaning behind the transidiomatic practice in Dutch. This, however, is rejected as well because it's "really different" (turn 8). When I then press her to express how it's different by asking her how the use of "talk about it" or some other alternative would come across to her, she positions this as so strange that her only reaction to reading such a phrase in Dutch by another user would be to think "why are you using THOSE kinds of words." In the

Attitudes Toward Transidiomatic Practices 159

end, *laviefantasque* rejects the entire idea of using some sort of Dutch alternative to "discuss" with a "no" with strongly falling intonation (turn 14), and laughter that positions it as absurd (turn 16).

Excerpt 5.7 comes from the 31-year-old German participant *hobbit*. It deals with a conversation in the *unserekleinestadt* community that deals with making song playlists in the Apple software iTunes.

Excerpt 5.7 "Playlist" (German community)

01 HB: ähm (.) da stolpere ich über das **playlist** überHAUPT nicht?

02 JD: ok

03 HB: weil ich das AUCH benutze? ((2-second pause)) jetzt so zum thema mir fällt kein deutsches wort ein ich wüsste auch [gar nicht (...) die deutsch

04 JD: [wie würdest du das (.) zum beispiel (...) in einer- einem gespräch mit deiner mutter bezeichnen. (.) AUCH **playlist**?

05 HB: ja wahrscheinlich. @@

06 JD: ok. und [würde sie das verstehen?

07 HB: [ich äh ich- ich überLEG grade. (..) ähhhh. ((2-second pause)) ich glaube ich würde das wesentlich kompliZIERter ausdrücken. wenn ich es nicht **playlist** nennen würde würd ich wahrscheinlich sagen ich hab hier muSIK zusammengestellt.

10 JD: o[kay.

11 HB: [oder sowas in der art. also ich hab- oder ich WÜRde das WORT vielleicht- wenn es (..) ich WÜRde es wahrscheinlich (.) entweder ich benutze es? oder ich benutze es GAR nicht in dem sinne dass ich (.) die formulierung ganz anders mache dass ich sagen würde (..) ich hab ne cd zusammengestellt oder ich hab muSIK [zusammengestellt.=

12 JD: [mhm

13 HB: =oder (..) mmm einfach nur (.) in kurz ich hab ne (.) liste [[gemacht oder so irgendwas.

14 JD: [[mhm

15 HB: aber (.) ich benutze eher **playlist** glaub [[ich. also.

16 JD: [[ok

17 HB: mir fällt jetzt auch grade gar nichts anderes ein gibts über- n vernünftiges deutsches wort dafür?

18 JD: wa- die ab- [abspiel- abspielliste?

19 HB: [@@@

20 JD: oder

21 HB: jach nee. @@@

22 JD: ok. @@@

160   5 The Why: Ideology, Positioning, and Attitudes toward English

```
01 HB:   um (.) i don't stumble over the playlist at ALL?
02 JD:   okay
03 HB:   because i use that TOO ((2-second pause)) now no german word occurs to me
         that has to do with that topic i wouldn't [even know (...) the german
04 JD:                                            [how would you (.) for example
         (...) what would you call it in an- a conversation with your mother. (.)
         ALSO playlist?
05 HB:   yeah probably. @@
06 JD:   okay. and [would she understand that?
07 HB:             [i uh i- i'm just thinking. (..) uhhhh. ((2-second pause)) i think i
         would express that in a much more COMplicated way. if i didn't call it playlist
         i would probably say i put some MUsic together here.
10 JD:   o[kay.
11 HB:    [or something like that. so i- or i WOULD use maybe i- the word- if it (..) i
         probably WOULD use (.) either i use it? or i don't use it at ALL in the sense
         that i (.) formulate it totally differently that i would say (..) i put a cd together
         or i put MUsic [[together.=
12 JD:                  [[mhm
13 HB:   =or (..) hmm just like (.) in short i put a (.) made a [list or something like that.
14 JD:                                                          [mhm
15 HB:   but (.) i would tend to use playlist i [[think. so.
16 JD:                                          [[okay
17 HB:   i can't think of anything else is there- a decent german word for that?
18 JD:   what the ab- [ab- abspielliste? ((literal translation of "playlist"))
19 HB:                [@@@
20 JD:   or
21 HB:   no way. @@@
22 JD:   okay. @@@
```

This excerpt begins very much in the same way that Excerpt 5.3 above from fellow German participant *sonnenkind* began: by saying that the word in question (playlist) isn't something that *hobbit* would particularly notice as unusual for two reasons: first, she would use the word as well, and second, there isn't a readily available German alternative. However, when I ask her in turn 4 how she might express the concept of a playlist to her mother, who does not speak English, it sets off a series of possible ways of coping with that situation that are quite different from the ones that Dutch participant *laviefantasque* came up with in Excerpt 5.6 above. First, she suggests that she would probably just say "playlist" after all (turn 5), then

Attitudes Toward Transidiomatic Practices   161

she moves on to suggest various paraphrases that she positions as "more complicated" such as "I put some music together" (turns 7 and 11), "I put a CD together" (turn 11), and "I made a list" (turn 13), before coming back around to the conclusion that she probably actually would just say "playlist," even with someone who doesn't speak English (turn 15). My suggestion of a potential direct translation in line 18 is met, similarly to *laviefantasque*'s response in Excerpt 5.6, with a strong negative response ("no way," turn 21) and laughter that positions the very idea as absurd.

Excerpt 5.8 comes from an interview with two 24-year-old Dutch participants, *luna_puella* and *isolde*, and it deals with a conversation about an excerpt from the *vragenuurtje* community in which *luna_puella* had posted a question about online dating.

Excerpt 5.8: "Internet dating" (Dutch community)

01 LP: als ik hier **ONline dating** had geschreven had ik het WEL los gedaan.
02 IE: **online [dating** is
03 LP: [want **online** is een bijvoeglijk NAAMwoord. en bijvoeglijke naamwoorden? en zelfstandige naamwoorden in deze context zou ik niet aan elkaar doen zoals ik **INternet** en **DAting** aan elkaar plak. maar **internetdating** is toch een HARTstikke nederlands WOORD geworden.
04 JD: @@ ja (.) oké.
05 LP: er is niet echt een nederlands alternaTIEF voor (.) dus je bent je er helemaal niet beWUST van dat je een engels woord geBRUIKT. [omdat het ZO INgeburgerd is.
06 JD: [ja.
07 IE: maar het KLINKT ook minder eng.
08 LP: ja.
09 IE: als je het hebt over **online dat**en (.) dat klinkt minder serieus dan *ik ben een relatie aan het zoeken via het wereldwijde **web***.
10 JD: @@@@[@@@@@@@@@@@@@@@@
11 LP: @@@@[@@@@@@@@@@@@@@@@
12 IE: [dan zou ik denken van (.) suCCES. weet je wel?
13 LP: JA @@@
14 JD: @@@
15 LP: dat WERKT gewoon niet. of de *digitale SNEL[weg* zoals het vroeger ook wel genoemd werd.
16 IE: [@@@@@@
17 JD: [@@@@@@
18 IE: daar let ik nog STEEDS op. en dan denk ik van (.) neeeee.

162   5 The Why: Ideology, Positioning, and Attitudes toward English

```
01 LP:   if i had written ONline dating here then i WOULD have written it as two
         words.
02 IE:   online [dating is
03 LP:          [because online is an ADjective. and adjectives? in this context i
         wouldn't put adjectives and nouns together in the same way that i put
         INternet and DAting together. i mean internetdating has comPLETEly
         become a dutch WORD.
04 JD:   @@ yeah (.) okay.
05 LP:   there isn't really a dutch eQUIValent (.) so you're not even really aWARE that
         you're USing an english word. [because it's SUCH a part of the LANGuage.
06 JD:                                 [yeah.
07 IE:   but also it SOUNDS less scary.
08 LP:   yeah.
09 IE:   if you're talking about online dating (.) that sounds less serious than *i'm
         looking for a relationship through the worldwide web*.
10 JD:   @@@@[@@@@@@@@@@@@@@@@@
11 LP:   @@@@[@@@@@@@@@@@@@@@@@
12 IE:          [if you said that i'd think (.) good LUCK. you know?
13 LP:   YEAH @@@
14 JD:   @@@
15 LP:   that just doesn't WORK. or the *digital SUper[highway* like they also used to
         call it.
16 IE:                                             [@@@@@@
17 JD:                                             [@@@@@@
18 IE:   i STILL pay attention to that. and then i think like (.) nooo.
```

The first six turns are primarily concerned with *luna_puella*'s explanation for why she wrote "internet dating" as a single word (i.e. according to Dutch rules) rather than preserving the two-word original English phrase. In turn 7, however, the conversation begins to moves down another track when *isolde* puts forward a different reason why people might want to use an English term for this concept rather than a native Dutch one: it "sounds less scary," a positioning that *luna_puella* immediately endorses. This is elaborated in turn 9, when *isolde* describes an English-origin expression as "less serious" than the Dutch paraphrase that she provides: "I'm looking for a relationship through the worldwide web." This paraphrase is so stilted that it immediately prompts raucous laughter from both myself and *luna_puella*, at which point *isolde* further

Attitudes Toward Transidiomatic Practices 163

positions the Dutch paraphrase as bizarre and stilted by saying "if you said that i'd think good LUCK." User *luna_puella* then takes this one step further in turn 15, offering up an even more stilted-sounding alternative that includes a Dutch translation of the old-fashioned expression "digital superhighway." It is notable that as in Excerpt 5.6 above, the only alternatives to the English suggested (and immediately rejected) by the participants in turns 9 and 15 are so deliberately stilted that this makes them easy to position as absurd and therefore reject outright as simply "sounding wrong." However, one somewhat more socially complex reasoning for using English is also provided here: the English sounds better because it contains an automatic connotation of being less scary and less serious. The deliberate stiltedness of the potential Dutch paraphrases obfuscates whether this "mildening" is being said to be a natural effect of transidiomatic practices, but as we will see, this idea of English as carrying less metaphorical weight than any possible Dutch equivalent is something we will see again and again throughout the Dutch data.

Finally, Excerpt 5.9 comes from an interview with the German participants *bienchen, menschenskind,* and *kakumo,* and it emerged as part of a discussion about when it is appropriate to use or inappropriate to use English as a part of an online conversation.

Excerpt 5.9 "White male privilege" (German community)

01 BC: was mir als beispiel einfällt is zum beispiel jetzt das ganze äh (.) vokabuLAR von der ich sach jetzt mal **net police**. halt zum beispiel ähm (.) ich GLAUbe (.) ich bräuchte viel mehr um gewisse konZEPTe wie zum beispiel jetzt (.) das erste was mir einfällt blöderweise is **white male privilege.**

02 MK: [ja.

03 JD: [mhm

04 BC: so und das- das is was ähm- da hab ich auf DEUTSCH noch nie drüber geLESen oder diskuTIERT (.) so.

05 MK: [mhm

06 BC: das heißt also ich würde AUtomatisch? auch wenn ich mit DEUtschen dadrüber REde auch in der FREIzeit? da die englischen begriffe [für verwenden

07 MK: [jaaaa?

08 BC: für dieses ganzen=

164   5   The Why: Ideology, Positioning, and Attitudes toward English

```
09 JD:   [mhm
10 BC:   =themen (.) cluster.
11 JD:   und wenn [du das
12 MK:           [ja.
13 JD:   wenn du das umschreiben müsstest?
14 BC:   das privileg des weißen mannes.
15 JD:   [mhm
16 MK:   [@@@
17 BC:   das klingt aber für MICH eher nach ähm
18 KK:   die BÜRde des [weißen mannes.
19 MK:                 [@@@@@
20 JD:                 [@@@@@
20 BC:   ja das- das klingt so nach äh (.) wir sind jetzt da wo die hutzis und die tutus
         oder warns die (.) tutus und die hutzis (.) sich gegenseitig um das privileg des
         weißen mannes im- kontrast zu
21 JD:   [@@@
22 KK:   [is
23 BC:   ähm (.) und dann halt im prinzip äh- ja.


01 BC:   what occurs to me as an example is for example that all that uh (.) voCABulary
         of the i'll just call it net police. the kind of um (.) i THINK (.) i would need
         much more in order to talk about certain concepts like for example now (.)
         stupidly the first thing that occurs to me is white male privilege.
02 MK:   [yeah.
03 JD:   [mhm
04 BC:   so and that- that's what um- i've never READ or TALKED about that in
         GERman (.) so.
05 MK:   [mhm
06 BC:   i mean i would automATically? even when i'm TALKing about it with
         GERmans even in my FREE time? i would automatically [use the english
         terms for that
07 MK:                                                        [yeaaaaah?
08 BC:   for that whole=
09 JD:   [mhm
10 BC:   =cluster (.) of topics
11 JD:   and if you had [to
12 MK:                  [ja.
13 JD:   if you had to say it in a different way?
14 BC:   the white man's privilege.
15 JD:   [mhm
16 MK:   [@@@
17 BC:   for ME that sounds more like
18 KK:   white man's [BURden.
```

19 MK:	[@@@@@
20 JD:	[@@@@@
20 BC:	yeah that- that sounds like (.) we're down where the hutzis and the tutus or was it the (.) tutus and the hutzis (.) where the two groups are fight- about the privilege of the white man in- contrast to
21 JD:	[@@@
22 KK:	[it
23 BC:	um (.) and then in principle uh- yeah.

The example that *bienchen* comes up with for something where she would automatically use the English term rather than a German equivalent is "white male privilege." Her reasoning is that she's never read about the topic of racial or gender-related privilege in German (turn 4), so when she talks about it with Germans, she would always automatically use the English terminology. When I then ask her how she might express it "in a different way," she responds in turn fourteen with a direct German equivalent of "white male privilege," which prompts laughter from *menschenskind* and an analogy to the similar-sounding term "white man's burden" from *kakumo*. Without rejecting these assessments, *bienchen* positions a potential German equivalent of "white male privilege" as failing to come across as part of the wider societal discourse that she has taken part in exclusively in English. A German equivalent or paraphrase for the topic area's vocabulary does not have the desired connotations of the wider discourse on racial and gender-related power relations, instead evoking entirely different connotations of racial relations that she presumably *has* read and talked about in German, namely the Rwandan genocide.

While there is only room here to discuss four examples, it seems important to reiterate here that the stance that certain things just "sound better" in English is markedly more common in the Dutch community than in the German one. However, when it *is* used in the German community, there are no notable differences in terms of the *ways* the stance comes up in the two communities. Instead, there are more apparent differences *within* both communities in terms of the complexity of the stated reasonings for what it is that *makes* things sound better. In Excerpts 5.6 and 5.7, one of which comes from a Dutch participant and one of which comes from a German participant, both direct translations and paraphrased alternatives are rejected in part because of potential unwanted connotations or because they are too complicated, but mostly because they simply don't "sound right" in a way that's hard to put a finger on but vaguely absurd. In Excerpts 5.8 and 5.9, however, more complex explanations are given: there are cases where expressing something in the local language would make a topic sound too serious or would evoke connotations of an entirely different societal situation than the intended one.

Mixing is More Economical

The stance that transidiomatic practices are (or can be) shorter or simpler than remaining only within the local language also comes up in both communities. I will present two excerpts in this section, one from the German community and one from the Dutch one. The first of these, in Excerpt 5.10, is from the 29-year-old German participant *caroline*, and the context is a discussion about a short excerpt of conversation from the *unserekleinestadt* community in which one user expressed an opinion and another user responded with the English phrase "same here."

Excerpt 5.10 "Same here is totally short" (German community)

```
01 JD:    würdest du das auch sagen? äh schreiben?
02 CA:    ja. wahrscheinlich schon.
03 JD:    ok. was hat man also daran?
04 CA:    mh
05 JD:    w- warum sa- äh
06 CA:    es is kürzer. *mir geht es genauso*. oder (.) *das hab ich auch erlebt*. das is viel
          zu lang. same here is total kurz.
07 JD:    ok.
08 CA:    also ja das ist oft einfach (.) beQUEMer (.) das KURZe (.) knackige (.)
          ENGlische zu nehmen
```

Attitudes Toward Transidiomatic Practices 167

01 JD:	would you say that too? or write it?	
02 CA:	yeah. probably.	
03 JD:	okay. so what does that give you?	
04 CA:	mh	
05 JD:	wh- why sa- uh	
06 CA:	it's shorter. *it's the same for me*. or (.) *i've experienced that too*. that's much too long. **same here** is totally short.	
07 JD:	okay.	
08 CA:	i mean that's often just (.) more COMfortable (.) to use the SHORT (.) crisp-sounding (.) ENGlish	

When I ask whether she would also say "same here" in a similar sort of situation, her response is a non-committal "yeah. probably." When I then ask what the benefit is of transidiomatic practices in this situation, she positions it as simply "shorter," comparing it with paraphrased German expressions that she positions contrastively as "much too long."

A similar example can be found in the Dutch community in Excerpt 5.11, which comes from 22-year-old participant *mfpim*. It concerns the same conversation in the *vragenuurtje* community that discussed in Excerpt 5.6 above, about the transidiomatic use of "discuss."

Excerpt 5.11: "That's much longer" (Dutch community)

01 MP:	dit is gewoon zo lekker makkelijk. want als je het in het nederlands moet zeggen (.) dan zeg je van *eh ga er maar even over praten* en **discuss** is gewoon één klein zinnig woordje? dus dan zeg je dat dan liever denk ik.
02 JD:	oké. en als je dat in het nederlands zou MOETen zeggen?
03 MP:	ja (.) dan leg je het veel te lang uit.
04 JD:	hoe klinkt dat.
05 MP:	dan zeg je niet (.) leg uit (.) maar=
06 JD:	LEG UIT @
07 MP:	=maar ga er effe over praten met zn allen (.) weet je? en dat is veel langer.
08 JD:	ja.
09 MP:	dit is gewoon een makkelijke weg.

168   **5 The Why: Ideology, Positioning, and Attitudes toward English**

> 01 MP: this is just so comfortable and simple. because if you have to say it in dutch (.)
>   then you say like *uh go on and talk about it a bit* and **discuss** is just ONE
>   tiny little word that makes sense? so then you tend to say that instead i think.
> 02 JD: okay. and if you HAD to say that in dutch?
> 03 MP: yeah (.) then it takes too long to explain.
> 04 JD: what does that sound like.
> 05 MP: then you wouldn't say (.) explain (.) but=
> 06 JD: EXPLAIN @
> 07 MP: =but go on and talk about it all of you together (.) you know? and that is much
>   longer.
> 08 JD: yeah.
> 09 MP: this is just a simple way.

Participant *mfpim* begins by positioning the use of "discuss" as "comfortable" and "simple," two separate concepts that she associates by juxtaposing them. She then contrasts this comfort and simplicity with the Dutch paraphrases "go on and talk about it a bit" (turn 1) and "go on and talk about it all of you together" (turn 7), which she positions as taking "too long to explain" and being "much longer." This stance that the use of transidiomatic practices can be simply more economical than an exclusive use of the local language is quite common in both communities—more or less equally so—and it comes up in the same kinds of contexts in each.

Mixing is Useful for Distinguishing a Youth Subculture

The stance that transidiomatic practices are useful for distinguishing a youth subculture is expressed in both communities, but there are key differences between the two that are revealing of distinct underlying ideologies. This section will contain four excerpts, two from the German community and two from the Dutch community, that are illustrative of this difference. The first of these comes from an interview with 31-year-old *tinchen* and the 30-year-old *mistertinchen*. It concerns the same conversation in the *unserekleinestadt* community discussed in Excerpt 5.3 above, about the use of the term "outdoor shoes."

Excerpt 5.12 "They remind me of my grandparents" (German community)

01 TI: also **OUTdoor**schuhe find ich- find ich ähm
02 MT: klingt normal.
03 TI: klingt norMAL WEIL? (.) das ist- das- wie sie auch meistens vertrieben werden und wie man sie eigentlich [KENNen lernt.
04 JD: [mh-hm (.) mh-hm
05 MT: ja.
06 TI: also sonst (.) würd ich WANderschuhe sagen?
07 JD: mh-hm
08 TI: [aber
09 JD: [ist das das gleiche?
10 TI: ähm (.) also wahrscheinlich ist der- ist der SCHUH SCHON der gleiche aber äh (.) die meisten leute würden sagen WANderschuhe sind eher LANGweilig (.) und erinnern mich an die GROSSeltern und **outdoor**schuhe das ist dann (.) das machen auch JUgendliche
11 JD: ok @@
12 TI: nach dem motto

01 TI: i mean **OUTdoor** shoes i think- i think um
02 MT: it sounds normal.
03 TI: it sounds NORmal beCAUSE? (.) that's- that's how they're usually sold and the way you tend to get to [KNOW them.
04 JD: [mh-hm (.) mh-hm
05 MT: yeah.
06 TI: so otherwise (.) i would say HIking shoes?
07 JD: mh-hm
08 TI: [but
09 JD: [is that the same thing?
10 TI: um (.) probably the- the SHOE IS the same but uh (.) most people would say HIking shoes tend to be BORing (.) and remind me of my GRANDparents and **outdoor** shoes then that is (.) YOUNG people do that too
11 JD: okay @@
12 TI: as they say

170   5 The Why: Ideology, Positioning, and Attitudes toward English

In the first three turns, both *tinchen* and *mistertinchen* state that the English-origin term "outdoor shoes" sounds normal to them. In turn 3 *tinchen* also provides a reason why this is the case—it is the term that is most common at the time one first comes in contact with that type of shoe—and in turn 5 *mistertinchen* agrees with this assessment. In turn 6, then, *tinchen* offers up the alternative purely German-origin term "Wanderschuhe" ("hiking shoes"), and when I ask whether that's the same thing, her response is complex. She says that the physical shoe is probably the same, but that "most people" would say that "hiking shoes tend to be boring and remind me of my grandparents" while "outdoor shoes" are something that young people would wear as well. The basic ideology underlying this is clear: when transidiomatic practices are used to describe a particular type of shoe, it automatically grants that shoe a certain youthfulness that is lacking when the German term is used to describe the same shoe. However, crucial here is the fact that this stance is prefaced with "most people would say," which positions it as a stance that is out there in the world, but not necessarily her own. This is reinforced in turn 12 when *tinchen* adds "as they say" (or more literally "according to the motto"), further underscoring the positioning of this stance as something that is coming from other people and not from herself.

A similar but slightly different example, also from the German community, can be seen in Excerpt 5.13. It comes from *caroline*, whose first appearance in this chapter was in Excerpt 5.10 above. It comes from a conversation in *unserekleinestadt* in which a user ended a long post in German with the English-origin phrase "help anyone."

Excerpt 5.13 "The person seems younger to me" (German community)

01 CA: na **HELP anyone**. süß.
02 JD: findest du süß.
03 CA: @@@ ja würd ich persönlich nich machen? ((3-second pause)) ähm (..) aber es
         is eben auch sowas ganz einfach- wo jeder versteht was gemeint is. auch wenn
         man nich VIEL englisch kann. von daher find ichs auch nich schlimm? (.) ähm
         ((6-second pause)) n bisschen unnötig vielleicht in dem zusammenhang weil (.)

Attitudes Toward Transidiomatic Practices 171

> HILfe FRAgezeichen auch kurz is. aber (.) das is auch persönlicher geschmack dann.
> 04 JD: hat das ne andere wirkung?
> 05 CA: mm
> 06 JD: als hilfe? fragezeichen?
> ((4-second pause))
> 07 CA: mh (.) ja ich GLAUbe (.) die person wirkt dadurch JÜNGer auf mich.
> 08 JD: ok.
> 09 CA: also eher- also auch deutlich jünger als ich bin.
> 10 JD: ok. ((3-second pause)) w- wie alt würdest du diese person einschätzen
> 11 CA: ähm (. . .) ich glaub maximal anfang zwanzig?

> 01 CA: oh **HELP anyone.** cute.
> 02 JD: you think that's cute.
> 03 CA: @@@ yeah personally i wouldn't do it? ((3-second pause)) um (..) but again it's just such a simple- where everybody understands what's meant. even if you don't know a LOT of english. in that sense i don't think it's that bad? (.) um ((6-second pause)) maybe a little unnecessary in that context because (.) HELP QUEStion mark is also short. but (.) that's just personal taste then.
> 04 JD: does that have a different effect?
> 05 CA: mm
> 06 JD: than help? question mark?
> ((4-second pause))
> 07 CA: mh (.) yeah i THINK (.) the person seems YOUNGer to me that way.
> 08 JD: okay.
> 09 CA: so more- i mean also distinctly younger than i am.
> 10 JD: okay. ((3-second pause)) h- how old would you imagine this person
> 11 CA: um (. . .) i think early twenties at most?

Her first reaction is to describe the transidiomatic practice as "cute" (turn 1), an assessment that is simultaneously positive and trivializing. Then, when prompted, she elaborates in turn 3 by saying that she "personally wouldn't do it," but "everybody understands what's meant" so it's "not that bad." This phrasing again positions her stance as basically accepting but simultaneously distancing. She further positions this transidiomatic practice "a little unnecessary" as a result of the fact that it's possible to be just as economical without using English (which, in turn, contributes to the stance that using English for economy-of-language reasons is acceptable, while other reasons are less so).

172 5 The Why: Ideology, Positioning, and Attitudes toward English

Then, when I ask what effect the use of the transidiomatic practice has, she says that "the person seems younger" to her (turn 7), and specifically ("distinctly younger than I am"). When prompted for how old such a person could be, she says gives the "early twenties" as the upper limit.

A contrasting example from the Dutch community can be seen in Excerpt 5.14. It comes from an interview with the 25-year-old participant *duimelotje*, and it concerns a discussion about the excerpt that appears as 4.17, from the weekly *vraagvrije vrijdag* post in the *vragenuurtje* community.

Excerpt 5.14 "My mother tries to" (Dutch community)

```
01 JD:   da- dan zeg je dat- als je dat in het ENGels zegt? heeft het de Ene lading? en als je de-
         als je hetZELFde- preCIES hetzelfde in het NEderlands [zegt?
02 DU:                                                         [heeft t een ANdere lading.
03 JD:   dan heeft dat een ANdere lading dan is dat EIgenlijk best (.) [[NUTTig
04 DU:                                                                  [[mm mm
05: JD:  ja? ja oké.
06 DU:   ja alleen ik denk niet dat iedereen daar beGRIP voor zou hebben.
07 JD:   hoe- hoe bedoel je
08 DU:   nou als ik zoiets tegen mijn MOEder zou zeggen? (..) dan zou ze zoiets hebben
         van (.) WAT?
09 JD:   en (..) o- omdat ze dat- dat niet beGRIJPT? of omdat ze dat niet goed vindt.
10 DU:   omdat ze dat niet beGRIJPT.
11 JD:   hm.
12 DU:   als ik woorden zou gebruiken als zo hier- als ik zou zeggen **RAGE** (.) mijn
         moeders kennis van het ehm (.) jeugdige engels is niet groot genoeg om dat ah
13 JD:   oké.
14 DU:   uhm (.) ja.
15 JD:   en- maar- als ze dat WEL zou begrijpen zou ze dat- zou ze dat AFkeuren?
16 DU:   nee.
17 JD:   nee oké.
18 DU:   nee mijn moeder zegt altijd voor de grap (.) **like totally** @@ [dus=
19 JD:                                                                    [Oké.
         @@@@@@@@@@[@@@
20 DU:                [@@@@@@
21 JD:   dus ZIJ doet het OOK [[@@@@@@@@@@@@@
22 DU:                         [[ze proBEERT t wel @@@@
         ((2-second pause))
23 JD:   moet jij dan een beetje LACHen? STIEKem? ja.
```

Attitudes Toward Transidiomatic Practices 173

22 DU: ja. ja (.) niet eens stiekem hoor? gewoon in dr gezicht.

01 JD: the- then you're saying that- if you say it in ENGlish? it has ONE connotation? and if you t- if you say the SAME thing exACTly the same thing in
[DUTCH?
02 DU: [it has a DIFFerent connotation.
03 JD: then it has a DIFFerent connotation then it's ACtually totally (.) [[USEful
04 DU: [[mm mm
05: JD: yeah? yeah okay.
06 DU: yeah but i don't think that everyone would have an underSTANding for that.
07 JD: what- what do you mean
08 DU: i mean if i were to say something like that to my MOTHer? (..) then she would
be like (.) WHAT? @
09 JD: and (..) be- because she do- doesn't underSTAND that? or because she doesn't
like it.
10 DU: because she doesn't underSTAND it.
11 JD: hm.
12 DU: if i were to use words like this here- if i were to say **RAGE** (.) my mother's
knowledge of the um (.) youthful english isn't enough to uh
13 JD: okay.
14 DU: um (.) yeah.
15 JD: and- but- if she DID understand it would she- would she have a PROBlem
with it?
16 DU: no.
17 JD: no okay.
18 DU: no my mother always says as a joke (.) **like totally** @@ [so=
19 JD: [oKAY. @@@@@@@@@@
[[@@@
20 DU: [[@@@@@@
21 JD: so SHE does it TOO [@@@@@@@@@@@@@@@
22 DU: [she TRIES to @@@@
((2-second pause))
23 JD: does it make you LAUGH when she does that? SECretly? yeah.
22 DU: yeah. yeah (.) not even secretly? right in her face.

In the first five turns, I am busy making sure I understand what she's
been saying previously about the usefulness of transidiomatic practices in
order to make a distinction in connotations. In turn 6, however, she
counters with a possible downside: not everyone would "have an understanding" for these practices. As in English, this phrasing is ambiguous:

174   **5 The Why: Ideology, Positioning, and Attitudes toward English**

it might imply that there are people who don't like these practices, or it might imply that there are people who literally do not understand them. So when I ask for further explanation in turns 7 and 9, she confirms that it's the latter meaning she intended: there are people—like her mother— who would not understand the particular mixed code that is typical of *vraagvrije vrijdag*-style conversations (see Chapter 4 for a discussion of this style). When I then ask whether her mother would have an issue with this sort of transidiomatic practice if she did understand it, *duimelotje* says that she would not (turn 16), and then, by way of evidence, offers up an example of a type of transidiomatic practice that her mother actually would use herself. However, she also positions these practices as something that are not inherent to her mother and her mother's group by saying that she would use these practices "as a joke." This positioning is confirmed when I comment (with words and with my laughter) that it is amusing that her mother does this as well, and *duimelotje* responds by correcting my comment to "she TRIES to," and then confirms that she laughs at her mother for making these attempts. The positioning is clearly of the transidiomatic practices as delineating a youth subculture, both in terms of comprehension and in terms of what is acceptable as practice.

Similar but even more overtly drawn boundaries in terms of acceptable practice across the generations can be seen in Excerpt 5.15, which comes from the same interview with Dutch participants *luna_puella* and *isolde* that came up in Excerpt 5.8 above. The context is a discussion about whether the English-origin phrase "oh great" is necessarily always sarcastic when used in a Dutch conversation.

Excerpt 5.15 "It's just all wrong" (Dutch community)

01 LP: ligt aan de UITdrukking? maar sommige?
02 IE: ik denk onder JONGeren. als mijn moeder zou zeggen **oh great** dan zou ik echt
         waarschijnlijk staan te kijken van wat ZEG je me nou.
03 LP: ja. (.) en mijn moeder gebruikt nu af en toe het woord **gross** en dan denk ik
         MAM dat PAST helemaal niet bij jou. dat HOORT niet. en je-
04 IE: seriEUS? als mijn moeder **gross** zou zeggen (.) zou ik echt staan te kijken.

Attitudes Toward Transidiomatic Practices 175

> 05 LP: ik OOK. ik heb ook elke keer dat ze dat doet van DOE dat nou gewoon NIET. @@@
> 06 JD: @@@
> 07 LP: het KLOPT helemaal niet.

> 01 LP: it depends on the exPRESSion? but some of them?
> 02 IE: i think among YOUNG people. if my mother said **oh great** then i would probably be shocked like what are you SAYing to me.
> 03 LP: yeah. (.) and my mother now uses the word **gross** every now and then and then i think MOM that doesn't SUIT you at ALL. that's just not RIGHT. and you-
> 04 IE: SERiously? if my mother said **gross** (.) i would really be shocked.
> 05 LP: me TOO. and every time she does that i'm all PLEASE DON'T do that. @@@
> 06 JD: @@@
> 07 LP: it's just all WRONG.

The excerpt begins with *luna_puella* still trying to sort out the issue of sarcasm, but then *isolde* jumps in and positions this sort of transidiomatic practice as something that specifically happens "among young people." She then strengthens this positioning by bringing up her mother and saying that she would be "shocked" to hear something like that from her. This is affirmed by *luna_puella* at the start of turn 3, and she responds with her own example: sometimes her mother does use transidiomatic practices in conversations with her. Both participants react negatively to this idea: these transidiomatic practices simply do not belong to the generations prior to theirs.

In both communities, transidiomatic practices are positioned as something that is used to distinguish a specifically youth-oriented subculture. However, not only does this stance come up much more frequently in the Dutch community, within that same community the use of transidiomatic practices to distinguish a youth subculture also tends to be positioned as something the participants would do themselves. In the German community, on the other hand, the positioning is more distancing: other people use it this way (or perceive it this way), but I myself do not. This may be in part reflective of actual usage—i.e. transidiomatic practices might *actually* be used less frequently among people

176   5 The Why: Ideology, Positioning, and Attitudes toward English

older than their early twenties in Germany, while in the Netherlands they are also common among people who are in their mid-twenties or early thirties. However, given the way that this distancing goes hand in hand with many of the other stances put forward by the German community, it seems likely that this points to an underlying difference in ideologies regarding the position of English as well as possible actual usage.

Mixing is Useful for Making Distinctions in Meaning

The stance that was briefly alluded to in Excerpt 5.14 above—that mixing is useful for making distinctions in meaning such as making up for a lack in the local language or allowing users to express different kinds of connotations—is found exclusively in the Dutch community. This is remarkable in and of itself, but the fact that this is actually one of the most frequently expressed stances in the entire Dutch data set makes this even more so. This stance comes up so frequently, in fact—multiple times in each Dutch interview—that it was difficult for me to limit the illustrative excerpts in this section to four. I did narrow them down to several excerpts representing different takes on the ways that transidiomatic practices are perceived as useful for making a distinction in meaning, and the first of these comes from *laviefantasque,* who was introduced back in Excerpt 5.6. The context is a discussion of the excerpt analyzed in 4.15, in which a user posed a question about whether a particular image of a celebrity was acceptable by posting "Yay of Nay"?

Excerpt 5.16 "A sort of feeling" (Dutch community)

01 JD: **yay** of nee? oké. en WAARom staat dat-
02 LV: ja (.) ach. de rest is ook allemaal gewoon- ik kan net zo goed zeggen JA of NEE. ((3-second pause)) maar ik denk ook (.) omdat het weer zon soort van **feeling** van het is een (..) **yay** of het is een- als je zegt (.) JA of NEE (.) dat is meer een definitief (.) antwoord van (.) ja (.) heb je iets gedaan ja of nee? (.) dit is meer- heb je- vind je dit LEUK of vind je dit STOM
03 JD: oké

01 JD:	**yay** or no? okay. and WHY is that-
02 LV:	yeah (.) oh i dunno. the rest is all just- i can't really explain it YES or NO. ((3-second pause)) but i do think (.) because it's a sort of **feeling** like it is a (..) **yay** or it is a- if you say (.) YES or NO (.) that's more about a definitive (.) answer like (.) yeah (.) did you do something yes or no? (.) this is more- do you have- do you LIKE this or do you think this is STUpid
03 JD:	okay

In this simple example, the reason why "yay or nay" is positioned as unable to be rendered in Dutch as "ja of nee" ("yes or no") is that it would literally have different semantic content. User *laviefantasque* begins by arguing that "yay or nay" "is sort of a feeling," but then moves on to say that "ja of nee" would be "more about a definitive answer," whereas "yay or nay" is about gathering together the group's *opinions*: "do you like this or do you think this is stupid." When *laviefantasque* puts her finger on what makes for this distinction, that serves to position the use of transidiomatic practices to express it as useful.

The reasons for the usefulness of the transidiomatic practice in Excerpt 5.17, on the other hand, are presented as somewhat different, though they still have to do with a distinction in meaning. This excerpt comes from an interview with 28-year-old *niettemin* and 29-year-old *vogel*, and concerns a discussion about the excerpt analyzed in 3.8, dealing with a dress that would be "too much of a boob fest" on a large-breasted woman.

Excerpt 5.17 "I have an amusing image in my head" (Dutch community)

01 JD:	het Ene meisje heeft gezegd (.) eh ik wil dit JURKje (.) eh (.) eh
02 NT:	**too much of a boob** [fest? is echt iets wat je inderdaad HEEL mooi zo kunt LAten=
03 JD:	[ja
04 NT:	=[en daar hoef je niks meer aan te doen.

178   5 The Why: Ideology, Positioning, and Attitudes toward English

```
03 VO:     [ja.                          als je dat in het nederlands zou neerzet-
           ten dan zou het vies en goedKOOP gaan lijken. nou is het nog [[iets=
04 NT:                                                      [[een- een
05 VO:     =iets GRAPPigs. (.) gewoon een STATEment. als je dat in het NEderlands zet
           (.) dan is het gewoon iemand die aan het vertellen is hoe haar BORSTen te
           groot zijn voor de kleding.
06 NT:     [ja.
07 JD:     [oké. oké. [[dus het is-
08 VO:                [[nou (.) nou heb ik- nou heb ik een GRAPPig PLAATje in mn hoofd
           (.) in het nederlands zou ik denken HUH? (.) [TIETen.
09: NT:                                                 [@@@ ja (.) dan zie je uiers en
10 VO:     ja. dat soort dingen.
11 NT:     @@@ dat is geen goed idee.
12 VO:     ja.


01 JD:     the ONE girl said (.) um i want this DRESS (.) um (.) uh
02 NT:     too much of a boob [fest? really is something that you can just LEAVE there
           all perfect=
03 JD:                        [yeah
04 NT:     =[[and you don't have to change a thing.
03 VO:      [[yeah.                          if you put it down in dutch then it
           would start sounding DIRty and CHEAP. this way it's just [[something=
04 NT:                                                               [[a- a
05 VO:     =something FUNny. (.) just a STATEment. if you put it down in DUTCH (.)
           then it's just someone who's talking about how her BREASTS are too big for
           the clothing.
06 NT:     [yeah.
07 JD:     [okay. okay. [[so it's-
08 VO:                  [[this way (.) this way i have- this way i have a FUNNy IMage in my
           head (.) in dutch i'd think HUH? (.) [TITS.
09: NT:                                         [@@@ yeah (.) then you imagine udders and
10 VO:     yeah. that sort of thing.
11 NT:     @@@ that's not a good idea.
12 VO:     yeah.
```

The first attitude that's expressed here is by participant *niettemin* in turn 2, where she describes the expression "too much of a boob fest" as "something that you can just leave there all perfect and you don't have to change a thing." Participant *vogel* agrees in turn 3 with a "yeah," then adds that the Dutch equivalent would sound "dirty and cheap," and in turns 5 and 7

Attitudes Toward Transidiomatic Practices 179

further positions the English as sounding "funny," while positioning a potential Dutch equivalent as automatically missing that humour value. Participant *niettemin* agrees in turn 9, adding that what a Dutch equivalent would convey would be "udders." In other words, the transidiomatic practices allow the user to convey a certain desired mood and a mental image, while any Dutch equivalent would not only *not* transmit that desired mood and mental image, it would instead transmit a completely different, undesired mood and mental image that is less funny and more dirty.

An example of a somewhat different sort of use of transidiomatic practices to make a distinction in meaning can be seen in Excerpt 5.18. It comes from Dutch participant *duimelotje*, who was introduced in Excerpt 5.14, and again deals with a discussion of the *vraagvrije vrijdag* conversation from Excerpt 4.17.

Excerpt 5.18 "A kind of Alcoholics Anonymous welcome" (Dutch community)

01 JD: waarom is hier heel veel- zit hier heel veel engels tussen maar de laatste zin is alleen in het engels.
02 DU: ik denk dat hier in het nederlands niet Over zou komen.
03 JD: en waarOM niet
         ((2-second pause))
04 DU: nou (.) ik vin- ik vind WEL dat als je het LETTerlijk zou vertalen (.) verwelko-men is als een soort uh (..) anonieme alcohol[ISTen welkom
05 JD: [ja @@ ja.

01 JD: why is there so much- there's a lot of english in here too but the last sentence is just in english.
02 DU: i think this here wouldn't come acROSS in dutch.
03 JD: and WHY not
         ((2-second pause))
04 DU: well (.) i thi- i DO think that if you translated it LITerally (.) welcome is a kind of uh (..) alcoholics an[ONymous welcome
05 JD: [yeah @@ yeah.

When asked why the last sentence of the post is just in English, *duimelotje* says that it "wouldn't come across" in Dutch. Elaborating on

180   5 The Why: Ideology, Positioning, and Attitudes toward English

this in turn 4, she then says that the Dutch word "verwelkomen" ("to welcome") would come across as "a kind of alcoholics anonymous welcome," which positions any Dutch equivalent as being inherently associated with something that is too adult and too serious for the context.

Finally, one additional use of transidiomatic practices to make a distinction in meaning can be seen in Excerpt 5.19, which comes from an interview with Dutch participants *geraldina* (age 26) and *gauwd* (age 24). They were also discussing the example analyzed in Excerpt 3.8, dealing with a group order members were placing together from an online shop in the UK, and the transidiomatic practices used to characterize the prices as low.

Excerpt 5.19 "The Zeeman attitude" (Dutch community)

01 GE: en dit kan ik dan meteen UITleggen
02 JD: **sale**? (.) **cheap**.
03 GW: ja (.) dat is ook echt zon uitroep **OH CHEAP**
04 GE: **cheap**. preCIES. want als ik het- in het NEderlands zou zeggen (.) dan zou ik zeggen goedKOOP=
05 GW: oh goedKOOP @@@
06 GE: =en dat heeft weer de **attitude** van- van ZEEman goedKOOP (.) zeg maar. @@@
07 GW: @@@
08 GE: dus niet (.) **cheap** is van **HEY** goeie **DEAL** weet je? je kan er je VOORdeel mee behalen? terwijl van oh wat goedKOOP. dan (.) dat- dat heeft meer zoiets van (.) de HEma heeft de TISSues AFgeprijsd ik denk maar @@=
09 JD: @@@
10 GE: =ze zijn nu maar vijf en twintig cent per PAkje goedKOOP (.) weet je? en dat-dat zou ik niet voor kleding of zoiets gebruiken.

01 GE: and this one i can exPLAIN right away
02 JD: **sale**? (.) **cheap**.
03 GW: yeah (.) it's really a kind of exclamation **OH CHEAP**
04 GE: **cheap**. exACTly. because if i- if i say it in DUTCH (.) then i'd say inexPENsive=
05 GW: oh inexPENsive @@@
06 GE: =and again that has the **attitude** of- like ZEEman ((the name of an inexpensive Dutch clothing chain)) inexPENsive (.) let's say. @@@
07 GW: @@@
08 GE: so not (.) **cheap** is like **HEY** good **DEAL** you know? you can take adVANtage of it? whereas like oh how inexPENsive. then (.) that- that feels more like (.)

> | | HEma ((the name of an inexpensive Dutch department store chain)) marked DOWN the TISSues i just end up thinking @@= |
> | 09 JD: | @@@ |
> | 10 GE: | =now they're just twenty five cents a PACK inexPENsive (.) you know? and that- i wouldn't use that for clothing or something like that. |

This excerpt begins with me pointing out the things I want them to explain in turn 2: the use of the words "sale" and "cheap" as opposed to their Dutch equivalents. Participant *gauwd* begins by explaining that "oh cheap" is "really a kind of exclamation," or some sort of set phrase. Participant *geraldina* agrees with her, saying that the Dutch equivalent would be "goedkoop" (which translates as either "cheap" or "inexpensive"), and *gauwd* reacts to this by rephrasing the original exclamation as "oh goedkoop," and following this with laughter that positions this phrasing as absurd. In turn 6, then, *geraldina* positions the Dutch word "goedkoop" as having "the attitude of Zeeman," an inexpensive Dutch clothing chain, and in turn 8, she says it feels like the Dutch word has connotations of the inexpensive Dutch department store chain HEMA having "marked down the tissues," so she wouldn't use the Dutch term for clothing. In other words, the Dutch term immediately transmits the image of both more everyday and more *specifically Dutch* things that it would feel inappropriate to use to describe clothing from an online shop based in the UK.

These excerpts show that English is seen as being useful to make a literal distinction in semantic meaning, but also to convey an amusing mental image (and to avoid a less amusing one), to keep things light and thereby avoid associations with things that are too adult and serious for the context, and to avoid connotations that are too specifically Dutch for a desired international context. The common thread here is that at least for the Dutch community, English clearly is perceived as having a function of making distinctions in meaning that have to do with lightheartedness and a lack of seriousness, as well as a lack of localness. These stances will come up again and again in the sections that follow. The complete absence of this stance in the German community is also noteworthy, however—while

182   **5 The Why: Ideology, Positioning, and Attitudes toward English**

there are certainly positive stances expressed by German community members about the use of transidiomatic practices, none of them view these practices as useful by virtue of allowing them to make a distinction in meaning that it would not be possible to make using German alone.

Mixing is Bad

In this next section, I will analyze excerpts that exemplify a stance that mixing is negative. Identified subcategories within that consist of the stance that mixing is unnecessary, that mixing is unpleasant, that mixing is not understandable, that mixing is lazy, and that mixing is adversely affecting the local language.

Mixing is Unnecessary

The stance that transidiomatic practices are bad because they are simply unnecessary is especially common in the German community, but there are also occasional examples in the Dutch one. This section will encompass three excerpts, two from the German community and one from the Dutch one, that show the range in the ways this stance is expressed. The first of these can be seen in Excerpt 5.20, from 30-year-old *unsereklei-nestadt* participant *misery_chick*. It comes from a discussion about things that other people might use transidiomatic practices for that she would say completely in German.

Excerpt 5.20 "Because why" (German community)

01 MC: ich habe neulich EINgekauft und hab- wollte MILCHreis kaufen und auf unserer milchreis packung stand **milk** reis
02 JD: oh
03 MC: also ein englisches **milk** und dann ein deutsches reis @ zusammen auf der packung
04 JD: [hm
05 MC: [da habe ich- und an dieser stelle hab ich mich WIRKlich geÄRgert
06 JD: ok
07 MC: das fand ich ganz fürchterlich

Attitudes Toward Transidiomatic Practices   **183**

```
08 JD:    huh
09 MC:    weil waRUM. @@
10 JD:    ja und- und- und kannst mir erklären- kannst du das erklären (.) warum du das
          fürchterlich findest
11 MC:    na ja es ist so dass man dadurch schon mal ein falsches BILD bringt weil wenn
          das jetzt JUgendliche sehen die denken [dann reis ist **rice**
12 JD:                                           [mhm          ja ja ok
```

```
01 MC:    recently i was SHOPPing and i- i wanted to buy rice PUDDing ((literally:
          "milk rice")) and on our rice pudding label it said **milk** rice
02 JD:    oh
03 MC:    like an english **milk** and then a german rice @ together on the label
04 JD:    [hm
05 MC:    [so i- and this was a point where i REALLy got annOYED
06 JD:    okay
07 MC:    i thought that was completely awful
08 JD:    huh
09 MC:    because WHY. @@
10 JD:    okay and- and- and can you explain to me- can you explain that to me (.) why
          you find that awful
11 MC:    well it's because you end up putting the wrong IMage across because if
          YOUNG people see that now who then [think rice is **rice**
12 JD:                                        [mhm          yeah yeah okay
```

This excerpt begins with *misery_chick* talking about the label of the rice pudding that she bought recently which used the English-origin term "milk" together with the German-origin germ "Reis" to form the phrase "Milk Reis" rather than the fully German "Milchreis." What is particularly interesting here is that rather than merely saying "the rice pudding label," she refers to this as "our rice pudding label," which positions German speakers as having a certain kind of ownership over the products they buy. Her reaction to this was to get "really annoyed" (turn 5) and to find it "completely awful" (turn 7), and the explanation she presents for this is "because why" (turn 9). By providing this as the reason, she positions transidiomatic practices as something that can only be considered fully appropriate when there is a good reason for them, a stance that is recurring within the excerpts from the German

184   **5 The Why: Ideology, Positioning, and Attitudes toward English**

community. When I prompt her to explain more about why she finds this "awful," she then adds that she is worried that German "young people" might think that the German word "Reis" is spelled "rice," as in English. This fear echoes similar fears expressed within the German public discourse about the use of "anglicisms" (Spitzmüller 2005).

A similar but slightly more complex stance is expressed in Excerpt 5.21 by German participant *urlaubssommer*, who was first introduced in Excerpt 5.5 above. Here she is reacting to the conversation that appeared as Excerpt 3.2 earlier in this book, about "outdoor shoes" and "light hiking."

Excerpt 5.21 "You would have had no problem expressing that in German" (German community)

01 US: und ähm (.) **LIGHT** wandern @@
02 JD: @[@@
03 US: [@@@ find ich sehr sehr komisch. das hab ich noch nie so gesehen dass- also das hätte man problemlos auch einfach auf deutsch ausdrücken können=
04 JD: ja
05 US: =einfach irgendwie mit so- halt keine (.) lange wandertouren oder ganz ((3-second pause)) ja äh wie sagt man denn auf deutsch ((4-second pause) ja es fällt kein- kein ((5-second pause)) ach du meine güte ja LEICHT würde man ja da nicht sagen aber also (.) @ich versteh schon was sie meint@ [@@@
06 JD: [@@@ [[ja
07 US: [[ähmm
08 JD: wie FINDest dus
09 US: äh (.) so **out of place** [also das ähm
10 JD: [hm mhm
11 US: gehört da einfach GAR nicht hin

01 US: and um (.) **LIGHT** hiking @@
02 JD: @[@@
03 US: [@@@ i think that's really really weird. i've never seen that sort- i mean you would have had no problem expressing that in german=
04 JD: yeah
05 US: =just somehow with like- just no (.) long hiking trips or all ((3-second pause)) yeah uh how do you say that in german ((4-second pause)) yeah i can't think of- of ((5-second pause)) oh my goodness okay you wouldn't say LIGHT for that but so (.) @i do understand what she means@ [@@@

Attitudes Toward Transidiomatic Practices 185

```
06 JD:   [@@@ [[ja
07 US:        [[ummm
08 JD:   what do you THINK of it
09 US:   uh (.) so out of place [i mean that um
10 JD:                          [hm mhm
11 US:   doesn't belong there at ALL
```

Participant *urlaubssommer*'s first reaction to the use of the phrase "light hiking" in the *unserekleinestadt* conversation is to laugh, which I also respond to with laughter. She then explains her reaction further in turn 3 by saying that this phrasing is "really really weird," and then elaborating on that reaction by saying that it's weird because "you would have had no problem expressing that in German." As in the previous excerpt, this phrasing positions transidiomatic practices as requiring a good reason, in this case the lack of a German alternative. In turn 5 she then tries to go ahead and actually express this in German, but this attempt is full of extremely long pauses and false starts, and ultimately by her giving up and saying that she does "understand what she means" and laughing. This difficulty would seem to suggest that there is not, in fact, a simple way of expressing "light hiking" in German with no problems, but when I ask what she thinks of this usage, she persists in this stance by using the English-origin phrase "out of place" (turn 9) and saying that it "doesn't belong there at all" (turn 11).

Finally, one example from the Dutch community can be seen in excerpt 5.22, which comes from an interview with *vragenuurtje* participants *geraldina* and *gauwd*, as previously introduced in excerpt 5.19. It comes toward the end of the interview, in a conversation that begins with a question from me about whether or not it is important to take into account the fact that there are Dutch people who don't actually speak very good English.

Excerpt 5.22 "I get a little annoyed by that too" (Dutch community)

```
01 GE:   daarnaast zeg ik ook wel dat het interessant is om te kijken van (.) in welke
         mate wordt er rekening mee gehouden met bijvoorbeeld MEdia-uitingen.
```

186   **5 The Why: Ideology, Positioning, and Attitudes toward English**

	want dat zie ik steeds meer dat ze dat heel erg in het engels gaan doen. vooral op tV en KREten en al. ik weet dat mijn moeder echt- zich echt aan ERgert.
02 JD:	hm.
03 GW:	ik erger me er OOK een beetje aan.
04 GE:	ja?
05 GW:	ik hoeZO. dan is er bijvoorbeeld een muSEum? gaat over (.) OOnze culTUUR? ik verzin maar even wat?
06 JD:	hm? hmm?
07 GW:	en dan staat erop **the experience [of your lifetime**
08 GE:	[ja.
09 GW:	dan ik hoeZO. [[wie gaat hier nou HEEN?
10 GE:	[[ja.
11 GW:	alleen NEderlanders denk ik dan in [((small northern coastal town)) of zo.
12 GE:	[het moet toePASSelijk zijn.
13 JD:	hm. hm.
14 GW:	ja dat vind ik echt (.) heel STOM.

01 GE:	at the same time i also say that it's interesting to see like (.) to what extent people take for example MEdia expressions into account. because i see more and more that they're doing that sort of thing in english. especially on tV and BUZZwords and stuff. i know that my mother real- is really annOYED by that.
02 JD:	hm.
03 GW:	i get a little annoyed by that TOO.
04 GE:	yeah?
05 GW:	i mean WHY. like for example there's a muSEum? it's about (.) OUR CULture? like just for example?
06 JD:	hm? hmm?
07 GW:	and it says something like **the experience [of your lifetime**
08 GE:	[yeah.
09 GW:	then i'm like WHY. [[who are the ones GOing there?
10 GE:	[[yeah.
11 GW:	just DUTCH people i think then in [((small northern coastal town)) of zo.
12 GE:	[it has to be appROpriate.
13 JD:	hm. hm.
14 GW:	yeah i think that's really (.) completely STUpid.

Participant *geraldina* begins this excerpt in turn 1 by saying that her mother gets "really annoyed" by the use of transidiomatic practices on television and in slogans. Positioning this as her mother's attitude rather than her own allows her to comment on the existence of this stance without directly identifying it, but in turn 3 *gauwd* says that she too finds such practices annoying (weakening this stance with the modifier "a little," but still identifying that stance as her own rather than someone else's). In explaining where her annoyance comes from, her issues sound remarkably similar to those of German participant *misery_chick* above: like her, *gauwd* initiates the explanation by saying "i mean why," which assumes the stance that there needs to be a specific acceptable reason to use transidiomatic practices in this sort of instance. Then, as with *misery_chick*'s "our rice pudding label" the example *gauwd* provides is a "museum about OUR culture" (turn 5), in which the only customers are "Dutch people" from a small northern coastal town. This positions this hypothetical museum as something the Dutch have ownership over, and transidiomatic practices as therefore inappropriate because their use is only actually necessary when non-Dutch people are involved. Her co-participant *geraldina* ultimately agrees with this basic stance, responding to *gauwd*'s "I'm like WHY" with a "yeah" (turn 10) and ultimately with her own stance that transidiomatic practices are required "to be appropriate" in order to be acceptable (turn 12).

Though it is notable that this stance is far more common in the German community than in the Dutch one, it is just as important to note that when it *does* appear in the Dutch community, there are more similarities between the two communities than differences. In all cases, the stance is put forward that there are circumstances when it is acceptable to use transidiomatic practices. The main difference, however, has to do with the specifics of those circumstances: members of the German community are more likely to cite a lack of a common German-origin alternative as the only truly acceptable reason for using transidiomatic practices, while members of the Dutch community are more likely to find it unacceptable when the context of the transidiomatic practice specifically has something to do with Dutch culture or society.

Mixing is Unpleasant

Another stance that falls under the larger category of transidiomatic practices being bad is the stance that mixing is somehow unpleasant.

188   5 The Why: Ideology, Positioning, and Attitudes toward English

This occurs in both communities, though there are differences between them in terms of how the stance tends to be expressed. The first of two such excerpts, one from the German community and one from the Dutch community, can be seen in Excerpt 5.23. It comes from the same interview that was seen in Excerpt 5.12 above, with German participants *tinchen* and *mistertinchen*. The discussion is of the same conversation in *unserekleinestadt* that was discussed in several of the other above excerpts, about "outdoor shoes" and "light hiking."

Excerpt 5.23 "I don't like it at all" (German community)

01 JD: ja. und HIER? **LIGHT** wandern?
02 MT: gefällt mir überhaupt nich.
03 JD: mhm.
04 MT: ((clears throat)) also DIE vermischung gefällt mir nicht. die ANdere (.)
         OUTdoorschuhe is bekannt. das- das- also ich- kenn das. das äh **geo (.) caching**
         oder wie auch immer man es nennen möchte is AUCH bekannt? (.) **light** wan-
         wandern ähm (.) ich wüsste nicht wie ichs besser um[schreiben würde?
05 JD: [mh-hm mh-hm
06 MT: ((clears throat)) man- man bräuchte auch wahrscheinlich n paar worte MEHR?
07 JD: mhm
08 MT: aber mir passt die- die zuSAMMenstellung nicht. auch wenns in- in
         ANführungsstrichen is.
09 JD: ahso
10 MT: also (.) is ne reine geFÜHLSsache.
11 JD: mhm
12 MT: s gefällt mir nich.

01 JD: okay. and HERE? **LIGHT** hiking?
02 MT: i don't like it at all.
03 JD: mhm.
04 MT: ((clears throat)) i mean i don't like THAT mix. the OTHer (.) **OUTdoor**
         shoes is well known. the- the- i mean i- know that. the uh **geo (.) caching** or
         whatever you want to call it is well known TOO? (.) **light** hik- hiking um (.)
         i'm not sure how i would pa[raphrase that?
05 JD: [mh-hm mh-hm
06 MT: ((clears throat)) and you- you would probably need a few extra WORDS?
07 JD: mhm

08 MT:	but the combinAtion doesn't sit well with me. not even when it's in- in quoTAtion marks.	
09 JD:	ah okay	
10 MT:	i mean (.) it's purely a matter of oPINion.	
11 JD:	mhm	
12 MT:	i don't like it.	

Participant *mistertinchen*'s initial reaction to the "light hiking" phrase (which uses the English-origin word "light" in combination with the German word "wandern," or "hiking") is that he doesn't "like it at all" (turn 2). In turn 4, then, by means of clarifying what specifically he objects to about it, he says that he doesn't mind the phrase "outdoor shoes" (which also contains a mixture of English- and German-origin words) because it's "well known," and the term "geocaching" is also fine for the same reason, but he positions "light hiking" as different (which, going by the sequential order of elements in his phrasing, implies that this phrase is specifically different because it is *not* "well known"). In turn 8, he elaborates that "the combination," i.e. the mixing of two languages into a phrase, is part of what bothers him (despite the fact that he didn't have a problem with the "outdoor shoes" mix), and that the quotation marks don't mitigate that. Finally, he attempts to stop explaining his stance and says that this is "purely a matter of opinion" (turn 10), and that he simply doesn't "like it" (turn 12).

This contrasts in many ways with a similar sort of stance found in the Dutch community, which is exemplified in Excerpt 5.24 by *bucket*. It comes out of a discussion of the conversation excerpted in 4.17, about the *vraagvrije vrijdag* style in the *vragenuurtje* community.

Excerpt 5.24 "I'm not even gonna read that" (Dutch community)

01 JD:	nog een PAgina van vragen- van vraagvrije vrijdag. nog (..) NOG een [keer laviefantasque	
02 BK:	[WAUW JEEEH @@@	

190   **5 The Why: Ideology, Positioning, and Attitudes toward English**

03 JD: @@@ eh ((3-second pause)) **let's start early**.
04 BK: oh ja maar- ja. ja? @@@
05 JD: @@@ ((3-second pause)) en **ontd is bringing me so much LOLS right now**.
06 BK: ik WEET dus niet eens wat **ontd** IS.
07 JD: ja dat is een- een **community** (.) nog een andere [**community**.
08 BK: [oh.
09 JD: **brb have to rehost pics**
10 BK: nee dit is turbo- mijn MOEder zou zeggen TURbotaal
11 JD: turbotaal
12 BK: is een soort (.) STRAATtaal maar dan op internet. daar [@distantieer ik mij
        helemaal van@.
13 JD: [ja. DAT doe je niet.
14 BK: nee. @@ nee. (..) ik vind dat- nee. (.) ik heb echt gewoon daar een soort
        [[fysieke reactie op
15 JD: [[@@@@@
16 BK: van [NEE. @@@@@ ik.
15 JD: [@@@@@
16 BK: OH. irriTANT. ik LEES het dan gewoon al niet eens.
17: JD: ja oké.
18 BK: dan denk ik een beetje aan van die (. . .) meisjes (..) STANDaard STEreotype
        (.) **californian girls** met zon *i don't like it ohhh* nou [DIE doen dit
19 JD: [ja
20 BK: en WAARom zou je je DAARmee willen associëren of?

01 JD: another PAGE from ques- from question free friday. an (..) anOTHer one
        [from laviefantasque
02 BK: [WOW YAAAY @@@
03 JD: @@@ um ((3-second pause)) **let's start early**.
04 BK: oh yeah but- yeah. yeah? @@@
05 JD: @@@ ((3-second pause)) and **ontd is bringing me so much LOLS right now**.
06 BK: i don't even KNOW what ontd IS.
07 JD: yeah that's a- a **community** (.) another [**community**.
08 BK: [oh.
09 JD: **brb have to rehost pics**
10 BK: no that's turbo- my MOther would call it TURbo language
11 JD: turbo language
12 BK: it's a kind of (.) STREET slang but then on the internet. i [@distance myself from it
        completely@.
13 JD: [okay. you don't do THAT.
14 BK: no. @@ no. (..) i think that- no. (.) i really have a kind of [[@physical reaction to it@
15 JD: [[@@@@@
16 BK: like [NO. @@@@@ i.
15 JD: [@@@@@

Attitudes Toward Transidiomatic Practices 191

> 16 BK: OH. IRRitating. i'm not even gonna READ that.
> 17: JD: okay got it.
> 18 BK: then i think a little bit about like those (...) girls (..) STANDard STEreotypical (.) **californian girls** with like a *i don't like it ohhh* i mean [THEY are the ones who do this
> 19 JD: [yeah
> 20 BK: and WHY would you want to associate yourself with THAT i mean?

Participant *bucket*'s assessment of the *vraagvrije vrijdag* style is already clear from her sarcastic, mocking "WOW YAAAAY" in turn 2 at the very idea of looking at another page of it. I then go through the text of the weekly *vraagvrije vrijdag* post with her, pointing out the various transidiomatic practices I would like her to comment on, and she makes short, noncommittal to negative remarks that ultimately culminate in her assessment in turn 10: "no that's turbo language," which she compares to "straattaal" (or "street slang," i.e. a common term for a specific variety of Dutch largely spoken by urban youth in the north-western part of the country, strongly associated with the Surinamese community, and characterized by a heavy use of transidiomatic prac-tices). Bucket adds that she doesn't want anything at all to do with this type of language (turn 12), and that in fact she has a knee-jerk negative reaction to it that feels almost physical and makes her want to turn away and not even read those community conversations (turns 14 and 16). She then elaborates on where this reaction comes from by positioning this sort of language as something that "standard stereotypical Californian girls" might use and asking why anyone would want to associate themselves with that. This serves to iconize these practices as inherently associated with this particular group of young American women, and specifically as an essential part of what stereotypes them.

Though both the German and the Dutch communities contain examples of the stance that mixing is simply unpleasant, in the German community all kinds of transidiomatic practices are character-ized in this way, from simple common nouns to the kinds of strategic uses that were discussed in Chapter 4. In the Dutch community, on the

192   5 The Why: Ideology, Positioning, and Attitudes toward English

other hand, not only is this stance far less common, but it is also exclusively reserved to pass judgment on the particular *vraagvrije vrijdag* style that is limited to those weekly posts, a style that is characterized by an even higher than usual degree of mixing than what is typical in the *vragenuurtje* community, and used specifically to index an overall sense of transnationalism (see Chapter 4 for more discussion about this). This suggests that the stance that transidiomatic practices are simply generally problematic is not at all uncommon in the German community, while in the Dutch community it is only the most extreme examples of these practices that meet with a similar kind of negative reaction.

Mixing is not Understandable

The stance that mixing is not understandable—i.e. the counterpart to the stance that mixing *is* understandable, which was previously discussed above—only occurs within the German community. Because all of the excerpts that contain this stance are more or less similar, I will provide only one example, which is seen in Excerpt 5.25, from *urlaubssommer* (who was previously seen in Excerpts 5.5 and 5.21). The context is a discussion about the use of transidiomatic practices in the media.

Excerpt 5.25 "My grandma has no idea what that's supposed to mean" (German community)

```
01 US:   und bin da auch n BISSchen kritisch
02 JD:   ok?
03 US:   also (.) es is j- nich nur geSPROCHen zum beispiel auch im SUpermarkt wenn
         irgendwo geschrieben steht ähm (..) bei irgendwelchen obstbeschreibungen dass
         es halt *SWEET* ist und nich [süß dann=
02 JD:                                [mhm mhm
03 US:   =ärger ich mich halt SCHON n bisschen drüber
04 JD:   [mhm
05 US:   [weil ich zum beispiel denke meine Oma hat keine AHNung was das
         [[dann heißen soll
06 JD:   [[ja ok. (.) ja.
```

01 US:	and i'm also a LITTle bit critical of this	
02 JD:	okay?	
03 US:	i mean (.) it's like- not just SPOken for example in the GROcery store too when it says somewhere um (..) when they're describing some sort of fruit that it's *SWEET* and not [sweet ((the German term)) then=	
02 JD:	[mhm mhm	
03 US:	=i DO get a little annoyed by that	
04 JD:	[mhm	
05 US:	[because for example i think my GRANDma has no iDEa what [[that's supposed to mean	
06 JD:	[[yeah okay. (.) yeah.	

Participant *urlaubssommer* begins by saying that she's "a little bit critical" of these practices in the media because they're "not just spoken" but also appear "for example in the grocery store," such as in signs using the English word "sweet" to describe fruit as opposed to the German term süß. Then, in explaining further why she gets "a little annoyed by that" (turn 3), she evokes her grandmother as someone who wouldn't even be able to parse something like that properly. This stands in direct contrast to, for example, Dutch community member *bucket*'s stance in Excerpt 5.4 that essentially everyone in Dutch society understands enough English to get by, and you have to go back into the absolute oldest of generations to find anyone who doesn't. Interestingly, it usually is a grandmother— either the participant's own grandmother or someone else's—who is evoked in these stances among German community members as a person whose needs it is important to keep in mind when using transidiomatic practices, which allows these existing or hypothetical grandmothers to bear the weight of the complaint of there being too much English rather than the participants having to assume it themselves (and therefore perhaps come across as speaking insufficient English). Also interesting is the fact that this stance is evoked most often in assessing transidiomatic practices as they are used in public contexts, and much less frequently as they are used in the

194   5 The Why: Ideology, Positioning, and Attitudes toward English

unserekleinestadt community itself or in their own language use in other contexts.

Mixing is Lazy

Another stance is that mixing is lazy, or something to fall back on when one is not putting very much effort into one's language. This stance comes up in both communities, so this section will contain one representative excerpt from each community. The first of these is Excerpt 5.26, from German participant *sonnenkind,* already known from a number of excerpts above. The context is a discussion about how her own use of transidiomatic practices differs depending on who she's talking to.

Excerpt 5.26 "Because I do speak English it's somewhat easier" (German community)

01 SK: ich finde es schade dass ich es tatsächlich mache. (.) aber ich mache es halt trotzdem. (.) also es ist- es ist- ich finde ähm (.) da ich halt englisch SPRECHe ist es für mich teilweise EINfacher weil es wie gesagt sachen ausdrückt die ich sonst nicht ausdrücken kann und wenn jemand auch halt gut englisch SPRICHT dann weiss er besser was ich MEIne als wenn ichs deutsche umschreibe weil es eben genau das ist was ich sagen will.
02 JD: mhm mhm
03 SK: und wenn ich das auf anderen sprachen- mit anderen worten nicht genauso [sagen kann
04 JD: [mhm
05 SK: nicht genauso auf den punkt bringen kann

01 SK: i think it's too bad that i actually do do it. (.) but i keep doing it anyway. (.) i mean it's- it's- i think um (.) because i DO speak english it's somewhat EASier for me because like i said you can express things that i otherwise can't express and if someone SPEAKS english well then they know better what i MEAN than when i paraphrase it in german because it's exactly the thing that i want to say.
02 JD: mhm mhm
03 SK: and if i can't say that in other langua- with other words [just as well
04 JD: [mhm
05 SK: can't cut to the chase in the same way

Attitudes Toward Transidiomatic Practices   195

Participant *sonnenkind* begins by maintaining that it is "too bad" that she uses transidiomatic practices at all, and quickly moves on to assert that speaking English makes things "somewhat easier" for her because it allows her to "express things that I otherwise can't express." However, the immediate juxtaposition of the notion that it's "too bad" that she uses transidiomatic practices and the fact that her knowledge of English makes things easier for her positions the latter assertion as something negative rather than the positive assertion that it could initially be read as. Specifically, it positions English as a crutch that she falls back on with people who speak the language as well as she does, as opposed to doing the work it would require in order to find a way of saying the same thing in German.

This same stance is expressed much more overtly (and also at much greater length) in Excerpt 5.27, which comes from Dutch participants *niettemin* and *vogel,* who likewise already appeared in several previous excerpts. The context is a discussion of whether you need to speak English well in order to use transidiomatic practices in primarily Dutch conversations.

Excerpt 5.27 "In my eyes it's always a weakness when people do that" (Dutch community)

01 JD: maar geeft het wel- het gebruik van het engels door het nederlands heen- geeft het wel- geeft het WEL een beetje een gevoel dat iemand WEL goed engels beheerst

02 NT: nee. [nee (.) ik ben er ook inmiddels achter-

03 VO: [nee (.) alleen maar dat ze slecht zijn in hun NEderlands. @

04 NT: ja. (.) het verhult vaak een gebrek van ten eerste van de NEderlandse taal (.) en vaak ook van de ENGelse taal.

05 JD: oké.

06 NT: dat zie je snel genoeg.

07 VO: ja.

08 NT: het is een eh-

09 VO: nee. het is (.) in mijn ogen het is altijd een zwakte als mensen dat doen. het is altijd omdat ze iets anders niet kun[nen.

10 NT: [vanuit luiheid.

11 JD: maar jullie hebben in het begin gezegd dat je- dat je- dat je dat zelf ook doet.

13 NT: ja. [nee. uit luiheid (.) absoluut.

196 5 The Why: Ideology, Positioning, and Attitudes toward English

14 VO: [ja. (.) ja.

15 JD: hoe bedoel je LUIheid?

16 NT: het is MAKKelijker? soms om iets- een VAST bestaande engelse uitdrukking te gebruiken? (.) eh (.) een engels cliCHÉ? (.) dan een origiNEle NEderlandse formuLERing ervoor te bedenken. wat niet als een NEderlands cliché voorHANDen is.

17 JD: oké.

18 NT: dan [val je in vaste patronen-

19 JD: [maar (. . .) soms- soms is dat GEEN vaste uitdrukking. bijvoorbeeld **too much of a boob fest** (.) dat hebben we ook gelezen.

20 NT: nee. nee.

21 JD: ja (.) of **BOOBness** (.) ja?

22 NT: nee (.) maar dan kom je al-

23 VO: dat zijn dingen waar je een PLAATje bij kunt maken.

24 NT: ja (.) dan kom je al bij het gebruik van eupheMISmes (.) en inderdaad (.) op het moment dat je naar euphemismes gaat zoeken (.) wil je juist zo creatief mogelijk iets proberen uit te drukken (.) en dan kan een vreemde taal (.) welke dan ook [makkelijker zijn.

25 JD: [oké.   oké.

26 VO: ja maar dan is het nog steeds (.) tenminste als- als IK engels naar iemand anders toe gebruik? engels door mn nederlands gebruik? dan is ze geschrokken ((indicates *niettemin* with a gesture)). want dan is het omdat ik niet op tijd een fatsoenlijk nederlands alternaTIEF heb kunnen verzinnen? (.) of omdat ik gewoon niet goed weet hoe dat SNEL à la minute in een nederlandse zin kan verWERKen.

27 NT: nee.

28 JD: ja (.) ja.

29 VO: [dus

30 JD: [@@

31 VO: ik zal- in een tekst zal ik ook altijd de ZIN proberen aan te passen zodat het in het nederlands KLOPT? dan dat ik er een wngels woord doorHEEN moet gooien.

32 NT: nee.

01 JD: but it does give off- the use of english mixed through the dutch- it gives off- it DOES give off a little bit the impression that someone DOES speak english well

02 NT: no. [no (.) by now i've come to the conclusion-

03 VO: [no (.) just that they're bad at DUTCH. @

04 NT: yes. (.) it often conceals a lack in first of all the DUTCH language (.) and often also in the ENGlish language.

05 JD:	okay.	
06 NT:	you recognize that quickly enough.	
07 VO:	yeah.	
08 NT:	it's an um-	
09 VO:	no. it's (.) in my eyes it's always a weakness when people do that. it's always because they're not capable of anything di[fferent.	
10 NT:	[because of laziness.	
11 JD:	but you two said at the beginning that you- that you- that you do that yourselves too.	
13 NT:	yes. [no. out of laziness (.) absolutely.	
14 VO:	[yes. (.) yes.	
15 JD:	what do you mean by LAZiness?	
16 NT:	it's SIMPler? sometimes to just- to use a STANdard existing english expression? (.) uh (.) an english cliCHÉ? (.) than to come up with an oRIGinal DUTCH formulation. which doesn't eXIST as a DUTCH cliché.	
17 JD:	okay.	
18 NT:	then [you fall into these standard patterns-	
19 JD:	[but (. . .) some- sometimes it ISn't a standard expression. for example **too much of a boob fest** (.) we saw that one too.	
20 NT:	no. no.	
21 JD:	yeah (.) or **BOOBness** (.) right?	
22 NT:	no (.) but then you're already getting into-	
23 VO:	those are things that you can imagine a PICture of.	
24 NT:	right (.) you end up getting pretty quickly into the use of EUphemisms (.) and in fact (.) at the point where you're looking for euphemisms (.) that's precisely the point where you want to try and express things as creatively as possible (.) and then a foreign language (.) whichever one [can be easier.	
25 JD:	[okay. okay.	
26 VO:	okay but then it's still (.) at least when- when I use english in speaking to somebody else? use english mixed into my dutch? then she's startled ((indicates *niettemin* with a gesture)). because that happens because i didn't come up with a respectable alTERnative in time? (.) or because i simply don't know well enough how i can work it QUICKly one two three into a dutch SENtence.	
27 NT:	no.	
28 JD:	yeah (.) yeah.	
29 VO:	[so	
30 JD:	[@@	
31 VO:	i will- in a text i'll always try to adapt the SENtence so that it WORKS in dutch? rather than having to throw an english WORD into it.	
32 NT:	no.	

198   5   The Why: Ideology, Positioning, and Attitudes toward English

The excerpt begins with the assertion from me that the use of transidiomatic practices at least gives off an impression of facility with English, but this is immediately negated by both participants in turns 2 through 4, where both assert that it actually just suggests that they're bad at Dutch (and, as *niettemin* argues, that they may also in fact be bad at English). Participant *vogel* then elaborates in turn 9 with a stance that is unencumbered by any hesitations: in his eyes, it's "always a weakness" when people use transidiomatic practices, and that people only use them because "they're not capable of anything different." Then, without any sort of counterargument (which positions *vogel*'s assertion as something she is in full agreement with), *niettemin* adds the reason why she believes people do this: "because of laziness." I then remind them that they both said that they use transidiomatic practices themselves, but both still maintain that they too do this "out of laziness."

In turn 15, then, I ask what they mean by "laziness," and the answer comes from *niettemin* that this judgment specifically has to do with a perceived lack of originality: that English is full of standard expressions that Dutch people take on and use themselves when they should be doing the more difficult work of coming up with original words. Crucial here is that the problem is not the notion that they are using English per se, but the notion that they are using clichés that they have heard from somewhere else rather than coming up with their own phrasing. I then protest in turn nineteen that sometimes the transidiomatic practices in question aren't set phrases at all, but actually indications of a creative use of the language, reminding them of the "too much of a boob fest" phrasing as discussed in Excerpt 5.17 above (which the same pair of participants in fact evaluated quite positively). Participant *vogel* seems to falter in the vehemence of his stance at this point and seems willing to make an exception for the kinds of transidiomatic practices that allow you to "imagine a picture of," but *niettemin* stands firm, arguing that this sort of language use gets "pretty quickly into the use of euphemisms" and "that's precisely the point where you want to try and express things as creatively as possible" at which point a foreign language makes things "easier." Participant *vogel* then ends by saying self-critically that the only time he uses transidiomatic practices, it is because he failed to "come up with a respectable alternative in time" (turn 26), but that he always at least tries to "adapt the sentence so that it works in Dutch rather than having to throw an English word into it" (turn 31). This positions transidiomatic practices not as something reserved for people with a certain facility with English, but instead for people whose extensive contact with English has rendered them incapable of expressing similar things in their own language in any sort of elegant way.

The main difference between the way this stance is expressed in the two communities is likely attributable to the fact that transidiomatic practices mainly encompass single-word and single-compound borrowings in the German community, while the Dutch community tends to use many more larger expressions and quotes and even entirely original, unborrowed phrasings (see the discussion about this in Chapter 3). In Excerpt 5.26, German participant *sonnenkind* is therefore mostly referring to single words, usually nouns, while Dutch participants *niettemin* and *vogel* are referring to a much greater range of practices in Excerpt 5.27, and seem to largely be focusing their ire on my category (c), or what I term "larger expressions or quotes lifted in their entirety from everyday English-language interaction and used to effect in conversation." This ire is particularly aimed at the clichéd nature of these expressions and quotes rather than on the fact that they originated in the English language. The result, however, is still the same stance, and in both communities the use of transidiomatic practices is expressed as a weakness, and the *users* of transidiomatic practices seen as unwilling to do the intellectual work that finding a local-language equivalent for the English expression requires.

Mixing is Adversely Affecting the Local Language

Based on what is known about the differences between the public discourses about influence from English in Germany and the Netherlands (see Chapter 2), my expectation was that the stance that mixing is adversely affecting the local language would be limited to the German community. Surprisingly, this is not the case: it is found in both communities. However, there is still a distinct difference between the

200   5   The Why: Ideology, Positioning, and Attitudes toward English

two in terms of how it is talked about. This section presents one representative excerpt from each community, the first of these again coming from German participant *sonnenkind*. It comes from a larger discussion prompted by my question about whether it is important to keep in mind that there are people who don't speak English well (or even at all).

Excerpt 5.28 "No more German words are being invented" (German community)

01 SK: ich- ich habe schon am anfang gesagt dass ich das nicht GUT finde? und trotzdem merk ich das selber grad WIE ich hier spreche und drauf ACHte dass ich durchaus einige englische worte einfach in meinen sprachgebrauch HAbe die ich einbau ohne es zu MERken (.) und das finde ich eigentlich tatsächlich schade weil ich finde (.) das eigentlich wichtig dass ein land SEIne sprache hat und die nicht mit anderen sprachen vermischt sondern eben dass die sprache so BLEIBT also natürlich wandelt sich eine sprache immer dass muss sie ja auch aber (.) ähm (.) also ich finde es schade dass sie so verschwindet und durchs englische- ja ins englische eingeht und es keine neue entwicklung- gar keine WOrte mehr auf deutsch erfunden [werden=

02 JD: [mhm

03 SK: =sondern nur einfach die englischen worte übernimmt und das find ich zum beispiel sehr schade.

04 JD: findest du dass es verSCHWINdet?

05 SK: ähm (.) nein aber es gibt diese neue entwicklung für die es eben einfach keine deutschen worte mehr GIBT und die nicht mehr er- erfunden werden (.) also es verschwindet nicht NOCH nicht aber es gibt halt (..) also momentan ist die tendenz hmm vor allem die leute die GROsse firmen haben die macht haben immer gerne die **business** worte so auf englisch halt [einführen (.)

06 JD: [mm mm

07 SK: auch eben **business** sagen zum beispiel das heisst hier **business**. das sage ich auch.

08 JD: geschäft

09 SK: ja das würde aber komisch klingen und **business** das klingt halt- das klingt halt GUUUUT und (.) HIP und moDERN

01 SK: i- i said already back at the beginning that i don't think this is a GOOD thing? and yet i still notice myself especially right now AS i'm speaking here and am paying attENtion that i absolutely DO have some english words in my language use that i incorporate without NOticing (.) and i really do think that's

> unfortunate because i think (.) it's actually important that a country has its OWN language and doesn't mix it with other languages but instead that the language STAYS like that i mean of course a language changes that has to happen but (.) um (.) i mean i think it's too bad that it's disappearing like that and is getting- is being adopted into english and that there's no new development- no more WORDS being created in [german=
>
> 02 JD: [mhm
>
> 03 SK: =but it's just taking the english words over and for example i think that's really too bad.
>
> 04 JD: do you think it's disaPPEARing?
>
> 05 SK: um (.) no but there's this new development that means there ARE no more german words and that no more are being cre- created (.) i mean it's not disappearing not YET but like there are (.) i mean at the moment the tendency hmm most of all the people who have BIG companies who have power they like to introduce these **business** words like in [english (.)
>
> 06 JD: [mm mm
>
> 07 SK: and like i mean saying **business** for example it's called **business** here. i say that too.
>
> 08 JD: business ((the German term))
>
> 09 SK: yeah but that would sound weird and **business** that just sounds- that just sounds GOOOOD and (.) HIP and MOdern

In turn 1, *sonnenkind* reiterates the stance that she's voiced in several other excerpts: that it is not only possible for a language to remain in a pure state uninfluenced by other languages, but that this is the most desirable outcome. The generic way that she voices this stance throughout, however (e.g. "it's important that a country has its own language and doesn't mix it with other languages"), suggests that this is not German-specific for her, but a generalizable ideology that would hold true for any language. This is remarkably in tune with both the German tradition of the way particular languages are thought to belong to particular nation states, as well as with the German wider public discourse on the role of English (see Chapter 2 for both of these discussions). As a part of voicing this stance, she criticizes her own use of transidiomatic practices ("I absolutely do have some English words in my language use that I incorporate without noticing, and I really do think that's

202   5 The Why: Ideology, Positioning, and Attitudes toward English

unfortunate"), saying that this is something she has only noticed about herself through talking about her language practices with me in the interview.

Toward the end of *sonnenkind*'s first turn and continued in turn 3, then, there is a shift toward a somewhat more radical stance: that "it's too bad that it's disappearing like that and is getting- is being adopted into English and that there's no new development- no more words being created in German but it's just taking the English words over." I prompt her to elaborate on this in turn 4, in response to which she first reiterates that the issue is the tendency to take on English words instead of creating German words in response to anything new, then clarifies that it's "not disappearing," but the "not yet" she tags onto this (turn 5) positions English as a threat with potentially dire consequences. She further characterizes this as a "new development," which positions this threat as imminent. She then gives a glimpse into who she believes is in control of this trend—"the people who have big companies, who have power"—which positions mere users of the language as helpless against the onslaught of English words controlled by representatives of these corporations. Finally, when I respond to her "business" example by offering up a possible German alternative, she objects on the grounds that the German would "sound weird," while using transidiomatic practices makes the same thing sound "good and hip and modern." Especially in light of her previous self-criticism, this assessment serves to position the entire trend toward the use of transidiomatic practices as a certain dangerous and sinister manufacture of consent, in which corporations are convincing ordinary German citizens to use English words that are, in the long run, not good for them.

An analogous but still noticeably different take on the same stance can be seen in Excerpt 5.29, which comes from the interview with *laviefantasque* from the Dutch community. This took place toward the beginning of the interview, as part of the conversation that resulted from my question about what her general opinions are about the use of transidiomatic practices.

Attitudes Toward Transidiomatic Practices 203

Excerpt 5.29 "As such it really is sad" (Dutch community)

01 LV: ik had wel een interessant geSPREK met iemand laatst (.) die zei van (.) het is wel (.) jammer dat er (.) mensen die dan in nederland geboren worden en opgegroeid worden (.) dat ze hun- ja (.) hun eigen taal verLIEzen. en ja natuurlijk heb je altijd wel taalveranderingen en dingen en (.) daar was ik VROEGer natuurlijk ook wel (.) MEER (.) mening over (.) als nu.

02 JD: en hoe VOND je dat

03 LV: nou dat vond ik wel als je zegt (.) van eh ((3-second pause))) hij is (.) langer dan ik en dan zeg je (.) *langer als mij*.

04 JD: hm.

05 LV: één leraar twee leraars? (.) kom op het is twee leraren. (.) maar dan denken ze niet na en weet je wel (.) gewoon **plural s** eraan PLAKKen (.) dan denk ik jaaa (.) jaaaaa (.) huh (.) weet je wel?

06 JD: vind je- vind je dat er wat aan is? of

07 LV: nou dat (.) als mensen veel meer die engelse woorden gebruiken (.) dat je dan je creativiteit met de nederlandse taal verLIEST (.) als je dan zegt van ja (.) ik ga geWOON (.) makkelijk de engelse termen overnemen.

08 JD: en dat vind je ook. (.) of niet.

09 LV: ehm ((2-second pause)) ja ik weet het niet eigenlijk. [ik ben er niet helemaal over uit.

10 JD: [oké.

11 LV: ik vind het aan de ene kant (.) ja dat geBEURT nu eenmaal talen gaan nu eenmaal SAmen (.) een taal verandert sowieSO daar kun je TOCH niks aan doen (.) of je het nu leuk vindt of niet leuk vindt (.) maar (.) ja. (.) moet dat dan (.) per se de ENGelse taal zijn of (.) [KAN de nederlandse taal-

12 JD: [mm

13 LV: ja (.) je kan- eigenlijk vind ik- ik blijf ik me wel verBAzen (.) dat- dat de nederlandse taal op zich ook wel heel mooi kan zijn? [[terwijl ik me vroeger daar toch echt tegen AF aan het duwen was?=

14 JD: [[hmm? ja.

15 LV: =omdat ik toch echt beWUST gewoon dacht van nu ga ik engels praten. (.) of nu ben ik in deze context en wil ik [DIT doen

16 JD: [ja.

17 LV: of een boek per se in het ENGels lezen of een film per se in het ENGels zien? want nederlandse films zijn allemaal stom en nederlandse boeken zijn allemaal stom? maar het is ook wel MOOI dat daar een cul[[tuur gewoon is.

18 JD: [[hm.

19 LV: en dichters of zo (.) dat die daarmee bezig zijn. en ja (.) de- de- de mensen die (.) dan later opgroeien zonder dat- ja (.) dat zal ook wel niet. (.) maar @@ die zien daar dan veel minder in (.) en dat is op zich ook wel jammer. (.) ja.

204   5 The Why: Ideology, Positioning, and Attitudes toward English

01 LV: i did have an interesting converSAtion with someone recently (.) who said like (.) it actually is (.) too bad that there (.) are people who were born and raised in the netherlands (.) that they're- you know (.) they're LOsing their own language. and yeah of course you always have language changes and things and (.) of course i USED to agree with that (.) MORE (.) than i do now.

02 JD: and what did you THINK of that

03 LV: well i did agree when you say (.) like uh ((3-second pause))) he is (.) taller than i am and then you say (.) *taller than me*.

04 JD: hm.

05 LV: one teacher two teachers ((with the plural s)) (.) come on it's two teachers. ((with the plural en)) (.) but then they don't think about it and you know (.) just SHOVE a **plural s** onto it (.) and then i think yeeeah (.) yeeeeeah (.) huh (.) you know?

06 JD: do you- do you think there's something to that? or

07 LV: well that (.) if people use a lot more english words (.) that you then end up LOsing the creativity with the dutch language (.) if you then say like (.) i'm JUST gonna (.) mindlessly take over the english terms.

08 JD: and you think that too. (.) or don't you.

09 LV: um ((2-second pause)) yeah i'm not sure honestly. [i haven't figured it all the way out yet.

10 JD: [okay.

11 LV: on the one hand i think it's (.) like that just HAPPens languages just fuse toGEther (.) a language changes ANYway you can't do anything aBOUT that (.) whether you like it or not (.) but (.) yeah. (.) does that (.) necessarily have to be the ENGlish language or (.) [is it POSSible for the dutch=

12 JD: [mm

13 LV: =language- yeah (.) you can- i actually think- i keep being surPRISED (.) that- that the dutch language can also be really beautiful in its own way? [[whereas i used to keep pushing it aWAY?=

14 JD: [[hmm? ja.

15 LV: =because i just CONsciously thought like now i'm gonna speak english (.) or now i'm in this context and i want to [do THIS

16 JD: [ja.

17 LV: or read a book in ENGlish at any cost or watch a movie in ENGlish at any cost? because dutch films are all stupid and dutch books are all stupid? but it really is WONderful that the cul[[ture is there.

18 JD: [[hm.

19 LV: and poets and stuff (.) that they work on things that have to do with that. and yeah (.) the- the- the people who (.) then end up growing up without that- yeah (.) i'm sure that won't happen. (.) but @@ they will end up thinking a lot less of it then (.) and as such that really is sad. (.) yeah.

Attitudes Toward Transidiomatic Practices   **205**

In turn one, *laviefantasque* begins by voicing a stance that she attributes to an unnamed "someone": the idea that the Dutch are "losing their own language." This contextualization of the stance as someone else's makes her its animator rather than its author, which in turn allows her to put it on the table for discussion while keeping it at arm's length. She does add two assessments to this stance in her own voice, however: "you always have language changes and things" and "I used to agree with that more than I do now," which both serve to distance her even further from the stance she has voiced, without being entirely clear about how she actually feels about it. Both assessments are also modified by the adverb "natuurlijk" ("of course"), which position her interactant—myself—as being on the same page as she is with respect to that stance, though it remains unclear at this point what that page is.

I then press her to tell me exactly how she feels about this stance, and she provides two examples where she does in fact perceive there as having been undue English influence: in the realm of the use of the object case rather than the subject case in the comparative phrase "taller than I am" vs. "taller than me" (turn 3) and in the use of the plural -s over the plural -en (turn 5). It is unclear whether these are actually grammatical developments in Dutch that are taking place under increasing influence from English, since both forms have been in free variation in Dutch for a good long time, but *laviefantasque* positions this as a fact, and states that she "did agree" with the original stance-taker about it in this respect (turn 3). This time the vehemence in the stance is positioned as her own, in other words: she's the one who's saying "come on it's two teachers" and talking about people "shoving a plural s onto it." In turn 6, however, when I press her still further to take a clearer stance, she responds with a series of relative clauses beginning with "dat" ("that"), which leave things unclear whether the ideas in the stance are part of the original stance-taker's wording or whether they could actually be hers (turn 7). When I then press her again to take a clear stance, she says that she's "not sure" how she feels about it and that she hasn't "figured it out all the way yet," leaving her ambivalence intact.

In the rest of the excerpt, then, she channels that ambivalence into a nuanced assessment that doesn't come down clearly on one side or the

206   5 The Why: Ideology, Positioning, and Attitudes toward English

other about whether influence from English is positive or negative, but still manages to communicate a clear stance that is both her own and also reflective of a particularly Dutch ideology regarding the position of English. She talks first about how influence from outside Dutch "just happens" to the point where languages even "just fuse together" and "you can't do anything about that whether you like it or not," but at the same time, she questions whether English really should have that role or whether some of the functions that have been relegated to English should actually stay with Dutch (turn 11). This ambivalence is strongly reminiscent of the debate in wider Dutch society about whether domain loss is something that should be resisted or merely accepted (see Chapter 2). She juxtaposes this with her own realization—which she positions as a change that has happened within her ("I keep being surprised" and "I used to keep pushing it away," turn 13)—that Dutch is something that she should actually be valuing for itself rather than always relegating it to second place to English in her own mind and her own practices (cf. turns 15 and 17). This realization is further juxtaposed with the importance of Dutch cultural products like poetry ("it really is wonderful that the culture is there," turn 17). She briefly flirts with a more radical stance that future generations might end up losing their language altogether ("the people who then end up growing up without that," turn 19) before dismissing that idea as unlikely ("I'm sure that won't happen," turn 19). But she ends nonetheless by positing the danger that future Dutch generations "will end up thinking a lot less of it" because of the heavy use of transidiomatic practices, positioning this as an unfortunate development.

This stance is similar to the attitude that the use of transidiomatic practices is inherently lazy in the sense that both stances zero in on these practices as something that occurs when people are resorting to English and not giving their own language a chance. However, this position takes the notion one step further by positing that people end up actually failing to learn their own language properly because of these lazy habits, and that this is having an adverse effect on certainly the local language and perhaps even the local culture. In addition, it is the case in both communities that the ordinary language user is positioned as someone without any real agency, i.e. as someone who these developments are simply happening to rather than something they have real control over. The difference between the two communities, of course, is that in the German community the influence from English that is being criticized is solely limited to the lexical, while in the Dutch community the concern has more to do with the notion of losing facility with one's own language when so many grammatical and interactional functions have changed under English influence. This is not surprising given the actual demonstrated differences in usage as discussed in Chapters 3 and 4, but it is still indicative of the distinct ideologies that underpin those differences: the German notion that even lexical influence is already cause for concern, while the Dutch have a greater tendency to accept influence from other languages except when it results in domain loss: and even then, resisting this influence is a contestable point (see the discussion about this in Chapter 2).

Mixing is Rule-Governed

In this next section, I will analyze excerpts in which a stance is taken that mixing is—or at least should be—rule-governed in some way. Identified subcategories within that consist of the stance that mixing should not involve "incorrect" English, the stance that the kind of mixing that goes on in the business world is problematic, and finally stances dealing with differences between how to mix the languages properly face-to-face interaction as compared with online.

The Issue of "Incorrect" English

The stance that "incorrect" English should not be a part of transidiomatic practices is found in both the *unserekleinestadt* and the *vragenuurtje* communities, but there are differences between the ways in which it is presented in each. In this section I analyze two contrasting excerpts, beginning with Excerpt 5.30, which comes from the interview with Dutch participants *luna_puella* and *isolde*. It emerged within my discussion with them toward the beginning of the interview about whether or not they have noticed the use of transidiomatic practices generally.

208   5 The Why: Ideology, Positioning, and Attitudes toward English

Excerpt 5.30 "Oh honey, please don't do that" (Dutch community)

01 LP: ik had ook toen ik stuDEERde (.) had- had ik ook een medestudent? en dan praatte ik met een aantal vrienDINNen die allemaal redelijk GOED engels spra-spraken. dan gooiden we wel HEEUL veel engels door het eh- door het nederlands heen soms dat we eigenlijk bijna alleen maar engels spraken? en dan was er één meisje dat ook meedeed (.) en dan dacht ik af en toe *ach meiske (.) doe dat nou gewoon NIET*.

02 IE: ja [@@@

03 JD: [@@@ hm. hm.

04 LP: we vinden je HEEL LIEF maar praat maar @gewoon NEderlands@. @@@

05 JD: ja (.) omdat- omdat ze niet zo goed EN[gels sprak.

06 LP: [nee inderdaad.

07 JD: oké.

08 LP: dat ze af en toe- dat er of (.) TAALfouten inzaten of dat gewoon haar UITspraak niet mooi was. en dan-

09 JD: oké. (.) moet- moet je dan echt GOED ENGels kunnen spreken [om- om

10 LP: [het MOET natuurlijk niet (.) ik bedoel (.) het- het is haar niet verBOden [om het te doen maar=

11 JD: [ja (.) eh

12 LP: =ik dacht het zou @FIJNer zijn als ze het NIET zou doen@.

13 JD: oké.

01 LP: i also had back when i was a STUdent (.) i had- i also had a classmate? and i'd always talk with a bunch of FRIENDS who all spo- spoke reasonably GOOD english. and we'd tend to throw LOOTS of english into our uh- into our dutch to the extent that we sometimes actually were almost speaking just english? and there was one girl that participated too (.) and i'd sometimes tend to think *oh honey (.) PLEASE don't do that*.

02 IE: yeah [@@@

03 JD: [@@@ hm. hm.

04 LP: we think you're REALLy SWEET but please just @stick to speaking DUTCH@. @@@

05 JD: right (.) because- because her english wasn't that [GOOD.

06 LP: [no exactly.

07 JD: okay.

08 LP: that there were sometimes- that either there were (.) GRAMMar errors in it or that just her pronunciAtion wasn't very nice. and then-

09 JD: okay. (.) do you need- do you then really need to be able to speak GOOD ENGlish [to- to

10 LP: [you don't HAVE to of course (.) i mean (.) she's not forBIDDen [to do it but=

Attitudes Toward Transidiomatic Practices

> 11 JD: [right (.) uh
> 12 LP: =i thought it would be @more PLEASant if she DIDn't do it@.
> 13 JD: okay.

Beginning in turn 1, *luna_puella* recounts interactions with a fellow student whose attempts to participate in transidiomatic practices among friends are positioned as having fallen flat. She is not specific about what exactly contributed to that falling flat, however, recounting only her younger self's reaction that the friend should have stuck to speaking only Dutch. Her laughter positions both the friend's attempts and her own reaction as amusing, however, which leads me to interpret this as the friend's English having been deficient (turn 5). In turn 6, *luna_puella* confirms that this was indeed the case ("there were grammar errors in it or that just her pronunciation Wasn't very nice"). Through this positioning of grammar errors and an unattractive, probably overly Dutch-sounding pronunciation as not being part of transidiomatic practices, the stance emerges that there are norms for using transidiomatic practices that some people fail to adhere to.

A contrasting excerpt in the *unserekleinestadt* community can be seen in Excerpt 5.31, which comes from the interview with German participant *caroline*, previously seen in Excerpts 5.10 and 5.13. The context is a discussion resulting from my more general question about the kinds of transidiomatic practices that bother her and the kinds that do not.

Excerpt 5.31 "I tend to find that annoying instead" (German community)

> 01 CA: mich störts DANN wenn ich das gefühl habe (.) dass ähm (.) jemand d- viel englisch benutzt um sich zu profiLIERren (.) um COOLer zu sein (..) ähm (.) und- und wenn ich den eindruck hab derjenige weiß vielleicht gar nicht was die worte beDEUten. (.) die er benutzt.
> 02 JD: achso. hm.
> 03 CA: sowas @mag ich GAR nicht@.

210   5 The Why: Ideology, Positioning, and Attitudes toward English

04 JD: ok. ((2-second pause)) also man muss schon (.) GUT englisch sprechen (.) um (.) so irgendwie das RECHT zu haben=
05 CA: @@@
06 JD: =englisch auch im deutschen zu gebrauchen
07 CA: mh
08 JD: hab ich- hab ich (.) das richtig verstanden?
09 CA: also ich finde man muss jetzt kein englischexperte s- sein um zum beispiel **online** oder **joystick** zu sagen (.) aber man sollte wenigstens wissen was diese begriffe bedeuten. und je mehr englische begriffe man einfließen lässt desto- von so mehr- desto mehr worte muss man auch auf deutsch @erklären können find ich@. also manche leute machen das ja NUR so aus geHABE? und dann schmeißen sie worte ein die die IRgendwo mal gehört haben? (.) [oder auch so REdewendungen=
10 JD: [ja
11 CA: so **by the way** oder keine ahnung (.) [[solche sachen
12 JD: [[ja. und das findest du nicht gut.
13 CA: äh nur wenn sie, wenn sie das auch (.) nicht verstehen. [also wenn es jetzt jemand is
14 JD: [achSO.
15 CA: der zum beispiel (.) ähm (.) fließend englisch spricht? und dann einfach zwischendurch **by the way** sagt? weil ihm grad das deutsche nicht so schnell eingefallen ist wie das englische? find ich das völlig ok=
16 JD: ok
17 CA: =wenn es jemand ist der KEIne ahnung hat was das heißt und das eventuell auch noch falsch benutzt
18 JD: @@
19 CA: dann find ich das eher nervig.

01 CA: i ONly tend to get annoyed when i have the feeling (.) that um (.) someone w- is using lots of english in order to make a NAME for himself (.) to be COOLer (..) um (.) and- and if i have the impression that the person maybe doesn't even know what the words MEAN. (.) that he's using.
02 JD: oh. hm.
03 CA: i don't @like that sort of thing at ALL@.
04 JD: okay. ((2-second pause)) so you do have to (.) speak english WELL (.) um (.) in order to kind of like have the RIGHT=
05 CA: @@@
06 JD: =to use english in your german
07 CA: mh
08 JD: do i have- did i understand (.) that right?
09 CA: i mean i don't think you have to b- be an english expert to say for example **online** or **joystick** (.) but you should at least know what these expressions mean. and the more english terms you allow to flow into your language the

	more- like the more- the more words you also have to @be able to explain in german i think@. so many people JUST do that kind of as affecTAtion? and then they throw words in that they just heard SOMEwhere out there? (.) [or like things like expRESSions=
10 JD:	[yeah
11 CA:	like **by the way** or whatever (.) [[stuff like that
12 JD:	[[yeah. and you don't think that's good.
13 CA:	uh only when they, when they (.) don't underSTAND it. [so if it's somebody
14 JD:	[OHHH.
15 CA:	who for example (.) um (.) speaks fluent english? and then along the way just says **by the way**? because just then the german isn't occurring to him so quickly as the english? i think that's completely okay=
16 JD:	okay
17 CA:	=when it's someone who has NO idea what that means and who potentially is even using it incorrectly
18 JD:	@@
19 CA:	then i tend to find that annoying instead.

In turn 1, *caroline* begins by positioning her annoyance as resulting from what she perceives as the user's intentions, such as using transidiomatic practices to "make a name for himself" or "to be cooler." Later in the same turn, then, she posits that this results from an insufficient knowledge of the meanings of English words (presumably as they are used in their original, native-speaker contexts). Through this series of positionings, the stance is implied that it is important to speak English well in order to use transidiomatic practices properly, and as in the previous excerpt, I inquire about that directly (turns 4, 6, and 8). Participant *caroline*'s response is laughter, followed by a clarification that it is not the usage that bothers her as much as the user's perceived knowledge of the original English meanings of the words.

In both communities, the use of "incorrect" English in transidiomatic practices is something that is done by inept users of the language who are intending to use it in the same way more adept users do, but failing. However, in the Dutch community it tends to be brought up as an issue of perceived pronunciation or grammar errors, while in the German community incorrect usage tends to be associated with a lack of knowledge of the original meanings of specific English words. As in previous

212   **5 The Why: Ideology, Positioning, and Attitudes toward English**

sections, this distinction is reflective of the widespread tendency among German community members to conceive of transidiomatic practices as essentially limited to the lexical level, while the Dutch community members tend to both use and perceive them as more broadly based. In both communities, however, it seems to be the native-speaker norm (in terms of pronunciation, grammar, or lexical meanings) that is posited as the yardstick by which to measure appropriate transidiomatic practices.

English in the Business World

The stance that there is something inherently problematic about English as it is used in the business world in the two countries also occurs within both communities, but as in the previous section, there are differences between the two in terms of the way this stance emerges. The first of two contrasting excerpts can be seen in Excerpt 5.32, which comes from the interview with German participants *menschenskind, bienchen,* and *kakumo.* It emerged within a discussion about which kinds of transidiomatic practices they will tend to overtly notice, and which ones they tend to not even be aware of.

Excerpt 5.32 "Meeting English" (German community)

01 MK: also ich äh kenne eigentlich fast nur leute die das machen- eben- ne- mir fällt das richtige wort nicht ein jetzt nehm ich- dass es PASST aber manche leute machen das ja auch um so ich- ich kann so tolles **business**englisch und=

02 BC: [ja

03 MK: [=schmeißen dann

04 BC: **meeting**englisch.

05 MK: ja [genau.

06 JD: [und und

07 MK: und das fällt mir [[UNangenehm auf.

08 JD: [[was würde dir- was würde dir- äh was würde dir als BEIspiel davon auffallen

09 MK: ähm (. . .) bei meiner arbeit (.) da kommt so was wie ja wir müssen jetzt **MEETen** und mal die äh die **POINTS of INterest** und die

10 BC: das haben wir jetzt OUT[geSOURCT

Attitudes Toward Transidiomatic Practices   **213**

11 MK: [das haben wir jetzt **outgesourct** und die **big players** müssen wir mal ranziehen und er macht es halt auch oft (.) falsch. also man MERKT (.) er will halt n englisches wort weil es COOL klingt (.) aber es passt überhaupt nicht da REIN? und das fällt direkt also das is wie so- wenn man irgendwie fährt mit dem auto aus der garage raus macht so *krrk* so dieses und ich sitz dann nur immer so und es tut @irgendwie so [weh@ und

12 JD: [@@

13 MK: weil ich merk er macht das nicht weil er- weil er das geWOHNT ist oder so? sondern weil eher so ich nehm jetzt dieses englische wort weil- das hab ich jetzt letzte woche gehört und das klingt so toll und ich will jetzt alle beEINdrucken

01 MK: i mean i uh actually almost only know people who- do that- once in a while- the right word isn't occurring to me so i'm going to say- where it FITS but some people do do that to like i- i can speak such a great **business** english and=

02 BC: [yeah

03 MK: [=then they throw in

04 BC: **meeting** english.

05 MK: yeah [exactly.

06 JD: [and and

07 MK: and i notice that [[and find it unPLEASant.

08 JD: [[what would- what would- uh what would you notice of that sort of thing as an exAMple

09 MK: um (. . .) at my workplace (.) it comes up like yeah we have to MEET and like the uh the **POINTS of INterest** and the

10 BC: we OUT[SOURCED that

11 MK: [we **outsourced** that and we have to get the **big players** in on things and he even does it (.) wrong a lot of the time. like you NOtice (.) he just wants an english word because it's COOL (.) but it doesn't fit IN there at all? and i notice that right- i mean it's like- when you're driving your car out of the garage and it makes a *rrrr* like that and i always just sit there and it's @just somehow so pain[ful@ and

12 JD: [@@

13 MK: because i notice he's not doing that because he- because he's USED to it or something like that? but just because oh i'm using this english word now because- i heard it last week sometime and it sounds so cool and i want to imPRESS everybody now

Participant *menschenskind* begins in turn 1 with a contrast between people who use transidiomatic practices "where it fits" and people who do not, and by using them as the first example that occurs to her, she

214   **5 The Why: Ideology, Positioning, and Attitudes toward English**

explicitly positions users of "business English" (turn 1, from *menschens-kind*) or "meeting English" (turn 4, from *bienchen*) as falling into the latter category. Initially she simply characterizes this group's use of transidiomatic practices as something that she would both notice and find unpleasant (turn 7), but when pressed for an example, she and *bienchen* together provide several, all of which specifically have to do with business-related vocabulary (turns 9 through 11). By implication, she is then positioning herself as the sort of user of transidiomatic practices who use them "where they fit," a positioning that is reinforced by her reaction in turn 11 that compares business-English users' transidiomatic practices as analogous to a car's motor making a "painful" sound. In turn 13, *menschenskind* then positions these people as using transidiomatic practices without sufficient knowledge of English ("I heard it last week") and with the intentional goal of self-aggrandizement ("it sounds so cool and I want to impress everybody now").

There are many similarities to this in Excerpt 5.32, from the Dutch community, but some differences as well. It again comes from the interview with *vragenuurtje* participants *vogel* and *niettemin,* and it emerged within a general discussion toward the beginning of the interview about the kinds of transidiomatic practices that exist.

Excerpt 5.33 "Management language" (Dutch community)

01 VO: ik moet WEL zeggen ik vind het wel vaak verVElend- niet zozeer vervelend omdat het ENGels is (.) maar **management**taal bijvoorbeeld.

02 NT: **management.**

03 VO: dingen die wel DEgelijk makkelijk uit te drukken zijn in het nederlands maar waar dan nog steeds het engels gebruikt wordt dat vind ik wel STOrend.

04 JD: en- en wat- wat is dan de beDOELing van het ENGels? wat- wat- wat denk je? ((2-second pause))

05 VO: [ja.

06 NT: [het- het is een **manager** die zichzelf (.) interessanter wil laten klinken dan hij IS.

07 JD: oké. ja.

08 VO: ja. of de term ook alleen maar in het ENGels kent? (.) en dan eigenlijk stiekem geen idee heeft wat het in het nederlands beTEkent.

09 NT: ja. dat heb je ook.

01 VO:	i DO have to say i do think it's often annOYing- not annoying so much because it's ENGlish (.) but **management** language for example.
02 NT:	**management.**
03 VO:	things that absoLUTEly are easy to express in dutch but where english is still used anyway i do find that annOYing.
04 JD:	and- and what- what is the MEANing of the ENGlish then? what- what- what do you think?
	((2-second pause))
05 VO:	[huh.
06 NT:	[it's- it's a **manager** who (.) wants to make himself sound more important than he IS.
07 JD:	okay. got it.
08 VO:	yeah. or who only knows the term in ENGlish? (.) and then actually secretly has no idea what that MEANS in dutch.
09 NT:	yeah. you see that too.

In turn 1, *vogel* begins by positioning the use of transidiomatic practices in "management language" as annoying, though "not so much because it's English" (turn 1), but because they *could* be using Dutch if they wanted to (turn 3). In turn 6, *niettemin* then positions them as only doing this because English makes them seem "more important" than they are. In turn 8, however, *vogel* posits that they may also "secretly" be doing this because they only know the term in English and don't have any knowledge of a Dutch equivalent, an assessment that *niettemin* agrees with in turn 9.

In both communities, users' intentions are an important part of the assessment of business language as an inappropriate part of transidiomatic practices: whenever businesspeople are perceived as deliberately trying to make themselves look good, this usage is automatically and explicitly rejected. However, in the German community, the perceived annoyance also comes in large part as a result of the perception that businesspeople are using words they don't actually have sufficient knowledge of, while in the Dutch community it comes in large part as a result of the perception that these people only know the English word and might not be aware of a Dutch equivalent. This is a subtle distinction, but one that points toward a

216   5 The Why: Ideology, Positioning, and Attitudes toward English

concern in the German community that the main issue is insufficient adherence to the native-speaker-norm meanings of words, and in the Dutch community that the main issue is an inability to use one's own local language properly.

Differences Between Mixing Online and in Face-to-Face Interaction

Stances about potential distinctions between mixing online and in face-to-face interaction occur within both communities, though the tendency is to take opposite stances about whether or not these distinctions exist. The first of two contrasting examples can be seen in Excerpt 5.34, which again comes from the interview with German participant *sonnenkind*. It emerged within a discussion about the use of transidiomatic practices particularly among young people to portray oneself as youthful and hip.

Excerpt 5.34 "It wouldn't happen like that" (German community)

01 JD: äh ist das- ist das hauptsächlich im INternet so? oder auch im so- im no-normalen gespräch.
((3-second pause))

02 SK: hmm (.) also im normalen gespräch wäre es KOmisch wenn man einfach so (...) englische **statements** mit zu (.) ähm reinbringen aber es gibt halt wie gesagt worte die ich andauernd benutze weil die sind im normalen sprachgebrauch die einfach aus den englischen sind- schon so eingegangen ins deutsche dass ichs gar nicht MERke und da würd es- würd ich glaub ich darüber stolpern wenn man plötzlich die deutschen ein- (.) es gibt vielleicht deutsche worte die keiner benutzt da würd ich darüber stolpern das find ich auch komisch also zumindest auffällig und merkwürdig

03 JD: mm

04 SK: während man im INternet eben auch solche- solche sachen sagt (..) wie uhm (..) dass man auf englisch (..) uhm **goodbye** oder so was- auf englisch tschüss sagt-dass würde man- das fand ich im deutschen total komisch wenn jemand auf einmal auf englisch tschüss sagen würde anstatt tschüss oder bis bald [sagen würde

05 JD: [mhm mhm

06 SK: das würde so nicht passieren

01 JD:	uh is that- is that mainly on the INternet like? or also in a like- in a no-normal conversation.
	((3-second pause))
02 SK:	hmm (.) okay in a normal conversation it would be WEIRD to just like (. . .) bring english **statements** (.) um in but like i said there are words that i use constantly because they're just from the english- already so woven into the german that i don't NOtice it at all and there it would- i think it would trip me up if somebody suddenly used the german- (.) maybe there are german words that nobody uses there that would trip me up i think that's weird too or at least striking and curious
03 JD:	mm
04 SK:	whereas on the INternet people also just say the kin- kinds of things (..) like um (..) that you say in english (..) um **goodbye** or something like that- like bye ((german term)) in english- people would think that- i would think that was totally weird in german if somebody suddenly said bye ((german term)) in english instead of in german or instead of [see you soon ((german term))
05 JD:	[mhm mhm
06 SK:	it wouldn't happen like that

I begin by asking *sonnenkind* whether the practices she is talking about are limited to the internet, or whether you might also find them as part of a face-to-face conversation. She takes a while to respond, but ultimately positions the use of the same kinds of practices in a face-to-face interaction that would be commonplace in a social media-based interaction as "weird," something that would "trip her up," and something that "wouldn't happen like that."

By contrast, Excerpt 5.35 from the interview with Dutch participants *isolde* and *luna_puella* shows the opposite stance. It came up during a discussion about which *vragenuurtje* participants tend to use transidiomatic practices more than others.

Excerpt 5.35 "I just go ahead and use it" (Dutch community)

01 JD:	en- en zouden jullie dit soort dingen ook in **face to face** gesprekken zeggen?
02 IE:	[ja.
03 LP:	[ja ik wel.

218   **5 The Why: Ideology, Positioning, and Attitudes toward English**

```
04 JD:   ja?
05 IE:   ja. zelfs met mijn vriend heb ik soms complete engelse gesprekken. maar dan doe
         ik het niet met mijn MOOIe engelse accent? maar een beetje met mijn-
06 LP:   een beetje CASual (.) en maakt niet uit hoe het klinkt. @@@
07 IE:   waarschijnlijk een (.) *ik klink heel erg debiel en kinderlijk* accent.
08 LP:   ja. [@@@@@@@@
09 JD:       [@@@@@@@@
10 IE:   dat is veel SPEELSer altijd.
11 LP:   ja.
12 IE:   maar ik geBRUIK het gewoon. niet als ik tegen mijn begeLEIder praat? maar
         tegen VRIENDen gebruik ik wel altijd engels in mijn eh
13 LP:   ja. ik gebruik het met vrienden die het OOK doen en die het SNAPPen.


01 JD:   and- and would you also say these kinds of things in a **face to face** conversation?
02 IE:   [yes.
03 LP:   [i would yeah.
04 JD:   yeah?
05 IE:   yeah. even with my boyfriend sometimes i have complete english conversations.
         but then i don't do it with my NICE english accent? but a little bit with my-
06 LP:   a little bit CASual (.) and it doesn't matter how it sounds. @@@
07 IE:   probably a (.) *i sound completely moronic and childish* accent.
08 LP:   yeah. [@@@@@@@@
09 JD:         [@@@@@@@@
10 IE:   it's always more PLAYful.
11 LP:   yeah.
12 IE:   but i just go ahead and USE it. not when i'm talking to my BOSS? but with
         FRIENDS i do always use english in my uh
13 LP:   yeah. i use it with friends who do it TOO and who underSTAND it.
```

Both young women respond to my question in turn 1 by stating that they would, in fact, use the same sorts of transidiomatic practices in a face-to-face conversation that they tend to use in social media interactions. Participant *isolde* even says that she has conversations with her boyfriend that are completely in English, but that when she does that, she's not using her "nice English accent" (turn 5), but instead an accent that "probably" makes her sound "moronic and childish" (turn 7). Agreeing with this assessment, *luna_puella* characterizes this register as "a little bit casual and it doesn't matter how it sounds" (turn 6), because it's "always more playful" (turn 10). Both participants then specify that this use of transidiomatic practices isn't part of formal registers ("not when I'm talking to my boss," turn 12), but something that is limited to conversations "with friends" (turns 12 and 13) "who do it too and who understand it" (turn 13).

This final phrasing of *luna_puella*'s does, however, imply that there are nonetheless people who do *not* "do it too and understand it." This brings me to the point that while it is most typical within the German community to say that transidiomatic practices are limited to the internet and most typical within the Dutch community to say that they are common both online and in casual face-to-face interaction—stances that are representative of the generally most widespread use of transidiomatic practices in each community— the opposing stances are in fact also found among members of both communities. This suggests that although the differences *between* communities is most striking when it comes to this stance, there also exist important differences *within* communities.

Explanations for Transidiomatic Practices

In this section, I will present and analyze a series of representative excerpts that reveal the two communities' stances regarding the purposes of their own and others' transidiomatic practices. The subsections below represent the most common types of stances within the larger category of explanations for transidiomatic practices, namely those regarding perceptions of influences from outside the German-speaking and Dutch-speaking worlds, and those regarding perceptions of the use of English to evoke a specific characteristic or mood.

Perceptions of Non-Local Influences

This subsection deals with excerpts in which transidiomatic practices are explained as being a result of influences from outside the German-speaking and Dutch-speaking worlds. Identified subcategories within that category consist of the stance that transidiomatic practices result

220   **5 The Why: Ideology, Positioning, and Attitudes toward English**

from influence from the English-speaking internet, the stance that they result from influence from the English-speaking media, and the stance that they are specifically used to index particular English-speaking cultures and subcultures.

Influence from the English-Speaking Internet

The stance that transidiomatic practices result from influence from the English-speaking internet occurs in both communities. There are no clearly noticeable differences between the ways the communities express this stance, either, though in this case I still provide one excerpt from each community for the sake of completeness and to show this similarity. The first of these can be seen in Excerpt 5.36, which comes from the interview with Dutch participant *bucket*. It emerged within a discussion about the conversation quoted previously in Excerpt 3.8, in which the English word "topic" is used by one respondent to refer to the post and its comments.

Excerpt 5.36 "It's simply already integrated" (Dutch community)

01 JD: wat vind je van **TOpic**
02 BK: ja dat is een (..) gewoon een INternet term (..) ik weet ook (..) ja (.) mijn MOEder zit ook op een forum? en daar noemen ze het een DRAADje of zo
03 JD: een WAT?
04 BK: een DRAADje.
05 JD: een draa-
06 BK: een draadje?
07 JD: ik zou- ik zou gewoon ONderwerp zeggen.
08 BK: oh. @@ oh ja. NEE.
09 JD: nee?
10 BK: ja. @@@ nee. @@@
11 JD: **topic** is **TOpic**?
12 BK: maar dit is (..) JA. (..) ik denk er niet eens aan om dat te vert- om dat te verTALen naar (..) naar onderwerp. ((2-second pause)) want voor mij heeft **topic** in deze context ECHT het (..) de betekenis van- van draadje of van- wat dit is? (..) en heeft NIET (..) het is gewoon al geïntegreerd.

Explanations for Transidiomatic Practices 221

01	JD:	what do you think of **TOpic**
02	BK:	hm that's a (..) just an INternet term (..) i mean i know (..) okay (.) my MOther is on a forum too? and there they call it a thread ((Dutch term)) or something like that
03	JD:	a WHAT?
04	BK:	a THREAD.
05	JD:	a thr-
06	BK:	a thread?
07	JD:	i would- i would just say TOpic. ((Dutch term))
08	BK:	oh. @@ oh okay. NO.
09	JD:	no?
10	BK:	okay. @@@ no. @@@
11	JD:	**topic** is **TOpic?**
12	BK:	but this is (..) YEAH. (..) it wouldn't even occur to me to transla- to translate that to (..) to topic. ((Dutch term)) ((2-second pause)) because for me in this context **topic** REALLy has (..) the meaning of- of a thread or of- the thing that this is? (..) and it DOESn't have (..) it's simply already integrated.

Turn 1 begins with my question about what *bucket* thinks of the use of the word "topic" in the example in question. She starts by saying that it's "just an internet term," which not only positions this transidiomatic practice as having originated in the social media subculture, but the "just" also positions it as something trivial that we shouldn't be concerned about. She then offers up an alternate term used by the generation ahead of hers: *draadje* ("thread"), to which I respond by saying that I would actually tend to use the term *onderwerp* (the literal translation of "topic") if I were going to use a Dutch term. In response, *bucket* says "oh" with falling intonation—conveying surprise—laughs, and says "no" with both emphasis and falling intonation (turns 8 and 10). Together, this serves to position my alternative both as something that would never have even occurred to her, and as kind of ridiculous. Why this is ridiculous becomes clear in turn 12: the English word "topic" specifically refers to a social-media-discussion sort of topic rather than a topic in general, and so translating the word directly to Dutch wouldn't be appropriate at all. And this term is so "integrated" (turn 12) into social-media Dutch that it feels strange to her to even question it.

222   **5 The Why: Ideology, Positioning, and Attitudes toward English**

A similar but somewhat more complex example of this stance can be found in Excerpt 5.37, from the German community. It comes from the interview with *menschenskind, kakuro,* and *bienchen,* and came out of a discussion about a conversation in *unserekleinestadt* in which one person's long comment in German was followed by a comment containing only the English-origin word "same."

Excerpt 5.37 "Internet dialect" (German community)

```
01 MK:   also same das mach ich STÄNdig (.) wirklich
02 JD:   ja?
03 MK:   d- das [fällt mir auch nicht mehr auf
04 KK:          [was LUSTigerweise- wahrscheinlich wenn man diejenige drauf ansprechen würde (.) die wüsste nicht wo das HERkommt.
05 MK:   ja
06 KK:   weil das- letzten endes ist das nichts anderes als auch einfach ein (.) URaltes reLIKT aus den netzzeiten zu der zeit als das noch über die mailinglisten ging. das ist ja- das was berüh- was berühmt wurde als dieses- dieses berühmte LOL (.) me too (.) same here. selbes ding. einfach nur dasselbe druntergeschrieben und [dadurch (.) das is ja=
07 JD:          [ja (..) ja
08 KK:   =irgendwann äh auf- auf den ganzen- den ganzen- in den ganzen ähm (.) USEnetsachen sind ja grade diese poster komplett verSCHRIEN [gewesen
09 MK:                                                                           [ja
10 KK:   ne? weil das- dieses das [[datenvolumen so in die höhe getrieben hat
11 JD:                            [[jaa?
12 KK:   ja die- die ziTIERten die gesam- den gesamten text des vorgängers @@
13 JD:   achSO ja stimmt
14 KK:   und schrieb- schrieben [nur drunter same here oder me too.
15 JD:                         [ja das weiß ich auch noch (.) ja
16 KK:   in FOren fällt das nicht mehr auf? (.) weils nicht mehr so releVANT ist und weil die infrastruktur anders [ist aber es ist immer noch dasselbe phänomen
17 JD:                                           [mhm mhm            ja
18 MK:   [[das ist INternetdialekt
19 BC:   [[wieder was gelernt
20 KK:   das ist internet- genau
21 MK:   ich würde dabei eher WEniger sagen das ist ENGlisch das ist internetdialekt.


01 MK:   like same i do that CONstantly (.) really
02 JD:   yeah?
03 MK:   th- that [isn't even something i notice anymore
```

Explanations for Transidiomatic Practices 223

```
04 KK:          [which funnily enough- probably if you were to ask that person about
                it (.) she wouldn't know where that COMES from.
05 MK:     right
06 KK:     because that- in the end that's nothing other than just simply an (.) ANcient
           RElic from the internet times at the time when it was all still about **mailing
           lists**. like it was- that was fam- which became famous as this- this famous **LOL
           (.) me too (.) same here**. same thing. they just wrote the same thing under-
           neath and [that's how (.) that's like=
07 JD:                  [ja (..) ja
08 KK:     =at some point uh on- on all the- all the- in all the um (.) **USEnet** things it was
           exactly these **posters** who were completely noTOR[ious
09 MK:                                                         [right
10 KK:     right? because that- this drove up the [[volume of data straight through the
           roof
11 JD:                                             [[jaa?
12 KK:     right they- they QUOted the whole- the whole text of the previous person @@
13 JD:     oh RIGHT yeah that's true
14 KK:     and wrote- just wrote [under that **same here** or **me too**.
15 JD:                            [yeah i remember that too (.) yeah
16 KK:     people don't notice it anymore in FOrums? (.) because it's not as RElevant
           anymore and because the infrastructure is different [but it's still the same
           phenomenon
17 JD:                                                          [mhm mhm          ja
18 MK:     [[that's INternet dialect
19 BC:     [[i just learned something new
20 KK:     that's internet- exactly
21 MK:     i would actually tend to say that's LESS ENGlish than it is internet dialect.
```

Turn 1 begins with *menschenskind* saying that this sort of use of "same" is something that she does herself, and so frequently (turn 1) that she doesn't even notice it (turn 3). Then, beginning in turn 4, *kakuro* talks about what he perceives as the origin of this practice: its use in USENET or mailing-list conversations (both precursors to the modern-day social media) where the entire previous post was quoted and the person would say only a word or two of agreement. He positions this practice as something so deeply rooted in social media history ("ancient relic," turn 6) that it's inseparable from it, and when he's finished recounting its perceived history, *menschenskind* goes on to pronounce this practice as not actually English at all, but "internet dialect" (turns 18

224 5 The Why: Ideology, Positioning, and Attitudes toward English

and 21). As in the previous excerpt from the Dutch community, this stance maintains that there are certain transidiomatic practices that may technically be of English origin, but they both originated within and are so indelibly wrapped up with social media culture that it does not occur to people that they are also simple English-language words that are used in a non-social-media context as well.

Influence from the English-Speaking Media

The stance that transidiomatic practices result from influence from the English-speaking media also occurs in both communities. As with the previous section, there are no clearly noticeable differences between the ways the communities express this stance, but one excerpt from each is still discussed below. The first of these is Excerpt 5.38, which comes from the interview with German participant *caroline*. It emerged within a discussion toward the beginning of the interview prompted by my question about the extent to which she notices transidiomatic practices in German conversations.

Excerpt 5.38 "Watching TV shows in English before they come out in German" (German community)

01 CA: auch je (.) JUgendlicher man sich ausdrucken- ausdrücken möchte desto mehr äh (.) angliZISmen sind drin [(.) egal ob sie richtig oder falsch sind?
02 JD: [ja   ja. ja.
03 CA: ähmm (.) und ich denke auch äh je mehr kontakt die menschen mit dem INternet haben (.) desto mehr anglizismen kommen auch vor wenn man viele sachen auf ENGlisch liest (.) auf englisch guckt- fernsehserien auf englisch guckt oder so (.) bevor sie auf deutsch rauskommen (.) und das hat ja dann auch so EINflüsse

01 CA: also the more (.) YOUthfully you want to express- express yourself the more uh (.) english terms are in it [(.) no matter whether they're right or wrong?
02 JD: [ja   ja. ja.
03 CA: ummm (.) and i think also uh the more contact the people have with the INternet (.) the more english terms also appear if you read a lot of things in ENGlish (.) watch a lot of things in english- watch television shows in english

> or something like that (.) before they come out in german (.) and that tends to
> have its influences

In turn 1, *caroline* evokes the stance, previously discussed with respect to Excerpts 5.12–5.15 above, that transidiomatic practices are used to construct and/or index a youth subculture. She doesn't stop there, though; she also positions transidiomatic practices as emerging as a direct result of social media use ("the more contact the people have with the internet, the more English terms also appear"), as discussed in the previous section, but also from "watching television shows in English […] before they come out in German." Since Germany practises dubbing for imported television shows, the idea here is that watching (presumably downloaded) television shows before the dubbing can occur exposes people to English practices that they wouldn't hear otherwise, and this has an influence on their own transidiomatic practices.

An even more directly formulated portrayal of this presumed cause-and-effect relationship can be seen in Excerpt 5.39, from *echinacea*. Again, it emerged within a discussion toward the beginning of the interview prompted by my question about the extent to which she notices transidiomatic practices in Dutch conversations and what she thinks of them.

Excerpt 5.39 "Now I hear all kinds of people saying 'get real'" (Dutch community)

01 EC: ja sommige mensen gebruiken het- eh- die proberen HEEL vaak een engelse zin en zo er in te schuiven.

02 JD: en- en waarom doen ze dat? (.) wat denk je?

03 EC: ik weet het- ik denk omdat ze missCHIEN (.) ja (.) bijvoorbeeld in NEderland is heel veel tV in het engels. bijvoorbeeld in DUITSland? en in- eh- FRANKrijk iTAlië SPANje word er NAgesynchroniseerd. maar in NEderland is bijna alles in het ENGels.

04 JD: klopt (.) ja.

226   5 The Why: Ideology, Positioning, and Attitudes toward English

05 EC: en dus we hebben wel een VOORbeeld van dat heel veel in het engels gebeurt? en natuurlijk (.) ik denk dat mtv daar een hele sterke rol in heeft. en ik denk dat mensen bepaalde zinnen kopiëren (.) kopieergedrag toch wel hebben. want (.) eh (.) bijvoorbeeld in **jersey shore** zegt één meisje- eh (.) zegt in het laatste seizoen (.) zegt ze super vaak **GET REAL**

06 JD: oké.

07 EC: en ik hoor nu allemaal mensen **get real** zeggen.

08 JD: opEENS?

09 EC: opEENS.

10 JD: en- en- en dat komt echt door deze SErie?

11 EC: ik denk het wel ja.

01 EC: yeah some people use it- uh- they try to put an english sentence and stuff like that in there ALL the time.

02 JD: and- and why do they do that? (.) what do you think?

03 EC: i know the- i think MAYbe because they (.) yeah (.) for example in the NETHerlands a lot of tV is in english. for example in GERmany? and in-uh- FRANCE ITaly SPAIN they DUB everything. but in the NETHerlands almost everything is in ENGlish.

04 JD: true (.) yeah.

05 EC: and so we do have an exAMple like that a lot of things happen in english? and of course (.) i think that mtv has a really strong role in that. and i think that people copy certain sentences (.) show copycat behaviour. because (.) uh (.) for example in **jersey shore** one girl- uh (.) in the last season she says (.) she says super often (.) **GET REAL**

06 JD: okay.

07 EC: and now i'm hearing all kinds of people saying **get real**.

08 JD: all of a SUDDen?

09 EC: all of a sudden.

10 JD: and- and- and that's really because of this SHOW?

11 EC: i think so yeah.

Turn 1 begins with *echinacea* talking about people's general transidiomatic practices, and in turn 2, I ask her why she thinks people use English words when speaking Dutch. Her response is to talk about the Netherlands as a country that subtitles its imported television, as opposed to many other countries, where such media is all dubbed (turn 3). This positions transidiomatic practices as something that comes up as a direct result of watching English-language media, and specifically, a result of doing so when the translations come in the form of subtitles that allow viewers to simultaneously listen to the original phrasings of the English. She then brings up the channel MTV as a specific originator of many of these practices, and provides an example from the reality television show *Jersey Shore*, where people "show copycat behaviour" in saying "get real" frequently (turns 5 and 7), just as one person does on the show. When I press her about whether this practice actually did specifically originate from the show, she positions it as something that began "all of a sudden" (turn 9), and as something she believes people did in fact pick up from the show (turn 11). This is the same stance that appears in the German community, with the only difference being that because the Netherlands subtitles imported shows, people don't need to be watching shows before they come out locally in order to have those influences, but are experiencing them every time they turn on the television.

Influence from Particular English-Speaking Cultures and Subcultures

The stance that transidiomatic practices result from influence from particular English-speaking cultures and subcultures occurs only within the Dutch community, and it comes up both extremely frequently and in many different ways. This section therefore contains seven excerpts dealing with different cultures and subcultures and the ways they are positioned as influencing Dutch community members' transidiomatic practices. The first four of these (Excerpts 5.40 through 5.43) deal with different ways in which African-American Vernacular English and/or African-American culture are positioned as influencing Dutch transidiomatic practices, while the three that follow on those (Excerpts 5.44 through 5.46) deal respectively with influences from US culture generally, from the language and culture of the US-based livejournal community ONTD, and from UK-English language culture generally. Excerpt 5.38 again comes from the Dutch participant *echinacea*, who we last saw in the immediately preceding excerpt. It emerged within a discussion toward the beginning of the interview prompted by my question about which transidiomatic practices she herself uses.

228   5 The Why: Ideology, Positioning, and Attitudes toward English

Excerpt 5.40 "English slang" (Dutch community)

01 EC: wat ik heel vaak zeg (.) en dat- dat is HEEL raar. ik zeg bijvoorbeeld **AIGHT**. en
dat is ook geen goed- dat is NIET eens goed [ENGels. maar-

02 JD: [en- en- en hoe zou je dat schrij-
ven? als je dat zou zeggen?

03 EC: A I G H T.

04 JD: oké.

05 EC: ja.

06 JD: en hoe- waar komt dat vandaan?

07 EC: @@ ik weet het niet. en iedereen (.) veel mensen zijn het van mij gaan
OVERnemen (.) dat ze zeggen ANNa ik begin nou **AIGHT** te zeggen (..)
bijvoorbeeld ik zeg van (.) oh ja hoe laat ben je hier? zeven uur? oké (.) **aight**.
aight. en dan zeggen zij OOK **aight**.

08 JD: wat- wat is dat voor taal?

09 EC: ja dat is- dat is engelse **SLANG**.

10 JD: ja.

11 EC: zo **YOOOO**.

12 JD: ja?

13 EC: ja. dat- dat doe- dat valt- valt me wel VAAK op- dat doe ik ook wel met- met
bepaalde vrienden zeggen we dan **YO WHAT UP**

14 JD: oké.

15 EC: **YO WHAT UP**

01 EC: what i say really often (.) and that- that's REALLy weird. for example i say
AIGHT. and that's also not- that's NOT even good [ENGlish. but-

02 JD: [and- and- and how
would you spell that? if you were to say that?

03 EC: A I G H T.

04 JD: okay.

05 EC: yeah.

06 JD: and how- where does that come from?

07 EC: @@ i don't know. and everybody (.) lots of people have started to take it OVER
from me (.) they keep saying ANNa i'm starting to say **AIGHT** now (..) for
example i say like (.) oh yeah how late will you be here? seven o'clock? okay (.)
aight. **aight**. and then they say **aight** TOO.

08 JD: what- what kind of language is that?

09 EC: yeah that's- that's english **SLANG**.

10 JD: right.

11 EC: like **YOOOO**.

12 JD: yeah?

13 EC: yeah. that- i do- i notice- i do notice that a LOT- i actually do that with- with
certain friends we then say **YO WHAT UP**

Explanations for Transidiomatic Practices 229

> 14 JD: okay.
> 15 EC: **YO WHAT UP**

In turn 1, *echinacea* begins by telling me that one practice she uses is to say "aight," a pronunciation of "all right" that is of AAVE origin. She then positions the fact that she uses this as "really weird," suggesting that she herself is puzzled by it, and the practice itself as "not even good English," suggesting that she thinks she probably *shouldn't* be using it. Then, in turn 6, I ask her where this practice comes from, and in response she laughs a bit (turn 7) and tells me she doesn't know its origin in her, but that she herself has become the origin in other people who have started using it under her influence (turn 7). I then ask what kind of language she thinks this practice represents (turn 8), and while she doesn't specifically name AAVE as the source of these practices, she does identify it as "English slang," which positions it as originating within some unidentified English-speaking subculture. Most fascinatingly, however, she then immediately juxtaposes this positioning with two other linguistic practices in her repertoire that also come from AAVE: the word "yo" (turns 11, 13, and 15), and copula deletion as seen in the phrase "what up" (turns 13 and 15). This immediate juxtaposition positions the three practices—"aight," "yo," and copula deletion—as related, and this in turn suggests that she is aware that they all come from the same English dialect, even as she's unable to identify which precise dialect that is. This suggests that in her own practice and in the practices of her friends, these AAVE-origin transidiomatic practices have been partly decoupled from their culture of origin, but not so completely that they are not still grouped together as part of the same whole. The indexing of African Americans as a group through these transidiomatic practices thus becomes blurred, but not to the point that the link is not there at all.

The second excerpt, also dealing with AAVE-origin transidiomatic practices, comes from Dutch participant *mfpim,* and emerges from a

230   5 The Why: Ideology, Positioning, and Attitudes toward English

discussion of one of her own posts and its comments that was previously discussed in Excerpt 4.9. The post in question begins with the AAVE-origin greeting "yo."

Excerpt 5.41 "Snobs or skaters or hip hop people" (Dutch community)

01 JD: en (.) het volgende voorbeeld is van jou. @@
02 MP: ja maar ik ben echt heel erg.
03 JD: @@
04 MP: ja (.) die **yo** is zeg maar ehm (.) dat doe ik bij bepaalde groepen mensen. bijvoorbeeld eh (.) kakkers (.) of **skaters** (.) of **hiphop**mensen. weet je wel? (.) een beetje van die groepjes (.) de meesten zeggen dan HOI of **YO** of (.) eh (.) *HAllo*?
05 JD: is dat engels of is dat nederlands?
06 MP: **nah** (.) dat is ook wel nederlands geworden. het is natuurlijk van het engelse (.) maar het is wel nederlands geworden.
07 JD: en is- hoort dat ook een- een beetje bij dezelfde groep?
08 MP: **yo**? ja.
09 JD: **skaters** enzovoort
10 MP: ja (.) ik weet niet (.) ik zie inderdaad niet heel veel meisjes die gebruiken **yo**? (.) meer een beetje als je- ja (.) een beetje **street** of best wel veel **hiphop** luistert. ik denk dat je het DAARvan overneemt.

01 JD: and (.) the next example is from you. @@
02 MP: yeah but i'm really totally bad.
03 JD: @@
04 MP: yeah (.) the **yo** is like um (.) i do that with certain groups of people. for example uh (.) snobs (.) or **skaters** (.) or **hip hop** people. you know? (.) it goes along with those little groups (.) most of them then say HEY or **YO** or (.) uh (.) *HEllo*?
05 JD: is that english or is that dutch?
06 MP: **nah** (.) that's become dutch too really. of course it comes from english (.) but it's become dutch.
07 JD: and is- does it belong- a little bit to the same group?
08 MP: **yo**? yeah.
09 JD: **skaters** et cetera
10 MP: yeah (.) i don't know (.) i don't actually see very many girls who use **yo**? (.) more a little if you- yeah (.) a little bit **street** or tend to listen to a lot of **hip hop**. i think that you take it over from THERE.

Explanations for Transidiomatic Practices **231**

Beginning in turn 4, *mfpim* immediately zeroes in on the "yo" at the beginning of her post. She positions this as a practice she reserves only for use "with certain groups of people," but the specific groups of people she gives as examples are extremely different from each other: on the one hand "kakkers" ("snobs"), which would seem to designate a group of people with a certain degree of money and clout, but on the other hand "skaters" (in the sense of people who use skateboards in skating parks) and "hip-hop people" (presumably in the sense of people who listen to that particular musical genre, but also perhaps in the sense of people who also take on certain aspects of international hip-hop culture, as discussed in Chapter 2), who generally seem to be representative of more economically disadvantaged and certainly culturally stigmatized groups. This suggests that for *mfpim*, the greeting "yo" indexes subcultures in general, but it has become decoupled from any particular subculture and, even more interestingly, even from its original status as part of a disadvantaged subculture.

This decoupling is strengthened by her characterization of "yo" as "going along with" groups that say "hoi" ("hey"), "yo," or "hallo" ("hello") with a deepened voice, the first and last of which clearly come from Dutch language and culture (or related subcultures) rather than from any English-origin culture. It is strengthened still further when I ask her whether she thinks of "yo" as English or Dutch (turn 5), and she says that while "of course" it comes from English, it's "become Dutch" (turn 6). However, when I ask directly whether she thinks of "yo" as being associated with "skaters et cetera" (turn 9), she responds "yeah," adding that the people who use "yo" tend to be "a little bit street or tend to listen to a lot of hip hop" and that it's those communities that have influenced its use. This brings things more in line with the word's AAVE origins, despite that language and community not being specifically named. As in the previous excerpt, this seems to suggest that there has in fact been a decoupling of certain AAVE-origin transidiomatic practices from their source culture, but that this decoupling is incomplete.

Excerpt 5.42 also deals with a discussion of *mfpim*'s post and its comments, and it comes from Dutch participant *bucket*.

232   **5 The Why: Ideology, Positioning, and Attitudes toward English**

Excerpt 5.42 "To get a taste of that sphere a bit" (Dutch community)

01 JD: wat is **yo**.
02 BK: **yo**. *YOOO*. ik denk dan (.) uh (..) **gangster** [eeeeh
03 JD: [**gangster** ja
04 BK: met zon handje. ((makes a sideways V-sign with her middle and index fingers, palm facing inward)) in nederland HEB je geen **gangsters** dus of tenminste geen- zoals- (..) ja. @@@ dus dat is gewoon een beetje tof TURbotaal. (..) weer.
05 JD: en [vind je dat=
06 BK: [nee. nee.
07 JD: =vind je dat- dat vind je dat vervelend? of- of- of
08 BK: nou (. . .) wat het OOK een beetje is? (..) ik doe dat- ik zeg OOK weleens [**yo**?
09 JD: [**yo**? oké.
10 BK: tegen vriendinnen? (..) één speciFIEK (..) maar (..) dat is om een beetje AAN te geven- zij heeft wel vrienden WEL in een beetje **yo yo** sfeer en die super tof zijn en zo? en dan DOEN we altijd alsof we ook zo zijn?
11 JD: mm-kay?
12 BK: door dan een beetje dat TAALgebruik aan te nemen? maar eigenlijk is het ÉÉN grote **sketch**. want wij zijn helemaal niet (.) **yo yo**? we zijn gewoon- (..) we hebben (..) @een universitaire opleiding@ en em @we komen echt niet [van de straat@ ik bedoel zij komt uit WASSenaar
13 JD: [ja ja
14 BK: ik bedoel [[dat
15 JD: [[@@@ ok snap ik wel
16 BK: [@@@@@@@@
17 JD: [@@@@@@@@ @snap ik al@
18 BK: dus umm? ja. dus dan doen we gewoon een beetje zo v- dat we dat sfeertje een beetje proeven? maar DIT
19 JD: maar wie- wie zegt er wel **yo** in nederland?
        ((2-second pause))
20 JD: ZONder zo te DOEN maar [meent het
21 BK: [ja gewoon meer voor- het ECHT zeggen.
22 JD: ja.
23 BK: ja (.) gewoon een beetje van die jongetjes- van die gastjes (..) wel een beetje van die- van die straat (.) schoffies. (.) denk ik. en dan vooral onderLING want mijn broertje is ook een straat (..) schoffie? maar die zegt dat echt niet bij ons thuis? maar wel met vrienden en dan doet ie ook **yo** (.) gast (.) zoie- (.) maar goed (.) ja.

01 JD: what is **yo**.
02 BK: **yo**. *YOOO*. i think then (.) uh (..) **gangster** [eeeeh

Explanations for Transidiomatic Practices   233

03 JD:	[**gangster** yeah
04 BK:	with a hand gesture like this. ((makes a sideways V-sign with her middle and index fingers, palm facing inward)) so in the netherlands you don't HAVE any **gangsters** or at least none- like- (..) yeah. @@@ so that's just a little bit of cool TURbo language. (..) again.
05 JD:	and [do you think that's=
06 BK:	[no. no.
07 JD:	=do you think- you think that's annoying? or- or- or
08 BK:	well (...) what it is a little bit TOO? (..) i do that- i say **yo** sometimes [TOO?
09 JD:	[**yo**? okay.
10 BK:	to my friends? (..) one speCIFic (..) but that's a little bit to INdicate- she does have friends from a little bit the **yo yo** sphere and who are super cool and stuff like that? and then we ACT as if we were like that too?
11 JD:	mm-kay?
12 BK:	by taking on a little bit of that LANGuage usage? but it's actually nothing but a **sketch**. because we're not like (.) **yo yo**? we're just- (..) we have (..) @a university degree@ and um @we really don't come [from the street i mean she comes from WASSenaar ((a very upper-class western small town))
13 JD:	[ja ja
14 BK:	i mean [[that
15 JD:	[[@@@ okay i get it
16 BK:	[@@@@@@@@
17 JD:	[@@@@@@@@ @i already got it@
18 BK:	so umm? yeah. so then we just act a little like- that we get a taste of that sphere a bit? but THIS
19 JD:	but who- who really does say **yo** in the netherlands? ((2-second pause))
20 JD:	withOUT ACTing but [who means it
21 BK:	[yeah just more for- who say it for REAL.
22 JD:	yeah.
23 BK:	yeah (.) just a bit like those young boys- like those young guys (..) it's more a little bit of those- of those street (.) punks. (.) i think. and then mostly among each OTHER because my brother is also a street (.) punk? but he really doesn't say that at home with us? but he does with friends and then he does **yo** too (.) dude (.) like tha- (.) but okay (.) yeah.

When I ask *bucket* directly about the "yo" in turn 1, she responds first by simply saying the word, and then by pronouncing it loudly and in a tone that comes across as imitative of the way it is frequently used in hip-hop culture: elongated, enthusiastic. She then immediately juxtaposes

234   5 The Why: Ideology, Positioning, and Attitudes toward English

this with her immediate association: "gangster" (turn 2), and the use of a particular hand gesture also seen within the hip-hop community (turn 4). This serves to iconize these linguistic and cultural practices as essentially relevant to a particular group. She qualifies this, however, by saying that gangsters (or at least gangsters of this particular sort) don't actually exist in the Netherlands, laughing, and dismissing this as "a little bit of cool turbo language." This is actually extremely insightful, since *bucket*'s use of the expression "turbo language" always tends to refer to transidiomatic practices that have been "Dutchified" in some way (see Excerpt 5.24 above, in reference to the *vraagvrije vrijdag* style), and that is certainly the case here.

When I ask her in turns 5 and 7 whether the use of "yo" is a practice that she finds annoying, however, she positions it as something that she herself actually uses sometimes (turn 8), in particular with one specific friend and in order to index belonging (or, in reality, pretending to belong) to a certain group of young people who are positioned as being "from a little bit the yo yo sphere and who are super cool and stuff like that" (turn 10). She positions them as being able to index this group by "taking on a little bit of that language usage," even though in reality "it's nothing but a sketch" because she and her friends have university degrees and come from stereotypically wealthy places. This constructs a stance in which the use of "yo" is, in fact, associated with traits that are connected to African-American hip-hop culture, such as being "super cool" and coming from "the street," but the group of people she and her friend are pretending to be a part of are not American but Dutch. The result is positioned as a way of getting "a taste of that sphere a bit" (turn 18) without actually committing to it (or, perhaps, being able to commit to it even if they wanted to, due to their wealthier origins and academic pursuits).

Finally, when I ask her to identify the groups that "really do say yo" in the Netherlands—i.e. those who do really commit to the sphere in question and really "mean it"—she identifies this group as "street punks" who use this sort of language "only among each other." This suggests that even in the case of people who really belong to the group in question, the "yo" greeting functions as a way of positioning themselves as a group member whenever it is directly relevant to the role they are taking up in the moment, rather than being a variety identified with a

Explanations for Transidiomatic Practices 235

group that they belong to by virtue of their racial or ethnic origins (which would of course be an identity that would be much more difficult to put on and take off again). To *bucket* and her friends—and perhaps even her brother—"yo" and its associated cultural practices are therefore part of not a distinctly identifiable dialect (English or Dutch), but nonetheless part of a distinctly identifiable linguistic style.

The final excerpt dealing with *mfpim*'s post and its comments is Excerpt 5.43, and it comes from the interview with Dutch participants *niettemin* and *vogel.*

Excerpt 5.43 "A white black person" (Dutch community)

```
01 NT:   dit is een exTREEM [geval.
02 VO:                    [die is echt (.) nou (.) echt verschrikkelijk.
03 NT:   dit is een extreem voorbeeld van=
04 JD:   extreem van?
05 NT:   =van apart taalgebruik. [@@@@@@@@
06 VO:                          [heel veel ENGels en allemaal engelse TERmen (.) en
         ja.
07 NT:   ook- ook haar NEderlands is VRIJ apart.
08 JD:   oké.
09 NT:   ja.
10 JD:   maar [dat is mij ook opgevallen [[dat zij HEEL veel engels gebruikt?
11 VO:        [dat is een blanke NEger [[sowieso. @@
12 NT:                                 [[ja oké.
13 JD:   maar- maar dan op een ANdere manier dan laviefantasque.
14 NT:   ja. [nee maar (.) en ook
15 VO:       [ja. zij komt uit een andere ACHtergrond. dat is- dat is een blanke neger.
16 NT:   ja. (.) zij [[gebruikt straat[[[taal.
17 VO:               [[ENGels (..)  [[[STRAATtaal allemaal dingen die ze eigenlijk niet
         snapt.
18 NT:   en ze is ook heel actief om dat allemaal over te brengen op die manier maar (.)
         ja.


01 NT:   this is an exTREME [case.
02 VO:                     [she is really (.) like (.) completely awful.
03 NT:   this is an extreme example of=
04 JD:   extreme of?
05 NT:   =of weird language use. [@@@@@@@@
```

06 VO:		[lots and lots of ENGlish and all kinds of english TERMS (.) and yeah.
07 NT:	her- her DUTCH is pretty unusual too.	
08 JD:	okay.	
09 NT:	yeah.	
10 JD:	but [i noticed that too	[[that she uses a LOT of english?
11 VO:	[that's a white BLACK person [[anyway. @@	
12 NT:		[[yeah okay.
13 JD:	but- but then in a DIFFerent way than laviefantasque.	
14 NT:	yeah. [no but (.) and also	
15 VO:	[yeah. she comes from a different BACKground. that's- that is a white black person.	
16 NT:	yeah. (.) she [[uses street [[[slang.	
17 VO:	[[ENGlish (..) [[[STREET slang all things that she doesn't actually get.	
18 NT:	and she's also constantly actively trying to put that across like that but (.) yeah.	

When presented with *mfpim*'s post and a couple of its comments, *niettemin* and *vogel* both have immediate and very strong negative reactions. In turn 1, *niettemin* identifies *mfpim* as "an extreme case" (turn 1), while *vogel* identifies her as "completely awful" (turn 2). The reasons for the negative reaction become clear over the course of the next several turns: she has "weird language use" (*niettemin*, turn 5), specifically in a way that involves "lots and lots of English" (*vogel*, turn 6), while "her Dutch is pretty unusual too" (*niettemin*, turn 7). Participant *vogel* then sums it up by referring to her as "a white black person" (turns 11 and 15), which serves to simultaneously iconize those practices as essentially associated with some community of non-white people (while leaving it unstated—and perhaps even irrelevant—whether this community in question is American or Dutch), and also position *mfpim* as a phony ("white") member of that community. This positioning further exhibits recursiveness in the sense that a contrast that is meaningful on one level (*mfpim*'s use of language practices that both are and are not associated with a black community) onto the level of her skin colour, turning her into a person who is simultaneously white (her actual skin colour) and black (the skin colour that is evoked through some of her transidiomatic practices).

Explanations for Transidiomatic Practices   237

These particularities of *mfpim*'s language practices are then attributed by *vogel* to her "different background" (turn 15), though again, the authenticity of this background is immediately called into question in the last three turns. Participant *niettemin* refers to *mfpim* as a person who uses "straattaal" or "street slang" (which, again, is a reference to a particular variety strongly associated in the Netherlands with the Surinamese community, many of whom themselves are non-white), but *vogel* positions this "street slang" in *mfpim*'s case in particular as something that, along with English, "she doesn't actually get" (turn 17), but is simply making use of in order to falsely claim an identity that doesn't belong to her. Participant *niettemin* then not only does not disagree with this assessment, but responds by characterizing *mfpim* as someone who in fact also makes a big show of being part of this community that she does not actually legitimately belong to (turn 18). This positions *mfpim* as someone who may be portraying herself as an insider through the use of certain transidiomatic practices—specifically "English" and "street slang"—but as doing so unsuccessfully enough that this lack of success is noted (and scorned) by other members of the *vragenuurtje* community.

Excerpt 5.44 deals with the ways that transidiomatic practices can index American culture in general and the results of this for the local interaction in the *vragenuurtje* community. It comes from 27-year-old Dutch participant *tesvel*, and it emerged within a discussion of a post and its comments that was previously discussed in Excerpt 4.15, in which community members give their reactions to a picture of former child singer Jan Smit in an underwear ad on a bus shelter.

Excerpt 5.44 "We tend to think of Americans as hysterical here" (Dutch community)

01 JD:	en (.) dan komen de reacties (.) namelijk *nee ew sorry maar die domme jantje heeft geen penis* (.) ja. *oké ik vind hem niet schockerend maar **i don't wanna see***.
02 TV:	ja.
03 JD:	en (.) dat kun je wel in het nederlands zeggen hè? je- je kunt zeggen (.) *maar ik wil het NIET ZIEN* (.) *zoiets wil ik NIET ZIEN*
04 TV:	ja maar

5 The Why: Ideology, Positioning, and Attitudes toward English

05 JD: wat- wat maakt het uit? wat doet dat anders hier.
06 TV: nou vooral in combinatie met de- met=
07 JD: hmhm.
08 TV: =met DIT erachter (.) is dit gewoon- eigenlijk vind ik het eerder raar dat zij niet HEEL deze ZIN in het engels gedaan heeft (.) want hier begint- gaat zij in hysterische modus.
09 JD: jaja.
10 TV: en dit is typisch de hysterische modus vind ik.
11 JD: hmhm. oké. dus het engels ook?
12 TV: ja dan- ja. want ik eh
13 JD: het komt een beetje hysterischer OVER. het engels.
14 TV: ja op- op deze manier zeker. ehm. ja ik- ik denk- het komt op MIJ hysterischer over.
15 JD: oké.
16 TV: ehm (.) misschien omdat het- omdat het bij ons toch een beetje leeft dat ameriKAnen hysterisch zijn.
17 JD: hmm.
18 TV: of zo. of KUNNen zijn. ehm
19 JD: en dat- dit hier- dat is ameriKAANS?
20 TV: ja.

01 JD: and (.) then the reactions come (.) like *no ew sorry but that stupid little jan doesn't have a penis* (.) yeah. *okay i don't find him shocking but **i don't wanna see***.
02 TV: yeah.
03 JD: and (.) that's something you CAN say in dutch right? you- you can say (.) *but i DON'T want to SEE it* (.) *i DON'T want to SEE that kind of thing*
04 TV: yeah but
05 JD: what- what makes the difference? what does it do differently here.
06 TV: now especially in combination with the- with=
07 JD: hmhm.
08 TV: =with THIS after it (.) this is just- i actually tend to think the opposite that it's weird that she didn't do this WHOLE SENTENCE in english (.) because this is where the- she goes into hysterical mode.
09 JD: yeah yeah.
10 TV: and this is typical hysterical mode i think.
11 JD: hmhm. okay. so english too?
12 TV: yeah then- yeah. because i uh
13 JD: it comes aCROSS a little bit more hysterically. english does.
14 TV: yeah in- in this way absolutely. um. yeah i- i think- it comes across as more hysterical to ME.
15 JD: okay.

16 TV:	um (.) maybe because the- because we tend a little bit to think of amERicans as hysterical here.
17 JD:	hmm.
18 TV:	or like. or CAN be. um
19 JD:	and that- this here- that's amERican?
20 TV:	yeah.

In the first five turns, I provide *tesvel* with examples of the excerpt of the transidiomatic phenomenon I'm zeroing in on (turn 1), suggest possible Dutch alternatives (turn 3), and then ask outright what the users get out of the transidiomatic practices that would be missing from my proposed Dutch alternatives (turn 5). Her initial response is to say that it's actually stranger that there is any Dutch in the sentence in question at all, because the sentence comes after the poster "goes into hysterical mode" (turn 8). This positions these transidiomatic practices as something that are inherently wrapped up with "hysterical mode," a positioning that I question her on directly in turns 11 and 13. She responds in turn 14 by saying that yes, English serves to make things more hysterical, adding in turn 16 that this is due to the fact that "we tend a little bit to think of Americans as hysterical here."

It is worth noting that all of these positionings are qualified in some way: "in this way absolutely" (turn 14) positions the hysterical connotation as something that is present in certain uses of transidiomatic practices but possibly not others, "it comes across as more hysterical to me" (turn 14) positions the hysterical connotation as something that could conceivably not read that way to others, and "or can be" (turn 18) positions Americans themselves as capable of more than just the hysteria they're being associated with in the local interaction. This positioning therefore exhibits iconicity in that the linguistic practices described here are being essentialized as part of American culture, but it does not exhibit erasure, because it allows for there to be people and linguistic practices that do not fit within this stereotype. This serves to soften the absoluteness of the

240   5 The Why: Ideology, Positioning, and Attitudes toward English

positionings without entirely disassociating American English from hysteria. The fact that this these practices are specifically identified as belonging to American English at all is also notable, however, because unlike with the AAVE-origin practices discussed in the previous four excerpts, there is nothing in the form of these practices that might suggest that they are specifically American rather than British or international English. I address this issue with a question to *tesvel* in turn nineteen: "that- this here- that's American?" and she responds with a clear, unqualified "yeah" with falling intonation. This assuredness is particularly interesting in light of this particular user's tendency to qualify any absolute assessments she makes elsewhere in the excerpt, which helps strongly position the practices in question as having specifically American-English connotations, even in the absence of specifically American-English forms.

Excerpt 5.45 again zeroes in on a smaller community, dealing with the ways that transidiomatic practices can be used in the *vragenuurtje* community to index the specific styles of American language and culture that are found in the celebrity-gossip-related livejournal community Oh No They Didn't (ONTD). This excerpt comes from the interview with *gauwd* and *geraldina*, and it emerged within a discussion about the specific *vraagvrije vrijdag* style as exemplified by the conversation discussed earlier in Excerpt 4.17.

Excerpt 5.45 "You borrow the joke whether it's conscious or unconscious" (Dutch community)

01 JD: en de LAATste ZIN? is altijd [alleen maar in het engels?
02 GW: [@@
03 JD: **we welcome sparkly fonts (.) gifs (.) big fonts (.) rage (.) anonymous joy**
         squee (.) chuck bass ANYthing.
04 GW: hm.
05 JD: waarom
06 GE: **oh no they didn't.**
07 GW: @@
08 GE: **oh no [they didn't. oh no they didn't.=**
09 JD: [hoe komt dat over?
10 GE: ken- ken je die [[**com- community?**

Explanations for Transidiomatic Practices   241

11 JD: [[ja? (.) ja? (.) jaja.
12 GE: daar heb je sowieso inderdaad **free for all friday.** (.) en ik weet dat DIE groep
ook heel veel op **oh no they didn't** zit? dus het komt daarvan OVER en- dus
het is OvergeNOmen (.) en daar hebben ze ook altijd als laatste (.) zin effe- eh-
ehm- of een THEma inderdaad te zetten of=
13 GW: ja.
14 GE: =**reminder** (.) **no porn** (.) **no blablabla.** (.) ehm dus (.) eh- eh- je neemt de
grap OVER zeg maar (.) zij het bewust onbewust. maar als ik het zo ZIE dan
relateer ik het automatisch aan dat ja.

01 JD: and the LAST SENtence? is always [just in english?
02 GW: [@@
03 JD: **we welcome sparkly fonts** (.) **gifs** (.) **big fonts** (.) **rage** (.) **anonymous joy
squee** (.) **chuck bass ANYthing.**
04 GW: hm.
05 JD: why
06 GE: **oh no they didn't.**
07 GW: @@
08 GE: **oh no [they didn't. oh no they didn't.**=
09 JD: [how does that come across?
10 GE: do you- do you know the [[**com- community**?
11 JD: [[yeah? (.) yeah? (.) yeah yeah.
12 GE: you actually have **free for all friday** there anyway. (.) and i know that THAT
group also spends a lot of time on **oh no they didn't**? so it comes OVER from
there- so it's been BORRowed (.) and there you always have as the last (.)
sentence like- uh- um- like to set a TOPic or=
13 GW: yeah.
14 GE: =**reminder** (.) **no porn** (.) **no blablabla.** (.) um so (.) uh- uh- you like
BORRow the joke (.) whether it's conscious or unconscious. but when i
SEE that like that then i relate it automatically to that yeah.

The first five turns are taken up with me constructing the question of
why the last sentence of the *vraagvrije vrijdag* post is always entirely in
English. The simple answer, then, as provided by *geraldina* is that it is a
specific imitation of the style found in the Oh No They Didn't livejournal
community (turns 6 and 8) and its own analogous Free For All Friday
weekly post (turn 12). This is positioned as happening because the group
of community members responsible for making the *vraagvrije vrijdag* posts
"also spends a lot of time on Oh No They Didn't," so they are positioned

242   5   The Why: Ideology, Positioning, and Attitudes toward English

as making very specific reference to the style that is typical there. This, in turn, results in the *vragenuurtje* community's own specific style that is particular to the *vraagvrije vrijdag* post and its comments (see discussion in Chapter 4). The purpose of this indexing is to "borrow the joke," and it is left open that this borrowing might be conscious, but it might actually be unconscious (turn 14). In either case, however, the result is for *geraldina*—and more than likely others—to "relate it automatically to that," constructing a direct relationship both in language and in culture between Oh No They Didn't's Free For All Friday and *vragenuurtje*'s *vraagvrije vrijdag*.

Finally, Excerpt 5.46, from the interview with *echinacea*, deals with the ways that transidiomatic practices can also be used in the *vragenuurtje* community to index a specifically UK-English language and culture. It comes from a discussion about a subthread on a post that asked what the various things are that community members are irritated by, and while the discussion in Excerpt 5.46 deals specifically with *echinacea*'s own comment, it is relevant that another poster has previously brought up the fact that she is irritated by "people who stay standing on the left of an escalator."

Excerpt 5.46 "It's typically English actually" (Dutch community)

01 JD: DAT vond ik ook echt HEEL interessant van je. het gaat om- eh- ja. ja mensen die LINKS op de ROLtrap blijven staan. ja?

02 EC: ja.

03 JD: en JIJ zegt *ik ben ook voor een bordje **please stand on the right***

04 EC: ja omdat je (.) dat is dus (.) in engeland heb je- heb je- in de **subway** en zo- heb je die bordjes van **please stand on the right**. en-

05 JD: en dus- dus dit bordje als- als het er daadwerkelijk was- zou het in het engels zijn.
((5-second pause))

06 EC: nee die zou dan gewoon in het nederlands moeten (.) maar omdat die bordjes er niet in- in het nederlands ZIJN weet je wel zo van- *eh dat is iets typisch ENGels eigenlijk*.

07 JD: oké.

08 EC: en dan-

09 JD: dus- dus- dus dat vind je dan ENGels- dus zeg je dat dan ook in het ENGels (.) ook al zou het bordje-

10 EC: ja.

Explanations for Transidiomatic Practices 243

11 JD: als het er was (.) in het NEDerlands. vind-
12 EC: gewoon in het nederlands.
13 JD: oké
14 EC: maar ab- absoluut (.) want (.) en misschien in het aRABisch erbij of zo maar
15 JD: @@@
16 EC: maar bijvoorbeeld als ik (.) ehm (.) op het station in ((small town in the southern Netherlands)) ehm (.) dan pak ik gewoon de TRAP die gewoon een stuk LANGer is dan de roltrap (.) gewoon omdat er ALtijd mensen stilstaan op die roltrap waardoor ik mijn bus naar SCHOOL mis.
17 JD: hm. hm.
18 EC: en dan denk ik ook altijd (.) AHHH kunnen we niet zon BORDje krijgen met **PLEASE stand on the RIGHT** of mag ik iedereen gewoon met een HONKbalknuppel even van die ROLtrap AFsmijten?
19 JD: maar je- je verwacht niet dat ze deze eventuele bordjes echt in het ENGels zouden maken?
20 EC: hm?
21 JD: je verwacht niet dat deze bordjes- dus als ze er daadWERKelijk WAren
22 EC: nee dat zou niet de eis zijn. (.) nee.
23 JD: oké.

01 JD: THIS is something that i also found VERY interesting from you. it's about- um- yeah. yeah people who stay standing on the LEFT of an EScalator. yeah?
02 EC: yeah.
03 JD: and YOU say *i'm also for a sign **please stand on the right***
04 EC: yeah because you (.) so that's (.) in england you have- you have- like in the **subway**- you have those signs like **please stand on the right.** and-
05 JD: and so- so this sign if- if it were really here- it should be in english. ((5-second pause))
06 EC: no then it should just be in normal dutch (.) but because those signs aren't in- AREN'T in dutch you know like- *oh that is typically ENGlish actually*.
07 JD: okay.
08 EC: and then-
09 JD: so- so- so you think that's ENGlish- so you say it in ENGlish too (.) even if the sign would-
10 EC: yeah.
11 JD: if it were there (.) in DUTCH. do you-
12 EC: just in normal dutch.
13 JD: okay
14 EC: but ab- absolutely (.) because (.) and maybe in ARabic alongside it or something like that but
15 JD: @@@
16 EC: but for example if i (.) um (.) at a station in ((small town in the southern Netherlands)) um (.) then i just take the STAIRS which is just a little bit

		LONGer than the escalator (.) just because there are ALways people standing on the escalator and they make me miss my bus to SCHOOL.
17 JD:		hm. hm.
18 EC:		and then i always think (.) AHHH can't we get one of those SIGNS with **PLEASE stand on the RIGHT** or can i just push everybody off the escalator with a BASEball bat?
19 JD:		but you- you don't expect that they would make these possible signs in ENGlish?
20 EC:		hm?
21 JD:		you don't expect that these signs- like if they were REALLy THERE
22 EC:		no that wouldn't be the requirement. (.) no.
23 JD:		okay.

In the first three turns, I outline the main question I'm asking *echinacea*: if the issue is Dutch people being irritated by other Dutch people standing on the left of Dutch escalators in Dutch train stations, then why did she portray the sign that she wanted to put up as reading, in English, "please stand on the right" (turn 3)? Her answer is to make specific reference in turn 4 to the signs that she's indexing by using the English-origin phrase: the ones in the London Underground reading "please stand on the right." But when I ask her whether this means the hypothetical sign she'd like to see in Dutch train stations should therefore be in English (turn 5), she is startled into silence for a full five seconds. When she then responds in turn 6, she says that no, the signs in question would of course be in Dutch, but that she used English to refer to them when she talked about them in the community in order to strategically and deliberately index the ones in the London Underground, i.e. to say "oh that is typically English actually." However, when she comes back around to referring to these hypothetical signs again in turn 18—signs that she portrays as being hung in a train station in a small town in the southern Netherlands—she again uses English, so I double-check in turn 19 that she still doesn't intend for them to actually appear in English. Her response is that no, that "wouldn't be the requirement" (turn 22). This set of positionings simultaneously serves to index the Londonness of the hypothetical sign while also fully localizing it to its immediate Dutch context.

In all of the above excerpts there is a deliberate, strategic use of transidiomatic practices to index some particular community that the speaker personally does not belong to (sometimes with more specificity regarding which precise community it is, and sometimes with less, but it is always clear that some specific non-local community is intended). As such, this usage can legitimately be called crossing. However, among *vragenuurtje* community members, both the practices and the indexing are also localized in the sense that the strategic use of the practices in question is always used to carry out some locally specific act. By complicating their indexing in this way, these practices have therefore been creatively reterritorialized, retaining bits of the cultures and societies that originally gave rise to them while simultaneously being semiotically rearranged. This makes it all the more intriguing that this particular stance—that of transidiomatic practices being used to index a specific non-local community—does not appear in the interviews from German community members at all.[1] This could suggest a simple lack of awareness that transidiomatic practices are being used like this, but it may in fact represent a lack of actual use in this way. If the latter of these explanations is the case, then this would suggest there may be less openness on the part of German community members to using English in this creatively reterritorialized fashion.

Perceptions of the use of English to Evoke a Characteristic or Mood

In this next section, I will analyze excerpts that exemplify a stance that transidiomatic practices are used not to index a particular English-origin culture or subculture, but instead to express a certain more general characteristic or mood for interactional effect. Identified subcategories consist of the stance that transidiomatic practices are used to convey worldliness,

---

[1] The closest the German data comes to this is one interview in which the participants talk frequently about the way their transidiomatic practices have been influenced by the (international, but largely US-, and certainly English-based) geek and fandom subcultures. However, the way the stance is presented in that interview is more analogous to the way the internet and televised media are seen as influences elsewhere in this chapter, as opposed to the notion that transidiomatic practices are specifically used strategically to index those subcultures.

246   **5 The Why: Ideology, Positioning, and Attitudes toward English**

the stance that they are used to convey modernity and/or a lack of old-fashionedness, the stance that they are used to perform a sort of theatricality, and the stance that they are used to evoke a lack of seriousness.

Worldliness

The stance that transidiomatic practices are used specifically to evoke a sense of worldliness can be found in both communities. While there are no clearly noticeable differences between the ways the two communities express this stance, one excerpt is still presented from each for the sake of completeness and transparency. The first of these can be seen in Excerpt 5.47, which is a simple example that comes from the interview with German participant *misery_chick*. It emerged within a discussion of how and when people begin using transidiomatic practices.

Excerpt 5.47: "When you want to be cooler, more cosmopolitan" (German community)

01 JD: ähm die leute die- die mehr englisch gebrauchen als du- äh machen sie das schon ihr ganzes leben lang
02 MC: nein
03 JD: oder fängt das irgendwann mal an
04 MC: das fängt irgendwann an
05 JD: und- und- und weißt du- weißt du wann (.) äh also zum beispiel ein fünfjähriges kind macht das nicht
06 MC: nee auf GAR keinen fall
07 JD: ein zehnjähriges kind?
08 MC: auch (.) wohl AUCH noch nicht ich denke das fängt mit der puberTÄT an (.) wenn man anfangen will cooler zu sein WELToffener zu sein nicht mehr so KLEINbürgerlich wie (.) ich bin halt aus ((name of small western german city)) nein ich bin aus-
09 JD: und englisch ist also automatisch ein zeichen für weltoffenheit
10 MC: ja. und- und cool
11 JD: und cool

01 JD: um the people who- who use more english than you do- uh have they been doing that for their whole lives
02 MC: no
03 JD: or is there a time when that starts

04 MC:	that starts at a particular time
05 JD:	and- and- and do you know- do you know when (.) uh so for example a five year old child doesn't do that
06 MC:	no CERtainly not
07 JD:	a ten year old child?
08 MC:	also (.) probably not yet then EIther i think that starts at PUberty (.) when you want to start being cooler more cosmopolitan not so PETTy bourgeOIS like (.) oh i'm from ((name of small western german city)) no i'm from-
09 JD:	and so english is automatically a sign of cosmopolitanism
10 MC:	yeah. and- and cool
11 JD:	and cool

In the first seven turns, I am attempting in various ways to nudge *misery_chick* into pinpointing when young people first tend to begin using transidiomatic practices. She first confirms that they haven't been doing that for their whole lives (turn two), then that a five-year-old child doesn't do it yet (turn 6), and finally that a ten-year-old child doesn't yet either (turn 8). She then goes on to position transidiomatic practices as something that is inherently connected with the period that starts in the teenage years "when you want to start being cooler, more cosmopolitan, and not so petty bourgeois" by first stating that directly and then by portraying it as the imagined thought processes of a hypothetical young teenager: not wanting to be from a small western German city, but an unspecified somewhere else, a place that is implied as bigger and more worldly (turn 8). There are no overt markers of mockery in this portrayal such as a sing-song voice or laughter, but the "oh I'm not from ((small western German city))" phrasing still reads mockingly due to the content, because of course the hypothetical person whose voice is being animated here actually *is* from that small western Germany city and can't really ever be otherwise. This positions the "English is worldly" stance as one that *misery_chick* is on the outside of, as a somewhat older young adult who remembers what that was like. I then ask her to confirm whether English is "automatically a sign of cosmopolitanism," and she confirms this with no hesitations and falling intonation (turn 9) before adding "and cool." This juxtaposition not only confirms that English is inherently linked to

248 **5 The Why: Ideology, Positioning, and Attitudes toward English**

both cosmopolitanism and coolness, but that the two characteristics are also linked with each other; to be cosmopolitan is to be cool. The same stance, though somewhat more subtly expressed, can be seen in 5.48, which comes from the interview with Dutch participants *geraldina* and *gauwd*. It comes from the discussion toward the beginning of that interview about the different transidiomatic practices that they themselves take note of.

Excerpt 5.48 "Just speak proper Dutch, not that English nonsense" (Dutch community)

01 GE:		ik heb meZELF eigenlijk al engels aangeleerd toen ik vrij klein was door het kijken naar de teleVIsie en **all fresh** dat zal jij waarschijnlijk ook hebben.
02 GW:		[hmhm.
03 JD:		[mm.
04 GE:		**all fresh** (.) bel**AIR** (.) **bbc NEWS** (.) die kun je thuis ook AANzetten (.) dus dan gaat het NOG makkelijker dat ik op een gegeven moment toen was ik- toen zat ik nog niet eens op de middelbare school maar toen ging ik al veel beter engels spreken dan mijn OUders.
05 JD:		jeh
06 GE:		dus ik zat **bbc** te kijken en mijn moeder vroeg of er een andere zender op mocht want zij begreep het niet.
07 JD:		mm?
08 GE:		en ik had toen ook weleens dat ik toen (.) eh (.) ONbeWUSt (.) soms om interessant te zijn want je bent twaalf jaar oud=
09 GW:		ja. @@@
10 GE:		=engelse TERrmen gebruikte en zij werd daar BOOS over. ze zegt geralDIna je bent NEderlands. praat gewoon fatsoenlijk nederlands NIET dat ENGelse ONzin? en ik beGREEP dat nooit. (.) ik had echt zoiets van (.) waarom word je zo in dat [HOEKje geZET weet je?
11 JD:		[en- en- en hoe VINDT ze dat vindt- vindt ze dat- vindt ze dat pretenTIEUS? of vindt ze dat
12 GE:		ik- ik denk dat het te maken heeft met nationaLISme wa- waarschijnlijk? eh dat je hebt- dat je toch iets hebt van *je behoort trots te zijn op waar je vandaan komt en daarom de taal in ere te houden*?
13 JD:		hm.
14 GE:		aan de ene kant? ehm (.) want dat heeft ze ook altijd eigenlijk een beetje doorgevoerd
01 GE:		i taught mySELF english already when i was pretty little through watching TElevision and **all fresh** you probably watched that too.
02 GW:		[hmhm.

03 JD:	[mm.	
04 GE:	**all fresh** (.) **belAIR** (.) **bbc NEWS** (.) you can turn those ON at home too (.) so that makes it Even easier to the extent that at a certain point when i was- i wasn't even in high school yet but at that point i was already speaking much better english than my PArents.	
05 JD:	yeah	
06 GE:	so i was sitting there watching **bbc** and my mother asked if i could change the channel because she didn't understand it.	
07 JD:	mm?	
08 GE:	and back then it also sometimes so happened that i (.) uh (.) subCONsciously (.) sometimes out of self importance because you're twelve years old=	
09 GW:	yeah. @@@	
10 GE:	=used english TERMS and she got ANgry about that. she says geralDIna you're DUTCH. just speak proper dutch NOT that ENGlish NONsense? and i never underSTOOD that. (.) i was really all (.) why are you being [DEmonized in THAT way you know?	
11 JD:	[and- and- and what does she THINK of that does- does she think it's- does she think it's preTENtious? or does she think it's	
12 GE:	i- i think that has to do with NAtionalism pro- probably? uh that you have that- that you're supposed to be all *you should be proud of where you are from and that's why you should honour the language*?	
13 JD:	hm.	
14 GE:	on the one hand? (.) because that's actually how she always approached it	

In the first five turns, *geraldina* sets the scene for this personal narrative from her childhood: herself as a 12-year-old girl who has made an effort to learn English through her own extracurricular interests. The consequences of this are then portrayed over the course of the next several turns: her mother asks her to change the channel while she is watching the BBC (turn 6), and ultimately snaps at her when she uses English words and tells her "Geraldina, you're Dutch, just speak proper Dutch, not that English nonsense" (turn 10). She portrays her mother's reasons for this behaviour initially as having to do with her own lack of comprehension (turns 4 and 6), but ultimately as a sense of "nationalism" (turn 12), i.e. anger or outrage at the transidiomatic practices that her daughter uses because they are read as meaning that she has distanced herself from her own culture.

250   **5 The Why: Ideology, Positioning, and Attitudes toward English**

These two excerpts indicate that transidiomatic practices always convey a sense of worldliness, but the nature of this worldliness is always filtered through the eyes of the beholder. This means that the young teenagers portrayed in both excerpts interpret this worldliness as an obvious positive thing that is associated with being cool, but the somewhat older *misery_chick* herself, looking back on that period, can observe it with more of a slightly mocking distance, while *geraldina*'s mother can view it as something that is even overtly negative. In all cases, English is the vehicle to express worldliness, but there are local identity consequences for doing so, and these vary widely.

Modernity

The stance that transidiomatic practices are used specifically to evoke a sense of modernity can also be found in both communities, and again I will present one from each. The first of these, from the German community, can be seen in Excerpt 5.49. It comes from the interview with *sonnenkind*, and it emerged as part of a discussion of a post requesting help with the iTunes software that is more or less entirely in German but ends with the English phrase "help anyone."

> **Excerpt 5.49 "Help me sounds cool I'm modern" (German community)**
>
> 01 JD: was hältst du DAvon. **help anyone**
> 02 SK: ja @
> 03 JD: KENNST du das- hast du das schon mal geSEHN oder-
> 04 SK: ja ich kenne- dass das viele leute dann- solche sachen (.) auf ENGlisch schrei-
> ben? ähmm (. . .) ja. (..) es ist einfach- wahrscheinlich ist es KÜRZer und klingt
> wieder neuer und hipper wie auch mit dem **itunes**. es ist ja auch- da gibts ja
> auch kein deutsches wort es ist ja auch ähm (.) ein englisches produkt? und ähm
> es- (. . .) hat es- es hat mehr glaub ich den charakter dass es leute drauf
> HINweist dass es leute SEHN und sie- sie reagieren eher drauf als wenn da
> steht (.) *hilft mir bitte irgendwer* oder so das das klingt halt (.) ähm COOLer
> einfach *hilft mir doch bitte helft mir* das klingt so als ob man SELBer das
> nicht weiss also das klingt ja HILFlos als ob man selber schwach ist **help me**

Explanations for Transidiomatic Practices 251

> klingt cool ich bin modern ich bin cool (.) so (.) ist es einfach- hat mehr **pep** sozusagen

01 JD: what do you think of THAT. **help anyone**
02 SK: yeah @
03 JD: are you aWARE of that- have you ever SEEN it before or-
04 SK: yeah i'm aware- that lots of people then- write things like that (.) in ENGlish? umm (. . .) yeah. (..) it's just- probably it's SHORTer and again it sounds newer and hipper just like with **itunes**. it's also- there also isn't a german word it's also um (.) an english product? and um it- (. . .) it has- i think it has more of the character that it INdicates to people that people SEE it and they- they're more likely to react to it than if it says (.) *is somebody please going to help me* or something like that that just sounds (.) um just COOLer *just help me please help me* that sounds like you don't know it yourSELF i mean that sounds HELPless like you're weak yourself **help me** sounds cool i'm modern i'm cool (.) so (.) it's just- it has more **pep** in other words

After my question about whether *sonnenkind* has seen this sort of transidiomatic practice before, she first says in turn 4 that she has, and then immediately launches into an explanation for why someone might use it. A large number of possible reasons are given in this single turn, but there is a pervading sense of English implying a sense of newness and modernity. By contrast, a German equivalent is not just less new and less modern, but actually uncool, helpless, and weak.

The same stance can also be seen in the Dutch community in Excerpt 5.50, which comes from the interview with Dutch participants *isolde* and *luna_puella*. It comes from a discussion of the example previously analyzed in Excerpt 4.4, in which the English word "lame" is used in the sense of describing a person or thing that is uncool.

Excerpt 5.50 "Lots of Dutch has become old-fashioned" (Dutch community)

01 IE: **lame** is gewoon een makkelijk [WOORD.
02 LP: [ja.

5 The Why: Ideology, Positioning, and Attitudes toward English

03 IE: ik zou ook niet weten hoe ik het in het nederlands- oh ja (.) dat is best wel [FLAUW? (.) SUF?
04 LP: [suf
05 JD: suf (.) ja.
06 LP: suf is denk ik wel de beste vertaling? (.) maar
07 IE: **lame** (.) dekt de lading beter.
08 LP: suf is weer zo JAren VIJFtig [MEIsjesboek. @@@@@
09 JD: [@@@@@@@@@@@
10 IE: ja (.) suf is gewoon een suf woord weet je wel?
11 LP: suf is zo *de olijke tweeling vindt hun nieuwe (..) **boarding school** kamer suf* @@
12 JD: @@@@@
13 LP: en ik kwam NIET op het nederlandse woord voor **boarding school** (.) dat is dan ook weer wel erg. [@@@@@@@@@@@@@@@@
14 IE: [@@@@@@@@@@@@@@@@@
15 JD: [@@@@@@@@@@@@@@@@@
16 LP: KOSTschool. (.) ik weet dat het dat IS. (..) maar het duurde even. @@
17 IE: **lame** dekt- is lekker KORT weer (.) en
18 LP: dat is weer zoiets (.) het is VLOTTer dan (.) het NEderlandse equivalent.
19 IE: ja. (.) suf is gewoon een SUF woord.
20 LP: ja suf is LElijk.
21 IE: suf KLINKT ook gewoon suf
22 LP: [@@@@@
23 JD: [@@
24 IE: alsof er een STOFlaagje op ligt of zo (.) [[zo klinkt suf.
25 LP: [[ja. @@@@@@@
26 JD: en dan hier de laatste.
27 LP: **this made my day obviously**? ja (.) **made my day** is (.) ja opnieuw weer iets dat lekker vast zo te zeggen valt.
28 IE: een vaste uitdrukking.
29 LP: in het nederlands zeg je *het heeft mijn dag goed gemaakt* (.) maar
30 IE: ja (.) of *mijn dag kan niet meer stuk* (.) maar dat is ook een beetje oubollig.
31 LP: ja veel nederlands is oubollig geworden (.) wat erg eigenlijk van je eigen taal. @@
32 JD: @@@
33 LP: *WE RAAAKEN JE KWIJT* @@@

01 IE: **lame** is just a simple little [WORD.
02 LP: [ja.
03 IE: i wouldn't even know how to say it in du- oh yeah (.) that is totally [BLAND? (.) DULL? ((both are ordinary Dutch words, but they were also used in the youth language of earlier generations))
04 LP: [dull
05 JD: dull (.) yeah.

Explanations for Transidiomatic Practices   253

06 LP:	dull really is the best translation (.) but	
07 IE:	**lame** (.) encompasses the meaning better.	
08 LP:	again dull is all BOOK for [GIRLS from the FIFties @@@@@	
09 JD:	[@@@@@@@@@@@	
10 IE:	yeah (.) dull is just a dull word you know?	
11 LP:	dull is like *the rascally twins find their new (..) **boarding school** room dull* @@	
12 JD:	@@@@@	
13 LP:	and i COULDn't think of the dutch word for **boarding school** (.) again that's bad too. [@@@@@@@@@@@@@@@	
14 IE:	[@@@@@@@@@@@@@@@@	
15 JD:	[@@@@@@@@@@@@@@@@	
16 LP:	BOARDing school ((Dutch term)). (.) i know that it's THAT. (..) but it took a bit. @@	
17 IE:	**lame** fits- it's nice and SHORT again (.) and	
18 LP:	we're back to that again (.) it's QUICKer than (.) the DUTCH equivalent.	
19 IE:	yeah. (.) dull is just a DULL word.	
20 LP:	yeah dull is UGly.	
21 IE:	dull just SOUNDS dull too	
22 LP:	[@@@@@	
23 JD:	[@@	
24 IE:	as if there were a layer of DUST on it or something like that (.) [[that's how dull sounds	

25 LP:		[[yeah. @@@@@@@
26 JD:	and then here the last one.	
27 LP:	**this made my day obviously**? yeah (.) **made my day** is (.) yeah again just something that it's just fun to say like that.	
28 IE:	a set expression.	
29 LP:	in dutch you say *it made my day good* (.) but	
30 IE:	yeah (.) or *now there's nothing that can break this day* (.) but that's also a little bit old fashioned.	
31 LP:	yeah a lot of dutch has become old fashioned (.) how awful about your own language. @@	
32 JD:	@@@	
33 LP:	*WE'RE LOOOOSING YOU* @@@	

In her attempt to explain why the original poster might choose to use the word "lame," *isolde* begins by arguing the positive side of the English-origin term—that it's "just a simple little word" (turn 1)—but she turns very quickly to coming at it from the other angle and

254   **5 The Why: Ideology, Positioning, and Attitudes toward English**

positioning Dutch as deficient. In turns 3 and 4 she and *luna_puella* work together to come up with two possible equivalents, "flauw" (or "bland") and "suf" (or "dull"), which—like "lame"—are both ordinary Dutch words, but they were also adopted as youth-language words of generations previous to theirs. In turn 6, then, *luna_puella* pronounces "dull" as "the best translation," but ends that turn with a "but," thereby positioning the word as not being quite right. In turn 7, *isolde* maintains that the English-origin word "lame" is still better because it "encompasses the meaning better." What follows then in turns 8 through 25 is a playful negotiation between the two of them of why exactly the "dull" doesn't work, and many of the reasons they provide position the word as having inherently old-fashioned connotations. The word feels like a "book for girls from the fifties" (*luna_puella,* turns 8 and 11), and it even sounds old-fashioned phonetically, "as if there were a layer of dust on it or something like that" (*isolde,* turns 21 and 24). Then, in turn 26, I present them with another example, the use of "this made my day obviously" in a different excerpt. Again the two of them come up with two possible Dutch equivalents—"het heeft mijn dag goed gemaakt" ("it made my day good") or "mijn dag kan niet meer stuk" ("now there's nothing that can break this day"), but *isolde* pronounces them as "a little bit old-fashioned" (turn 30).

Then, in turn 31, *luna_puella* observes that this is actually the case with a lot of Dutch words, and then laughingly remarks that this is an "awful" thing to notice "about your own language"—that when transidiomatic practices have so thoroughly taken on the role of representing the modern connotations of life, any local-language terms for the same concepts are automatically rendered old-fashioned by contrast. Her final "we're losing you," which positions the Dutch language as something that is slowly slipping away, echoes the positioning of German community member *sonnenkind* in Excerpt 5.28 toward her own language, but *luna_puella*'s laughter positions it as a joke or at least something to be taken lightly rather than something to be seriously concerned about. This is very much in line with the ambivalence as seen in broader societal discourses about influence from English, and the notion that the Dutch are much less certain than the Germans tend to be whether this situation should be resisted or simply accepted.

Explanations for Transidiomatic Practices   255

Theatricality

The stance that transidiomatic practices are used to evoke a sense of theatricality is only found in the Dutch community. It is also extremely common—appearing in every single Dutch interview at least once—but a representative example appears in Extract 5.51. It comes from the interview with *bucket*, and it emerged as part of a longer discussion about differences between face-to-face conversations and social media ones.

Excerpt 5.51 "More of a kind of caricature" (Dutch community)

01 BK: wat ik bij mezelf merk als- als ik iets meer (..) als ik een HEEL dramatisch verha- of een theatraal verhaal. dat ik het dan EERder gebruik om het extra kracht bij te zetten (.) ehm (..) dus het heeft wel [iets theatraals of zo

02 JD: [oké dus het engels komt theatraler over?

03 BK: ja. (..) ja het is toch meer een soort typetje. (..) wat BLOEMiger of zo (.) maar dat is weer (..) om hetzelfde effect te hebben in het nederlands moet je heel goed- moet je HEEL veel weten van de nederlandse taal. of heel veel versch- andere en synoniemen om het een beetje leuk te maken? (..) en hetzelfde effect kan je eigenlijk ook bereiken door gewoon een engels woord (..) te gebruiken want ja dat is toch al een beetjuuh *whoooo* **fancy fancy**. @@@

04 JD: dus het KAN wel

05 BK: ja

06 JD: alleen in het nederlands?

07 BK: ja. (.) ja. dat denk ik maar dat kost wel veel MOE[ite. @@@

08 JD: [oké

01 BK: what i notice in terms of myself if- if i want to give something a bit more (..) if i'm telling a REALly dramatic sto- or a theatrical story. that i have MORE of a tendency to use it to add some extra power to it (.) um (..) so it does have [something theatrical or something like that

02 JD: [okay so english comes across as more theatrical?

03 BK: yes. (..) yeah it really is more of a kind of caricature. (..) more FLOWery or something like that (.) but again that's (..) in order to have the same effect in dutch you have to speak really good- you have to know a LOT about the dutch language. or a lot of diff- other and synonyms to make it a little bit nice? (..) and you can actually get the same effect by just using an english word (..) because of course that's already a littllllle *whoooo* **fancy fancy**. @@@

04 JD: so it IS possible

05 BK:	yes	
06 JD:	just in dutch?	
07 BK:	yes. (.) yes. i think that but it takes a lot of EFF[ort. @@@	
08 JD:		[okay

In turn 1, *bucket* begins with the observation that she uses transidiomatic practices when she's "telling a really dramatic or theatrical story," and this is positioned as being successful by virtue of the way English-origin words "add some extra power to it" and add "something theatrical" to it. When I ask her about this, she responds in turn 3 by saying that using English makes people come across as "meer een soort typetje," which I've translated as "caricature," but the Dutch term actually refers to the notion of a *fictional character* with strongly caricature-like qualities. This adds even further to the theatrical connotations of transidiomatic practices, positioning them as not just theatrical in the sense of melodramatic, but also theatrical in the sense of somehow being fictional (or at least as being not *quite* real). She adds at the end that it is indeed possible to get the same kinds of effects only by using Dutch, but that "you have to know a lot about the Dutch language" in order to achieve this (turn 3), and that doing so "takes a lot of effort" (turn 7).

Lack of Seriousness

The stance that transidiomatic practices are used to evoke a lack of seriousness is found in both communities, but it is much more prominent in the Dutch community. There is no especially noticeable distinction in terms of how it is voiced in the two communities, but again I will include one excerpt from each. The first of these is Excerpt 5.52, which comes from the interview with German participant *sonnenkind*. It is part of a discussion about a conversation in *unserekleinestadt* in which the English-origin term "cheers" is used as a closing to a post.

Explanations for Transidiomatic Practices   257

Excerpt 5.52 "Cheers sounds casual and nice and pleasant" (German community)

01 JD: hier
02 SK: **cheers** ja
03 JD: @@@
        ((4-second pause))
04 SK: äm (..) jaa (. . .) es ist einfach ähm deutsche (..) sache um tschüss zu sagen klingt auch ein bisschen komi- weil tschüss- (..) klingt es komisch oder bis BALD oder **whatever** es gibt halt **cheers** klingt wieder mal LOCKerer also es ist halt immer so dass das englische einfach LOCKerer klingt **cheers** klingt (.) locker und nett und und symPAthisch denn wenn man sagt *bis ballld* oder *tschüüüss* oder so dann klingt das halt wieder so- wieder so kastig so (..) deutsch halt @

01 JD: here
02 SK: **cheers** yeah
03 JD: @@@
        ((4-second pause))
04 SK: um (..) yeah (. . .) it's just um a german (..) thing to say bye it sounds a little bit wei- because bye- (..) it sounds weird or see you SOON or **whatever** there's just again **cheers** just sounds more CASual i mean it's always like that english just sounds more CASual **cheers** sounds (.) casual and nice and and PLEASant because if you say *see you sooon* or *byyyyye* or something like that then again it sounds so- so boxy so (..) i guess german @

After I present *sonnenkind* with the excerpt, she explains the use of the English-origin "cheers" for the closing of a post in turn 4 by saying that "it's just a German thing to say," then adding that a German equivalent would "sound weird" as well as "boxy, so . . . I guess German" (the German for "boxy" is "kastig," which is a word usually used more literally to describe cars, clothes, and furniture, but which seems here to refer figuratively to thinking). By contrast, she describes "cheers" as sounding "more casual" as well as "nice and pleasant." This positions the English-origin term as positive, but in a low-key way that is not at all serious, while a German equivalent would feel less flexible, less light and airy.

258   5 The Why: Ideology, Positioning, and Attitudes toward English

The same stance can also be seen in the Dutch community in Excerpt 5.53, which comes from the interview with Dutch participant *tesvel*. It originated in a discussion of the conversation previously excerpted in 3.8, in which a number of community members got together to put in a group order on *tesvel*'s credit card for clothing from a UK-based shop.

Excerpt 5.53 "English remarks go along with anticipatory excitement" (Dutch community)

01 JD: maar bij mij waren de maten (..) nu heb je de- de- de KLEren al.
02 TV: ja.
03 JD: bij MIJ waren de maten goed dus **pray pray**.
04 TV: @@@
05 JD: en DAAR wil ik echt een uitleg voor.
06 TV: @@@
07 JD: waarom **pray pray** en niet (.) niet hetzelfde in het nederlands?
08 TV: ehm- ja (.) het is- voor mn gevoel zitten al die engelse uitspraken heel erg in het- eh- het gebiedje van de voorpret en de=
09 JD: hmhm.
10 TV: =niet- niet perse het serieus geregel maar heel erg het meisjes- meisjesdingetjes van- eh- *oh past het wel* en- eh- ja (.) **no problem** dat doen we toch voor elkaar (.) het- het heeft voor mij wel een andere- eh (.) ja. het- het is een- ja (.) het gevoel van onder elkaar (.) het (.) ook samenspannend afwachten of zo?
11 JD: hmhm (.) ja.
12 TV: begrijp je wat ik bedoel?
13 JD: ja oké. maar ik heb ook het idee dat- misschien dat als je dit zou vertalen (.) dat- dat- dat zou heel anders overkomen.
14 TV: @@@ dus bidden [maar @@
15 JD: [bidden maar (.) ja. @@
16 TV: nou ik zou dat op zich best geschreven kunnen hebben (.) met zon KNIPoog erachter.
17 JD: heel gewoon.
18 TV: bidden maar (.) dat had ik nog best gedaan denk ik. want dat is- dat is juist weer zo serieus (.) dat is (.) eh- ja- dat het ook weer niet- niet serieus kan zijn. ja.

01 JD: but for me the sizes were (..) now you have the- the- the clothing already.
02 TV: yeah.
03 JD: for ME the sizes were right so **pray pray**.
04 TV: @@@
05 JD: and THAT's what i really want an explanation for.
06 TV: @@@

Explanations for Transidiomatic Practices 259

```
07 JD:    why pray pray and not (.) not the same thing in dutch?
08 TV:    um- yeah (.) it's- from my perspective all those english remarks are really
          strongly part of the- uh- the arena of anticipatory excitement and the=
09 JD:    hmhm.
10 TV:    =not- not really all the serious organizational stuff but a whole lot more the
          girly- girly things like- uh- *oh does it fit* and- uh- yeah (.) no problem we'll
          do that for each other (.) it- for me it does have another- uh (.) yeah. it- it's a-
          yeah (.) the feeling of conspiratorially waiting for something together as a group
          or something like that?
11 JD:    hmhm (.) yeah.
12 TV:    do you know what i mean?
13 JD:    yeah okay. but i also have the sense that- maybe if you were to translate this (.)
          that- that- that would come across really differently.
14 TV:    @@@ so like just [pray @@
15 JD:                     [just pray (.) yeah. @@
16 TV:    well i actually could have written that (.) with a little WINKy face after it.
17 JD:    just like that.
18 TV:    just pray (.) i actually would have said that i think. because that's- that's just so
          serious again (.) that is (.) uh- yeah- that again it doesn't- that it can't be serious.
          yeah.
```

In turn 1, I introduce which portion of the conversation I'm referring to, specifically the part that comes after *tesvel* has already received the clothing items on behalf of the others, and they're discussing whether the sizing is going to be right. In the original excerpt, *tesvel* says that for her the sizes were right, so "pray pray" (with the last two words in English), so in turns 5 and 7 I ask her about why she used English there rather than a possible Dutch equivalent. In response, she characterizes transidiomatic practices as strongly belonging to the the "anticipatory excitement" (turn 8) and "girly things" (turn 10) part of organizing this sort of group order rather than the "serious organizational stuff" (turn 10). When I ask her whether a Dutch equivalent would come across differently, she proposes "bidden maar" ("just pray," in turn 14), and then argues that the Dutch equivalent would actually have sounded just fine (turns 16 and 18), although in turn 16 she qualifies that statement by saying this would only work as long as she had "a little winky face after it" (i.e. ";)"). She elaborates on this in turn 18 by saying that the

Dutch equivalent works "because that's just so serious" that "it can't be serious." This positions the transidiomatic practices as appropriate for the lighter, less serious side of talking about the clothes they have ordered. A Dutch equivalent could in fact be rescued from its inherent overwhelming seriousness and even lent a sort of ironic non-seriousness with the addition of an emoticon that communicates this, but the English-origin terms convey that all on their own.

The characteristics and moods that the use of transidiomatic practices tend to be depicted as evoking—worldliness, modernity and/or a lack of old-fashionedness, theatricality, and a lack of seriousness—are not random or accidental. They all clearly originated as bits of the Anglophone cultures that originally gave rise to the words that eventually come to be used in the *vragenuurtje* and *unserekleinestadt* communities: English is worldly because it is associated with people in their own cultures who have travelled internationally and associate regularly with non-locals, English is modern because many new cultural and other products come from Anglophone countries, English is theatrical and unserious because Americans (and particularly young Americans) are perceived as being this way. However, as these practices are used in creatively reterritorialized ways, evoking these characteristics and moods means that the indexing of those original cultures is usually done with something other than a one-to-one correspondence, and likely often below the level of explicit consciousness. Additionally, all of these stances appear much more frequently (and in some cases even exclusively) in the Dutch community, which again points toward the likelihood of there being less openness on the part of German community members to using English in this creatively reterritorialized way.

Stances Regarding the Position of English

In this section, I will present and analyze a series of representative excerpts that reveal the two communities' stances regarding the position of English in their own societies and in the world. The subsections below represent the most common types of stances within that larger category, namely the stance that English is self-evident, the stance that English is a symbol for English-speaking countries, and the stance that English is a symbol of a larger internationalized world.

English is Self-Evident

The stance that English is self-evident is found in both communities, however there are major differences in both the frequency of occurrence and the ways the stance is realized between the two communities. This section will therefore include one excerpt from the German community and two from the Dutch, in order to best show those differences. An illustration from the German community can be seen in Excerpt 5.54, which is a simple example that comes from the interview with German participant *caroline*. It emerged within a discussion about the categories of things that tend to be said in English.

Excerpt 5.54 "Pretty natural" (German community)

01 CA: am anfang wurden ja viele sachen übersetzt so (.) drucker (.) maus (.) tastatur (.) aber ich glaub das nimmt immer mehr ab also ich glaub die neuen sachen sind dann halt- also heute sagen viele leute (.) und zum beispiel damals schon wars dann der **joystick**. der wurde auch nicht übersetzt.

02 JD: ok (.) stimmt (.) ja.

03 CA: und ähm (.) heute sagen auch viele leute **harddrive** statt festplatte. oder wir sagen alle- wir sagen **motherboard** [und nicht hauptplatine.

04 JD: [das stimmt (.) ja das hab ich auch bemerkt. hm. is mir auch aufgefallen ja.

05 CA: und so gibts dann immer son misch. masch. was jetzt ä=

06 JD: ja.

07 CA: =auf englisch bleibt.

08 JD: und wie FINDest du das.

09 CA: ähm (.) ich find es nicht SCHLIMM ich finds eigentlich recht naTÜRlich. weil (.) naja we- wenn die sachen die werden ja haupt- oft kommen die aus amerika zu uns.

10 JD: mhm

11 CA: und dann haben die eben den deutschen namen (.) noch nich. und haben erstmal n englischen namen. und dann isses irgendwie künstlich wenn man sich

262   **5 The Why: Ideology, Positioning, and Attitudes toward English**

> dann später (.) wenn sich bei einigen leuten der englische name schon EINgebürgert hat nochmal n DEUtschen erfinden.

01 CA: in the beginning lots of things were translated like (.) printer ((German term)) (.) mouse ((German term)) (.) keyboard ((German term)) (.) but i think there's less and less of that so i think the new things are then- i mean today lots of people say (.) and for example even back then it was the **joystick.** that wasn't translated either.

02 JD: okay (.) true (.) yeah.

03 CA: and um (.) today lots of people say **harddrive** instead of hard drive ((German term)). or we all say- we say **motherboard** [and not motherboard. ((German term))

04 JD: [that's true (.) yeah i've noticed that too. hm. it's occurred to me too yeah.

05 CA: and so then there's always this mish. mash. which is now=

06 JD: yeah.

07 CA: =staying in english.

08 JD: and what do you THINK of that.

09 CA: um (.) i don't think there's anything WRONG with it i actually think it's completely NAtural. because (.) well when- when the things they're usual- often they're coming from america to us.

10 JD: mhm

11 CA: and then they just don't have the german name (.) yet. and they do have an english name at first. and then it's somehow artificial to come back and (.) after the english name has already taken ROOT with some people come back and invent a GERman one.

Turns 1 through 7 are about *caroline*'s perceptions of the way that in earlier years, words for cultural and other products that arrived in Germany from Anglophone countries were translated or otherwise transposed into German terms, but now when even newer products arrive, the words for them are borrowed directly from English. Then, in turn 8, I ask her what she thinks of that, and her response is to say that this is "completely natural" by virtue of the fact that these products are "coming from America" to Germany. She even goes so far as to say that going back and creating a German word for English terms that have "already taken root" would be "somehow artificial." This positions these kinds of transidiomatic practices—nouns used for specific product items

Stances Regarding the Position of English 263

that originated in Anglophone foreign countries—as absolutely self-evident and refraining from using them in those cases as problematic.

The first such example from the Dutch community can be seen in Excerpt 5.55, which comes from *echinacea* and originated in the context of a discussion toward the end of the interview about the extent to which it is important or necessary to change one's transidiomatic practices in order to accommodate people who might not speak English well.

Excerpt 5.55 "Italians and Spanish people are missing out on that" (Dutch community)

01 EC: sommige nederlanders zeggen dan (.) ik kan geen engels. maar dan denk ik (.) we spreken alleMAAL engels. dat krijg je al (.) vroeger was- eh- waren KINdertelevisieseries (.) die zijn nu wel in het NEderlands. (.) toen WIJ opgroeiden (.) mijn generatie (.) was het OOK in het engels. KINdertelevisie.

02 JD: ja.

03 EC: dus TUURlijk spreek jij engels. ik zeg (.) je keek MTV de hele TIJD lang.

04 JD: hm.

05 EC: dus het KAN niet dat jij geen engels spreekt.

06 JD: hm.

07 EC: en dan uiteindelijk merk je (.) al is het dan met een zwaar accent of met foutief taalgebruik (.) maar uiteindelijk kan IEderEEN zich redden in het engels. en daar-

08 JD: en- en vind je dat goed zo?

09 EC: ik vind dat heel goed. ik vind dat wel een KRACHT van nederlanders. want bijvoorbeeld (.) eh (.) italiAnen en SPANjaarden MISSen dat.

10 JD: klopt.

11 EC: en (.) want die zijn iets- eh- daardoor echt wel **SCREWED**.

01 EC: some dutch people say (.) i can't speak english. but then i think (.) we ALL speak english. you already get that (.) back then there- uh- there were television shows for CHILdren (.) now they are in DUTCH (.) back when WE grew up (.) my generation (.) it was ALSO in english. CHILdren's television.

02 JD: right.

03 EC: so of COURSE you speak english. i say (.) you watched MTV all the TIME.

04 JD: hm.

05 EC: so it's not POSSible for you to not speak english.

06 JD: hm.

07 EC: and then finally you notice (.) even if it's with a heavy accent or language use full of mistakes (.) but in the end EVerybody can muddle through in english. and there-

264   **5 The Why: Ideology, Positioning, and Attitudes toward English**

08 JD: and- and do you think that's a good thing?
09 EC: i think that's really good. i do think that's a STRENGTH of dutch people. because for example (.) uh (.) itALians and SPANish people are missing OUT on that.
10 JD: true.
11 EC: and (.) because they're some- uh- really **SCREWED** because of that.

In turns 1 through 7, *echinacea* outlines her stance that there aren't any Dutch people—at least not in or around her generation—who can't at least "muddle through" in English. Then, beginning in turn 8, when I ask her whether she thinks this is a good thing, she positions this as not just "really good," but specifically as "a strength of Dutch people" that people from other societies (specifically southern European countries like Italy and Spain) are at a disadvantage for not having.

Finally, a slightly different sort of example of this from the Dutch community can be seen in Excerpt 5.56, which comes from *mfpim* and originated within a discussion about a conversation in *vragenuurtje* in which community members were all discussing the various things that irritated them.

Excerpt 5.56 "Germans who expect every Dutch person to speak German" (Dutch community)

01 JD: en op het EINde? (.) duitsers die- die verwachten dat elke nederlander wel duits spreekt (.) dat- dat irriTEERT me zegt ze (.) en- en-
02 MP: mij ook.
03 JD: ja?
04 MP: ja mij ook. ik werkte bij de albert heijn in ((name of beach town)) en daar waren natuurlijk heel veel duitsers? en de meeste duitsers die gaan er gewoon van uit dat jij- eh- ook duits kan.
05: JD: mm
06 MP: ja (.) om één of andere reden (.) ik weet het ook niet. en dan staan ze bij je KASSa en dan PRAten ze alles in het DUITS en dan zit jij zo van (..) hun gaan er echt gewoon van UIT dat jij gewoon duits kan
07 JD: ja dat heb je heel veel aan het strand hè?

Stances Regarding the Position of English 265

08 MP: ja maar de meeste duitsers zijn gewoon ook heel LUI en heel LAKS in LEren. die gaan er maar vanUIT dat iedereen hun TAAL leert. hun gaan de MOEIte niet doen. in ieder geval (.) dat zeiden mijn OUDers ook altijd.

09 JD: en- hoe is het dan als het een ENGelsman is? die verwacht dat je dan ENGels spreekt?
((2-second pause))

10 MP: ja (..) bij engels is het ANders (...) want engels leer je ook gewoon al vanaf groep ZES ZEven (.) dat is logisch. duits dat leer je echt pas op de middelbare SCHOOL en niet iedereen krijgt dat (.) en het ligt eraan wat voor niVEAU je doet. en engels is gewoon internatioNAAL, dat MOET je gewoon kunnen.

11 JD: ja (.) maar dan is het (...) oké. als er iemand denkt (.) ja (.) je moet MIJN taal spreken.

12 MP: jaaaa (.) het HEEFT natuurlijk (..) ik weet niet- het ligt er ook aan waar het IS hoor. het is soms ook wel stom als er echt engelsen naar je toekomen en van alles gaan vragen (.) en misschien kan je het inderdaad ook helemaal niet. maar (.) bij DUItsers is het gewoon wel ECHT zo.

01 JD: and at the END? (.) germans who- who expect every dutch person to speak german (.) that- that IRRitates me she says (.) and- and-

02 MP: me too.

03 JD: yeah?

04 MP: yeah me too. i worked at a supermarket in ((name of beach town)) and of course there were a whole lot of germans there? and most of the germans they just assume that you- uh- can speak german too.

05: JD: mm

06 MP: yeah (.) for some reason or another (.) i don't know either. and then they stand at your CASH register and then they SAY everything in GERman and you just end up all (..) they really just assUME that you just speak german

07 JD: yeah you get that a lot at the beach don't you?

08 MP: yeah but most germans are just completely LAzy and LAX in LEARNing. they just assUME that everybody's going to learn their LANGuage. they don't make the EFFort. at least (.) that's what my PArents always said.

09 JD: and- how is it if it's an ENGlishman? who expects you to speak ENGlish?
((2-second pause))

10 MP: well (..) it's DIFFerent with english (...) because you're already learning english starting in grade THREE FOUR (.) that's logical. german you only learn that in HIGH school and not everybody gets that (.) and it depends on what kind of LEvel you do. and english is just interNAtional. you HAVE to know that.

11 JD: okay (.) but then it's (...) okay. if somebody thinks (.) yeah (.) you have to speak MY language.

12 MP: okaaaay (.) of course it DOES (..) i don't know- it also depends on where it IS. it actually is sometimes stupid if english people really come up to you and ask

266   **5 The Why: Ideology, Positioning, and Attitudes toward English**

> all sorts of questions (.) and maybe you really don't speak it at all. but (.) with
> GERmans it's just REALLy like that.

I begin in turn 1 by pointing out the part of the *vragenuurtje* conversations where another community member had listed one of the things that irritated her as "Germans who expect every Dutch person to speak German." Rather than commenting on that community member's language use, however, *mfpim* says that she feels the same way as that other person (turns 2 and 4). She then provides an example from her own life to explain why she finds this irritating: when she worked in a town that got a lot of German tourists, most of them just spoke to her in German (turns 4 and 6), and she even attributes this tendency to Germans' "laziness" and their unwillingness to "make the effort" to learn another language (turn 8). At this point it is unclear whether these Germans are being criticized for being unwilling to learn and speak to her in Dutch, or to learn and speak to her in English, but the turns that follow suggest that it must be interpreted as the latter. Specifically, when I ask *mfpim* in turn 9 whether she feels the same way "if it's an Englishman" who expects her to speak English, there's a noticeably long pause, followed by a characterization of this as a situation that's "different" by virtue of the fact that Dutch people all actually speak English while not everyone speaks German, and that "English is just international anyway" and something that people "have to know" (turn 10). When I question her about the underlying principle in what she's saying by arguing that in both cases you've got someone saying that other people have to learn their language, she acknowledges my point, but only then (turn 12).

The stance that English is self-evident does in fact come up in the German community, but only within the very limited contexts of talking about loanwords for specific cultural or other products that originated in English-speaking countries. In the Dutch community, however, the perceived self-evident nature of the omnipresence of English is so strong that it's woven into practically every line of every interview, without even a single exception. This means that even when they are talking about how self-evident English is, the German community members are doing so by overtly defending the use of specific transidiomatic practices, while the Dutch community members are doing so by positioning the English language as something that is in every Dutch person's repertoire, and the use of the language—whether in transidiomatic practices or with respect to passive consumption or active use—as so obvious and natural that there's nothing *to* defend.

English is a Symbol of English-Speaking Countries

The stance that English is a symbol of English-speaking countries is found only in the German community, and the occurrences of this stance are similar enough that I will only discuss one excerpt in this section. This is Excerpt 5.57, which comes from German participant *sonnenkind* and which originated in a general discussion toward the end of the interview about what her perceptions were of the role and position of English in the world and in everyday German life.

Excerpt 5.57 "There are many English-speaking countries that I like" (German community)

01 JD: was bedeutet englisch für dich. (.) was- äh welche geFÜHLe (..) WECKT es in dir

02 SK: hmm (. . .) es gibt halt viele englischsprachige länder die ich mag und ich würd unglaublich gern nach australien oder neuseeland gehen? und deswegen wächst mir das gefühl von etwas- (.) äh von abenteuern etwas tollen- etwas schönen was ich mal erleben möchte. (.) und ähm ja manchmal mach ich das auch zum SPASS also nicht hier in hannover aber wenn ich woanders bin dass ich halt leute kennen lern und einfach so tue als wenn ich nicht aus deutschland komme. [und ich finde das=

03 JD: [mhm

04 SK: =einfach lustig also zu spielen als ob ich von irgendwo anders herkomme und mir die $stadt zeigen lasse von dem$?

05 JD: mhm

268   5 The Why: Ideology, Positioning, and Attitudes toward English

06 SK: einfach ähm (.) ja weils einfach LUSTig ist und dann ist eben englisch auch ne
gute SAche um so zu tun als ob man nicht aus deutschland kommt weil englisch
beherrscht ebenso gut dass die leute- vor allem die deutschsprachigen leute mir
das AB[nehmen würden
07 JD: [ja ja
08 SK: und ähm (..)
09 JD: und (.) sagst du dann (.) wo du herkommst?
10 SK: ja ich denk mir dann meist irgendwas aus (.) also- also-
11 JD: wo kommst du dann her
12 SK: aus **minnesota** meistens [@@
13 JD: ok   [@@@
14 SK: ja (. . .) da komm ich her (.) dann immer @@
15 JD: äh aber du- aber du würdest dann nicht sagen ich komm aus SCHWEden oder
so
16 SK: nein das würde ich nicht sagen weil dann würde ja die gefahr bestehen dass
jemand auf schwedisch kann und ich nicht (.) [@@
17 JD: ok   [@@
18 SK: ich kann halt kein schwedisch und das [[würd auffallen
19 JD: [[ja @@@@@ oder ja sowas wie tsche-
chien oder so
20 SK: ja ja aber da ist aber immer die gefahr das irgend [jemand zwei drei worte
KANN
21 JD: [ja ok
22 SK: also das würd ich halt nie sagen ich würd dann immer nur ein englischspra-
chiges land- also meistens eher auch aMErika weil (.) ähm (.) mein englisch
dann- schon durch die filme die ich gucke eher einen amerikanischen akzent
hab

01 JD: what does english mean for you. (.) what- uh what FEELings does it (..) STIR
up in you
02 SK: hmm (. . .) there are a lot of english speaking countries that i like and i would
dearly love to go to australia or new zealand? and that's why this feeling grows in
me of something- (.) uh of adventures something exciting something wonderful
that i want to experience. (.) and um yeah sometimes i do that too just for FUN
i mean not here in hanover but when i'm somewhere else that i meet people and
just act like i'm not from germany. [and i think that's
03 JD: [mhm
04 SK: completely fun to play as if i'm from somewhere else and $get them to show me
the city$?
05 JD: mhm
06 SK: just um (.) yeah because it's FUN and then also english is a good THING to
pretend that you're not from germany because everybody knows about the same

	amount of english that people- especially german speaking people BUY [that coming from me
07 JD:	[yeah yeah
08 SK:	and um (..)
09 JD:	and (.) do you tell them then (.) where you're from?
10 SK:	yeah i mostly just come up with something (.) i mean- i mean-
11 JD:	where are you from then
12 SK:	from **minnesota** mostly [@@
13 JD:	okay [@@@
14 SK:	yeah (...) that's where i'm from (.) always @@
15 JD:	um but you- but then you wouldn't say i'm from SWEden or something like that
16 SK:	no i wouldn't say that because then there would be the danger of someone speaking swedish and i can't (.) [@@
17 JD:	okay [@@
18 SK:	i don't speak any swedish and [[people would notice that
19 JD:	[[yeah @@@@@ or something like the czech republic or something
20 SK:	yeah yeah but there's always the danger that some[one KNOWS two three words
21 JD:	[yeah okay
22 SK:	i mean i would never say that i would always just pick an english speaking country then- i mean usually it would tend to be aMErica because (.) um (.) my english then- already because of the films i watch i tend to have more of an american accent

When I ask *sonnenkind* what English means for her, her first association is with English-speaking countries that she would like to visit (turn 2), but also with the experience of play-acting someone from an English-speaking country when she has the occasion to do so while she is visiting another German city (turns 2 through 12). When I ask where she pretends to be from when she does this, she names the US state of Minnesota (turn 12). When I then ask her whether she would ever consider pretending to be someone from some other non-English-speaking country and still use English (turn 15), she says she would not. She cites concern that her "mark" could conceivably speak Swedish or Czech as the reason for this (turns 16, 18, and 20), but the possibility of a random German person being able to speak sufficient English to

270   5   The Why: Ideology, Positioning, and Attitudes toward English

recognize her as a non-native-speaker would seem to be at least as great a risk. She finishes in turn 22 by saying that she would "always just pick an English-speaking country," and especially in combination with her initial comments about associating English with English-speaking countries she wants to visit, this positions English as first and foremost the language of those countries, and not of other European places like Sweden or the Czech Republic (or Germany).

It is notable that this stance does not come up in the Dutch community at all. This seems to be because the first associations with English for the Dutch are not people to meet and experiences to have in English-speaking countries, but with things that are much closer to home: television watched in their own Dutch homes dating back from when they were children, conversations had at their own Dutch schools or workplaces. For the Dutch community members, English is not first and foremost a foreign language belonging to Anglophone countries, but a language that is not just a vital but also a completely ordinary part of their everyday lives in the Netherlands. This is very much in tune with the findings of the survey research discussed in Chapter 2.

English is a Symbol of a Larger International World

The stance that English is a symbol of a larger international world is found in both communities, but there are again differences between the way the two communities express them, so this section will contain excerpts from both. The first of these is Excerpt 5.58, which comes from Dutch participant *duimelotje* and which originated in a general discussion about the style that is used in the weekly *vraagvrije vrijdag* posts.

> ### Excerpt 5.58 "I think she's more internationally oriented" (Dutch community)
>
> 01 JD   dat- dat heb je heel VAAK in tweeTAlige gemeenschappen (.) da- da- dat zo is
>   (.) bijvoorbeeld in montreal (.) in canada of zo
> 02 DU: ja in BELgië heb je dat natuurlijk [OOK.
> 03 JD: [ja

Stances Regarding the Position of English   271

```
04 DU:   van die franse ( . . . ) [[zinnetjes dr door
05 JD:                          [[ja. (.) ja. (..) O ja? Oké.
06 DU:   ja.
07 JD:   maar dat doet laviefanTASQUE bijvoorbeeld niet? @@@
08 DU:   nee (.) nee.
09 JD:   ja waarom niet? ja waarom- waarOM dan eigenlijk?
10 DU:   ik denk dat omdat laviefantasque- ah (.) je bedoelt FRANS praten?
11 JD:   ja.
12 DU:   omdat zij meer internatioNAAL georiënteerd is. en veel (..) bezig is met de
         ENGelse taal.


01 JD    you- you get that an awful LOT in biLINGual communities (.) tha- tha- that
         are like (.) for example in montreal (.) in canada or something like that
02 DU:   yeah in BELgium of course you get that [TOO
03 JD:                                          [ja
04 DU:   all those little ( . . . ) [[french sentences strewn throughout
05 JD:                              [[yeah. (.) yeah. (..) OH yeah? oKAY.
06 DU:   yeah.
07 JD:   but for example laviefanTASQUE doesn't do that? @@@
08 DU:   no (.) no.
09 JD:   yeah why not? yeah why- WHY NOT?
10 DU:   i think that because laviefantasque- uh (.) you mean speak FRENCH?
11 JD:   yeah.
12 DU:   because she's more interNAtionally oriented. and really (..) preoccupied with
         the ENGlish language.
```

I begin this excerpt by positioning transidiomatic practices as analogous to code-switching "in bilingual communities," and I name the Canadian city of Montreal as a typical example. In response, *duimelotje* says that this also happens in Belgium, where Dutch-speaking Belgians speak Dutch with "all those little French sentences strewn throughout" (turn 4). I then ask her in turns 7 and 9 to speculate about why her fellow participant *laviefantasque* (who had recently spent a number of years living in Belgium) didn't do this. Her response is to say that "she's more internationally oriented," which is immediately juxtaposed with the idea of being "really preoccupied with the English language" (turn 12). This positions the use of transidiomatic practices involving French as signifying a *lack* of an international orientation, while the use of

272   **5 The Why: Ideology, Positioning, and Attitudes toward English**

transidiomatic practices involving English is positioned as inherently more international, despite the fact that both are nominally foreign languages to a Dutch person.

A somewhat different take on this same stance can be seen in Excerpt 5.59, which comes from *hobbit* in the German community. Again, this came from the end of the interview where I was asking her about her perceptions of the role and position of English.

Excerpt 5.59 "With English I can talk to anyone in any country in the world" (German community)

01 JD: beDEUTet englisch für dich. ((2-second pause)) also (.) is das (.) ja so- womit verbindest du englisch.

02 HB: ähm ((4-second pause)) ich verbinde englisch DAmit (.) dass ich mich wirklich mit menschen auf der ganzen welt unterHALTen kann die auch aus nem ganz andern kulTURkreis stammen?

03 JD: mhm ok

04 HB: ähm ((2-second pause)) ich bin ganz froh englisch zu beHERRschen wie gesacht wenn ich mir meine MUtter angucke die kein englisch kann und wenn ich sehe was der [alles entGEHT.

05 JD: [mm

06 HB: und (.) wo sie dann nicht mehr MITkommt (.) find ich das immer irgendwie total TRAUrig

07 JD: mhm

08 HB: weil ich das geFÜHL habe (.) ähm (.) dass ich das- durch das englische doch mein horizont ganz erHEBlich erWEItern kann

09 JD: mhm

10 HB: und weil es auch viele dinge gibt (.) dies- dies eben auf deutsch gar nicht GIBT?

11 JD: mhm

12 HB: auch jetzt keine ahnung ähm (.) irgendwelche seis- jetzt auch irgendwelche SErien oder BUcher oder was weiß ich die gar nicht übersetzt worden sind (.) auch für mein studium hab ich teilweise bücher auf englisch gelesen weils die auf deutsch einfach gar nicht GIBT.

13 JD: mhm

14 HB: mh ((2-second pause)) ja. also is schon ((2-second pause)) ich finds toll das zu können? (.) is für mich halt so ne möglichkeit ein- einfach nochmal kommunikationsmittel

15 JD: und du ver- du verbindest es nicht mit ENGland oder (.) aMERika oder

16 HB: mhh

17 JD: ja mehr mit- [eher mit- also- di- DIE internationale [[sprache ist das und

18 HB:	[mh [[ja ich glaub eher ich glaub eher mit dem internationalen?
19 JD:	ok?
20 HB:	weil ich halt auch (.) vielleicht auch DEShalb- weil ich auch durchaus freunde in (..) SCHWEden (. . .) ISrael (. . .) südaMErika
21 JD:	ok
22 HB:	weiß der geier wo habe oder wie gesacht die zwei wochen die ich da in (.) in kenia war da wo man sich auch nur auf englisch unterhält [oder
23 JD:	[mhm
24 HB:	auch in THAIland (.) [[hab ich (.) englisch gesprochen und nich- nicht deutsch?
25 JD:	[[mhm mhm
26 HB:	klar für mich [is auch
27 JD:	[und und kein thailändisch @@@
28 HB:	nee @@@ mhh ((3-second pause)) aber ((2-second pause)) die sache is? (.) für mich? (.) mit ENGlisch kann ich eigentlich in JEdem land der welt? mit irgendwem reden.

01 JD:	what does english MEAN to you. ((2-second pause)) i mean (.) is it (.) yeah like- what associations do you have with english.
02 HB:	um ((4-second pause)) i associate english with (.) the fact that i can really TALK to people all over the whole world even if they come from a completely different CULtural sphere?
03 JD:	mhm okay
04 HB:	um ((2-second pause)) i'm really happy to have a commAND of it like i said if i look at my MOther who doesn't speak english and when i see what all she's missing [OUT on.
05 JD:	[mm
06 HB:	and (.) where she just doesn't keep UP (.) i always think that's somehow completely SAD
07 JD:	mhm
08 HB:	because i have the FEELing (.) um (.) that i- through english i can really exPAND my horIZon considerably
09 JD:	mhm
10 HB:	and because there are also a lot of things (.) that- that- just don't exIST in german at all?
11 JD:	mhm
12 HB:	also now no idea um (.) all kinds of sh- like various TELevision shows or BOOKS or whatever that never end up getting translated (.) for my university studies too to some extent i read books in english because they just dont exIST in german.
13 JD:	mhm

14 HB:	mh ((2-second pause)) yeah. so it's ((2-second pause)) i think it's great to know it? (.) for me it's just a possibility simp- simply again a method of communication
15 JD:	and you asso- you don't associate it with ENGland or (.) aMERica or
16 HB:	mhh
17 JD:	right more with- [more with- i mean- th- it's THE international [[language and
18 HB:	[mh [[yeah i think instead it tends to be with the international thing?
19 JD:	okay?
20 HB:	because like i (.) maybe THAT's why- because i definitely have friends in (..) SWEden (. . .) ISrael (. . .) south aMErica
21 JD:	okay
22 HB:	god knows where or like i said the two weeks that i was down in (.) in kenya where people also only speak english with each other [or
23 JD:	[mhm
24 HB:	also in THAIland (.) [[i spoke (.) english and not- not german?
25 JD:	[[mhm mhm
26 HB:	of course for me [it's also
27 JD:	[and- and not thai @@@
28 HB:	no @@@ mhh ((3-second pause)) but ((2-second pause)) the thing is? (.) for me? (.) with ENGlish i can ultimately- in ANy country in the world? i can talk to anybody.

In response to my question about what associations she has with English, *hobbit* (unlike *sonnenkind* in Excerpt 5.57) talks about the language as being associated not with English-speaking countries, but with the language's ability to enable her to "talk to people all over the whole world, even if they come from a completely different cultural sphere" (turn 2). She then contrasts this ability of hers with her mother's lack of the same ability, and positions the latter as "missing out" on a great deal of worldly experience as a result (turns 4 through 12). When I then ask in turn 15 whether this means she doesn't associate it with English-speaking countries at all, she agrees that her associations tend to be more with "the international thing" (turn 18) because speaking English means first and foremost that "in any country in the world" she can "talk to anybody." This is essentially the same stance that can be seen in *duimelotje*'s excerpt in 5.58, but when this is expressed in the Dutch community, it's always in a

Stances Regarding the Position of English   275

completely self-evident way that goes hand in hand with the idea that the use of English is self-evident (as explored in the previous section). By contrast, the German community is split. Whereas some of the participants associate English first and foremost with English-speaking countries, as *sonnenkind* does in Excerpt 5.57, other German participants' first associations are primarily with the way English opens speakers up to the entire world, which includes but is not limited to English-speaking countries. However, even when this latter stance is voiced by German participants, the completely self-evident nature that surrounds it in each and every one of the Dutch participants I interviewed is still absent.

Perhaps surprisingly, however, all members of both communities who expressed a stance about who English "belongs" to agreed that it is the provenance and possession of English native speakers first and foremost. Not only did no one express anything to the contrary despite having ample opportunities to bring up a stance like that, but whenever I asked any of the participants directly about the idea that a frequent creative use of English could imply that English could somehow be their language as well, the idea was always dismissed or at least strongly negated. An example of this can be seen in Excerpt 5.60, from Dutch participant *bucket*.

Excerpt 5.60 "Dutch is my first language and that's how it's always going to be" (Dutch community)

```
01 JD:   dat is wel een beetje JOUW TAAL. (..) of niet.
02 BK:   NEE.
03 JD:   nee?
04 BK:   nee (..) nee. (...) nee. hoewel ik t wel door de jaren door wel meer ben gaan
         waarDEren? omdat er juist ook heel van die dingen zijn die BEter een gevoel
         weergeven of beter de LAding dekken? (..) ik vind russell grant ook echt GE (.)
         WELdig? (.) gewoon zijn hele- hoe hij (.) gewoon met taal mensen om zn vinger
         windt (.) en super- verha- nou te gek? dus dan vind ik het echt geweldig? (...)
         maar (..) ik blijf toch gewoon wel- nederlands is wel gewoon mijn eerste taal en
         dat zal het ook altijd blijven.


01 JD:   it really is a little bit YOUR LANGuage. (..) or not.
02 BK:   NO.
```

03 JD:	no?
04 BK:	no (..) no. (. . .) no. although i have learned to appREciate it more and more? also precisely because there are lots of those things that reproduce a feeling BETTer or encompass a MEANing better? (..) i think russell grant is just AWE (.) SOME? (.) just his whole- how he (.) just wraps people around his finger with language (.) and super- stor- i mean so great? so i do really think that's completely awesome? (. . .) but (.) i really am still- dutch is just my first language and that's how it's always going to be.

The response to my implication in turn 1 is swift and strong: English is most decisively *not bucket*'s language. She then goes on to elaborate that while she approves of transidiomatic practices because they can sometimes "reproduce a feeling better or encompass a meaning better," and while she also has an appreciation for the way many native English-speaking artists use their language, it is simply a fact that Dutch is her first language and that's not something that will ever change. This positions English—and in fact any language—as necessarily the possession solely of its native speakers, despite high proficiency, deep affinity, or even daily use by non-native speakers. There is therefore a clearly articulated difference between the stance that English may be *used* by everyone by virtue of being an international language (which is universal in the Dutch community and a commonly expressed stance in the German community as well) and saying that it *belongs* to them (which is not present in either community).

Summary of Trends

The analysis in this chapter makes it clear that while the notion of differing proficiencies between German and Dutch young people may certainly be a widespread trend, it is far from a sufficient explanation for the differences seen between the two communities in terms of the transidiomatic practices analyzed in Chapters 3 and 4. Instead, the patterns that emerge in the two communities' differing attitudes toward transidiomatic practices and toward the position and role of English overall seem to suggest that the Germans are much more likely to question whether transidiomatic practices are appropriate and question whether the ubiquity of English in an increasingly internationalized world is a good thing. The Dutch, on the other hand, tend to regard English as a completely normal and natural part of their own local environment, a part that is so self-evident that it is ridiculous even to question it (even when talking about the downsides of this). The self-evidentness of English in both Dutch interaction and Dutch society is a stance that is ubiquitous in the interviews from the *vragenuurtje* community, and this stance strongly echoes the ideology of English that is typically found in wider Dutch society, one that is mostly unconcerned with the increased use of specific English lexical items and even uncertain how concerned it should be about the loss of previously Dutch-only domains. The Germans do certainly view English as a vitally necessary part of their lives, but for them it is still always positioned as a foreign language, while the Dutch position English as something different altogether: not as "their" language, because that is a title reserved for Dutch alone, but not as something entirely foreign, either. Because they position English as an international language that may be used by anyone rather than a foreign language that is mostly useful in interactions with foreigners, the participants in the Dutch community are much more likely than the Germans to incorporate it as a casual part of their language play and other more casual interactions.

The differing ideologies that are on display in this chapter have their roots in the differences between the primarily ethnic tradition of nationalism that emerged in Germany and the primarily civic tradition of nationalism that emerged in the Netherlands, and the ways that these underlying nationalist ideologies have come into play through the centuries within each country's language regimes have only reinforced these differences. On the other hand, however, it is clear that the young people in these two social media communities are not influenced solely by their countries' histories of nationalism, but also by a globalizing world and the different ways they interact with that world, and specifically by the different roles (in terms of its functional range and societal depth of use) that the English language plays internationally in their respective societies. Equally important as well is the fact that these sets of ideologies are not the be-all and end-all in either case, but the starting point. In both communities, these youth draw on their own countries' centuries-old national language ideologies and more recent conceptions of English as a global language, but they also call them into question and, ultimately, reshape them into something specific to them and their purposes. I will discuss these issues in more detail in Chapter 6.

6

English as a Trans-National Language

Drawing on two comparable social media communities, this book compares transidiomatic practices from two countries with both distinctly different ideological histories and distinctly different institutional and semi-institutionalized traditions, taking both the language practices themselves and that ideological backdrop into account. In this concluding chapter, I compare the findings from the data analysis in Chapters 3, 4, and 5, looking specifically at the differences between the two communities. In this comparative summary, I will dwell specifically on which of the two communities tends to use which kinds of transidiomatic practices in social media interactions, how the two communities use these practices differently for conversational effect in their interactions, the differing beliefs and ideas the two communities have about their own language practices and the role of English in general, and how all of these differences relate back to the two societies' separate ideological histories and state traditions. I will then return to the theoretical framework that I outlined in Chapter 2, and delineate the implications of these findings for a more generalized theory of global English in a globalizing, superdiverse world. Finally, I end by considering some

© The Author(s) 2017
J. Dailey-O'Cain, *Trans-National English in Social Media Communities*, Language and Globalization,
DOI 10.1057/978-1-137-50615-3_6

279

280 6 English as a Trans-National Language

implications of these findings for language policy in Germany and the Netherlands, as well as in other countries where global English plays a role.

Transidiomatic Practices in Social Media Interaction: The Who, the What, the How, and the Why

The first and most basic comparative observations that can be made about the findings come in Chapter 3, and these have to do with the differing amounts of English-origin transidiomatic practices used between the two communities. Specifically, it can not only be said that a great deal more of these practices are used in the Dutch community *vragenuurtje* overall than in the German community *unserekleinestadt*, but also that the types of practices that require a greater degree of knowledge of and creativity with the English language tend to be much more common in the Dutch community than in the German one. In addition, there is a greater tendency within the German community to flag the use of English-origin transidiomatic practices as being somehow unusual, and there is also a slightly lower tendency in the German community to choose English-origin usernames than there is in the Dutch one. These findings—especially when taken together—suggest that the members of the Dutch community generally regard a full spectrum of transidiomatic practices as a normal and appropriate part of their social media discourse, while this is not the case among most members of the German community.

Chapter 4 deals with the second set of comparisons that can be made regarding the findings. These comparisons have to do with differences relating to how members of the two communities use their transidiomatic practices, or in other words, which purposes these practices serve interactionally. What I found was that the young people in the Dutch community on the one hand frequently use language alternation as a tool to structure conversation, and on the other hand also tend to use transidiomatic practices in identity-related acts such as positioning. While it is also the case that these types of transidiomatic practices are used by particular individual young people in the German community, they are markedly less pervasive in that community as a whole. It is also apparent that the types of participant-related language alternation most clearly associated with evoking and aligning with the aforementioned wider transnational world of communication—such as the use of English-origin transidiomatic practices to indicate lightheartedness among strong affect, and language mixing to index a general sense of transnationalism—are limited exclusively to the Dutch community. These observations suggest that the members of the Dutch community are much more likely to use transidiomatic practices in ways that resemble the full diverse spectrum of discourse-related and participant-related forms of language alternation that have been found in face-to-face bilingual communities, such as the Spanish-speaking community in New York City or German-Italian bilinguals in Germany. This, in turn, suggests that members of the Dutch community have a much stronger tendency than members of the German community to view themselves as users of English, even when it comes to their day-to-day lives within their own country.

Chapter 5 presents the third and final stratum of comparisons that can be made between the two communities. This concerns not the language practices themselves, but community members' ideas and beliefs about those practices as revealed through an analysis of their language attitudes and ideological stances. These findings suggest that while the young people in the Dutch community tend to regard English as a completely natural and self-evident part of their own local environment, the young people in the German community are more likely to question whether the ubiquity of English in an increasingly internationalized world is a good thing. Furthermore, Dutch participants are much more likely than German participants to be both consciously aware of and accepting of the fact that they use English for a specific interactional effect (such as to do identity work by indexing specific non-local communities, or to distinguish a youth subculture). And while both Dutch and German participants observe that the local languages have in many cases lost their ability to communicate things like worldliness, modernity, and a lack of seriousness now that English-origin words

282   6   English as a Trans-National Language

and expressions tend to be used to do that work, the German participants are much more likely to be critical of this practice, while the Dutch participants tend to be simply accepting of it (or at the very most, a bit wistful). Finally, while the German participants do certainly all view English as an important and necessary part of their lives, they have a greater tendency to position it as an international language that is used primarily in interaction with non-Germans, while the Dutch participants are more likely to position it as something that has made an indelible mark on their own local society and can therefore be used to fully local ends.

In Chapter 2, I referred to Park and Wee's (2012: 25–6) discussion of how global English has come to be linked with *value,* both in the economic sense (i.e. the belief that competence in English can be converted into material gain), but also moral and ethical value (i.e. the way the use of English can point to a vague sense of good upbringing and moral integrity that is associated with and used to justify a higher social status). This linkage with value pervades the ways English-origin transidiomatic practices are characterized by participants in the two communities discussed in this book, even among those participants who are often critical of them. For example, it is no accident that English-origin transidiomatic practices are seen by participants in both communities as indexing a sense of worldliness and/or a sense of modernity specifically *because* the latter traits are associated with the Anglophone cultures that originally gave rise to the words and expressions used in such practices. But while this perceived value implied by the origin of these transidiomatic practices in predominantly Anglophone cultural contexts remains, the specific American or British cultural references that were originally strongly linked with those practices in their societies of origin have become abstracted away and recontextualized differently within each local cultural context. The result is a set of specifically local norms for how transidiomatic practices are to be used, a specifically local set of attitudes and ideologies that underlie that use, and transidiomatic practices themselves that are infused with new local meanings while still retaining the flavour of global culture.

These norms are not solely a result of preferences that have developed within the respective social media communities, however. Instead, they are embedded within broader social and cultural trends that have been present within the two societies since long before these specific social media communities evolved (cf. Deumert 2014: 144). In particular, both the different sets of transidiomatic practices on display in the two communities and the two sets of participants' largely differing explanations for those practices seem to be rooted on the one hand in the two different traditions of nationalism in Germany and the Netherlands, and on the other hand in the differing institutionalized and semi-institutionalized language practices that have become rooted within the two societies. The participants of the *unserekleinestadt* and *vragenuurtje* communities therefore are acting under the influence of their own countries' respective language regimes at the same time that they are calling parts of them into question through the distinctly transnational act of using transidiomatic practices. The result is two distinctly different approaches to the creation of localized social media spaces that are simultaneously national and transnational, and two different—but apparently equally tenable—approaches to addressing some of the ideological and pragmatic issues stemming from the emergence of English as a global lingua franca.

From Language Regime to Language Practice

I argued in Chapter 2 that sociolinguists who want to better understand how global English works differently in different local contexts need to keep three things in mind. First, while survey research can play an important role in pointing sociolinguists in the right direction regarding the burning questions that might be asked about the subject of transidiomatic practices, it is still always essential to situate a theory of global English within what we can learn from detailed analyses of actual language practices. Second, it is important to analyze not just the language practices themselves, but the specific indexicalities of those practices within each local community (for which a complete picture needs to take not just practices, but also ideas and beliefs about those language practices into account). Third, it is just as important to make sure any analysis of language practices and language attitudes can be understood against the backdrop of each complex and layered

284   6 English as a Trans-National Language

specifically *local* ideological context (consisting of long-standing influences from traditions of nationalism and other state traditions, as well as institutionalized and semi-institutionalized traditions of language policies) in which these practices and attitudes are embedded. The analysis in this book stands as my attempt to do each of those things in an integrated way, in an attempt to gain a better understanding of the transidiomatic practices in two particular national social media communities. However, there is more to be said about these findings that go beyond Germany and the Netherlands on the one hand, and beyond social media on the other. We can also gain key insights from them that have implications for a more general theory of global English.

When I first began talking with other people about the social media data in this book and some of the differences I was finding, many people—non-linguists and linguistic scholars alike—engaged me in conversations about specific single factors that they believed could explain those differences. One of these factors was the differing amount of English to which German young people and Dutch young people are exposed, or more specifically, the fact that English-language media are subtitled rather than dubbed in the Netherlands and/or the fact that English is more widely used in higher education in the Netherlands than in Germany. A second suggestion was that the relative sizes of the two countries could be a factor: with a population of around 82 million for Germany and less than 17 million for the Netherlands, there are simply many more speakers of German than Dutch. A third suggestion was that the status of each of these two languages within the world could also be argued to explain the differences, since German has historically had the status of a widely used lingua franca, while Dutch has never played this role.

However, it would be overly simplistic to presume a direct cause-and-effect relationship between any one of these societal factors and differences in the two communities' transidiomatic practices. After all, no one's language practices can be said to be explicitly determined by—for example—whether they hear the original English versions of translated American shows or not when they watch television! Additionally (and perhaps more importantly), semi-institutionalized language practices such as dubbing vs. subtitling do not themselves arise in a cultural vacuum, but are instead influenced by other social and linguistic practices and language ideologies in the society around them. So while it would be a mistake to discount the importance of any one of these factors, they all need to be seen within their wider societal context, as part of a complex interplay of influences.

I return, therefore, to the concept of a language regime that I introduced in Chapter 2 (e.g. Sonntag and Cardinal 2015). This concept allows analysts of language ideologies and language practices to take into account the ways that these are always influenced by state institutions and their historical traditions. Within such a model, state traditions serve to frame both language ideologies and language policies, and this framing, in turn, influences the ways that language users' practices emerge. However, the relationships between each of the components of the model are always dialectical ones, with language ideologies and language policies not only influencing, but being influenced by historical traditions of nationalism, institutionalized language practices, and other relevant factors, as well as each other. A visual conceptualization of this model can be seen in Fig. 6.1.

The two circles together form a given society's language regime. This language regime is made up partly of that society's language ideologies— i.e. its sets of beliefs regarding perceived language structure and use that are regarded as being universally true—at the centre, and partly of various parts of an additional circle of factors that both influence and are influenced by those language ideologies. These factors are:

- institutionalized practices such as the societal choice between dubbing or subtitling when translating non-local-language media, as well as the extent to which other languages are used (and commonly accepted as normal) within the workplace and in higher education,
- a given society's historical traditions of nationalism such as Germany's "state nation" tradition of ethnic nationalism and the Netherlands' "nation state" tradition of civic nationalism with pillarization, each of which has tended to conceptualize the local language as belonging to the nation in some sort of natural correspondence, but in often drastically different ways and with rather different effects,

286 6 English as a Trans-National Language

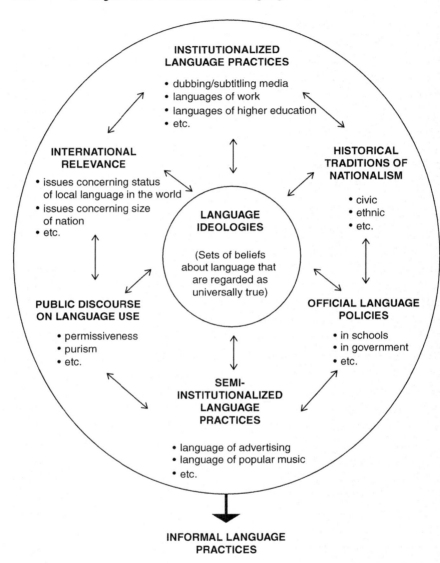

Fig. 6.1 The influence of a language regime on informal language practices

- official language policies regarding which languages are to be used within schools and within government,
- semi-institutionalized language practices such as the languages that tend to get used in sectors such as advertising and popular music,
- public discourse regarding the appropriateness of permissiveness and purism in language use, and
- factors concerning a given society's international relevance such as the size of the country, the number of speakers of its local language, and that language's status respective to other languages within an international context.

Within this model, each of these components crucially stands in a dialectical relationship to each of the others.[1] So, for example, a society's public discourse on language use is both influenced by and influences its language ideologies, both influenced and influenced by its historical traditions of nationalism, both influenced by and influences its official language policies, etc. Informal, everyday language practices—in social media as well as elsewhere—then emerge under the influence of all of these factors interacting simultaneously.

To return to the subtitling vs. dubbing example, then, this implies that a given Dutch young person's experience having always listened to the English soundtrack whilst watching subtitled Anglophone television shows cannot be seen in and of itself as being responsible for producing the kinds of language practices common in the *vragenuurtje* social media community. Such subtitling practices do, however, serve as one contributing factor that brings the English language into this particular Dutch young person's home and her daily life, which in turn promotes and spreads a language ideology that conceives of English as something that is and should be ever-present and ubiquitous; and this, taken in tandem with other interacting factors, influences that individual Dutch

---

[1] The conceptualization of this dialectical relationship is weakest when it comes to the international relevance component—it is difficult to claim, for example, that a society's historical traditions of nationalism literally influences the size of a nation—but it certainly can be said to influence how a nation *perceives* its size relative to other nations and how it deals with what that size might imply.

person's language practices. This relationship is always dialectical, however: the ideologies in Dutch society regarding the position of English may be reinforced by the constant presence of English in Dutch living rooms, but those same ideologies were also drawn on in establishing the normalcy of the semi-institutionalized practice of subtitling in the first place, and will undoubtedly continue to be drawn on if any changes to such policies are to be crafted in the future.

Implications for Language Policy

The influence of English in Europe has increased in recent decades, and there has been a commensurate increase in public debate about how European societies can and should deal officially with the language when it comes to their official policies. These developments affect European Union policies (such as the choice of the language or languages in which the EU is to conduct its business, and the extent to which it is important to make sure that English is not the sole language of EU governance), but they also have effects on policymaking within each individual European country as they make decisions about the extent to which English should be promoted or discouraged within schools, institutions of higher education, workplaces, advertising, print and broadcast media, and so on. Attempts are being made to balance practical considerations with long-term societal interests in considering matters such as the increasing influence of an English-origin lexicon within even formal monolingual contexts, as well as shifts in domains that used to belong exclusively to local languages but where these are now being increasingly encroached on by English as a lingua franca. However, much of this debate is being conducted either without reference to data, or only with reference to survey data. It is my hope that this book—with its attention to both actual language practices and beliefs and ideas about language among two European countries with distinctly different ideological traditions—will increase the knowledge of policymakers about topics such as how European users of English in different countries incorporate English into their everyday conversations, why they do it differently from each other, and what those differences in use imply about English and globalization.

In thinking about the implications of this book's findings for language policymaking, it is important to remember that influence from English is never ideologically neutral. In other words, despite indications that non-native-speaker users of English may often conceive it as such (e.g. Callahan 2005: 284), it is too simplistic to assume that the use of English outside of its native-speaker contexts can actually be said to have been denationalized to the extent that the language has become "a mere tool bereft of cultural capital" (House 2003: 560). When any local language gets "shot through" with English (Blommaert 2010: 60), there are always certain cultural and ideological connotations that are transmitted along with it. However, these connotations are always transformed by the local context, and may therefore play very different roles in that new context than they did in the Anglophone countries where they originated. This means that there are always sociocultural and ideological implications of choosing English-origin transidiomatic practices over local-language equivalents, but at the same time, there cannot be assumed to be a one-to-one correspondence between a higher frequency of the presence of English-origin transidiomatic practices within a particular society (or even a greater use of English as a lingua franca) and greater cultural imperialism. For policymakers, this means that it is important to strike a balance between a laissez-faire approach that assumes that whatever happens without intervention is necessarily the best way of dealing with influence from English, and the kind of blind panic that can often be seen in public discourses about purism and correctness in the face of influence from English in a transnationalizing world. An awareness of the dialectical interactions at work in issues surrounding global English as seen in Fig. 6.1 above—or in other words, the knowledge that each policy decision does not occur in a vacuum but is instead a part of a complex interplay of factors that will have implications for the use of both the local language and English as a transnational language—should be an important part of this balance.

This chapter serves as a summary and a synthesis of the issues raised in the rest of the book, but it also hints at directions for possible future developments. The data in this book comes from two social media

290   6   English as a Trans-National Language

communities and from interviews with community members about the language use in those communities, but a fuller picture of the role that global English plays in the lives of European young people will need to include the same kinds of data from different European countries (reaching north into Scandinavia, south into countries such as France, Italy, and Spain, and east into the former Eastern Bloc countries). This bigger picture will also have to deal with different kinds of data that will allow us to consider possible differences between spoken and written interactions, and between informal and formal ones. In that respect, this book is not meant to stand as any sort of definitive answer to the questions I posed in Chapter 1, but as a launching pad for further research, additional conversations, and greater knowledge.

Bibliography

Alfonzetti, G. (1998) 'The conversational dimension in code-switching between Italian and dialect in Sicily', in P. Auer (ed), *Code-Switching in Conversation: Language, Interaction, and Identity* (London, New York: Routledge), pp. 180–214.

Alvarez–Cáccamo, C. (1996) 'The power of reflexive language(s): code displacement in reported speech', *Journal of Pragmatics*, 25, 33–59.

Alvarez–Cáccamo, C. (1998) 'From "switching code" to "code-switching": towards a reconceptualization of communicative codes', in P. Auer (ed), *Code-Switching in Conversation: Language, Interaction and Identity* (London, New York: Routledge), pp. 29–50.

Ammon, U. (1998) *Ist Deutsch noch internationale Wissenschaftssprache? Englisch auch für die Lehre an den deutschsprachigen Hochschulen* (Berlin, New York: de Gruyter).

Anders, C.A., Hundt, M. and Lasch, A. (eds) (2010) *Perceptual Dialectology. Neue Wege der Dialektologie.* (Amsterdam, Netherlands: de Gruyter).

Androutsopoulos, J. (2006a) 'Introduction: sociolinguistics and computer-mediated communication', Journal *of Sociolinguistics*, 10, 4, 419–38.

Androutsopoulos, J. (2006b) 'Multilingualism, diaspora, and the internet: codes and identities on German–based diaspora websites', *Journal of Sociolinguistics*, 10, 4, 520–47.

© The Author(s) 2017
J. Dailey-O'Cain, *Trans-National English in Social Media Communities*, DOI 10.1057/978-1-137-50615-3

292   Bibliography

Androutsopoulos, J. (2007) 'Bilingualism in the mass media and on the internet', in M. Heller (ed), *Bilingualism: A Social Approach* (London, New York: Palgrave Macmillan), pp. 207–30.

Androutsopoulos, J. (2008) 'Potentials and limitations of discourse-centred online ethnography', *Language@Internet*, 5, article 9.

Androutsopoulos, J. (2010) 'Localizing the global on the participatory web', in N. Coupland, (ed), *The Handbook of Language and Globalization* (Malden, Oxford: Blackwell), pp. 203–31.

Androutsopoulos, J. (2011). 'From variation to heteroglossia in the study of computer–mediated discourse', in C. Thurlow and K. Mroczek (eds), *Digital Discourse: Language in the New Media* (Oxford: Oxford University Press), pp. 277–298.

Androutsopoulos, J. (2015). 'Networked multilingualism: Some language practices on Facebook and their implications', *International Journal of Bilingualism*, 19, 2, 185–205.

Androutsopoulos, J. and Hinnenkamp, V. (2001) 'Code-switching in der bilingualen Chat-Kommunikation: Ein explorativer Blick auf #hellas und #turks', in M. Beißwenger (ed.), *Chat-Kommunikationen* (Stuttgart: Ibidem), pp. 367–402.

Angouri, J. (2016) 'Online communities and communities of practice', in A. Georgakopoulou and T. Spilioti (eds) *The Routledge Handbook of Language and Digital Communication* (London, New York: Routledge), pp. 323–338.

Arnaut, K., Blommaert, J., Rampton, B., and Spotti, M. (eds) (2015) *Language and Superdiversity* (London, New York: Routledge).

Auer, P. (1995) 'The pragmatics of code-switching: a sequential approach', in L. Milroy and P. Muysken (eds), *One Speaker, Two Languages: Cross-Disciplinary Perspectives on Code-Switching* (Cambridge: Cambridge University Press), pp. 115–135.

Auer, P. (1998) 'Introduction: *bilingual conversation* revisited', in P. Auer (ed.) *Code-Switching in Conversation: Language, Interaction, and Identity* (New York, London: Routledge), pp. 1–24.

Auer, P. (2007) 'The monolingual bias in bilingualism research, or: why bilingual talk is (still) a challenge for linguistics', in M. Heller (ed.), *Bilingualism, A Social Approach* (London, New York: Palgrave Macmillan), pp. 319–39.

Bailey, B. (2007) 'Heteroglossia and boundaries', in M. Heller (ed.), *Bilingualism, A Social Approach* (London, New York: Palgrave Macmillan), pp. 257–74.

Bibliography 293

Baker, C. (1992) *Attitudes and Language* (Bristol: Multilingual Matters).

Barbour, S. (2005) 'Contemporary English influence on German—a perspective from linguistics', in G. Anderman and M. Rogers (eds), *In and Out of English: For Better, For Worse?* (Clevedon: Multilingual Matters), pp. 153–60.

Baron, N.S. (2000) *Alphabet to Email: How Written English Evolved and Where It's Heading* (London, New York: Routledge).

Baron, N. S. (2008) *Always On: Language in an Online and Mobile World* (Oxford, New York: Oxford University Press).

Barrett, R. (2006) 'Language ideology and racial inequality: Competing functions of Spanish in an Anglo-owned Mexican restaurant', *Language in Society*, 35, 163–204.

Barton, D. and Lee, C. (2013) *Language Online: Investigating Digital Texts and Practices* (London, New York: Routledge).

Bastardas-Boada, A. (2012) *Language and Identity Policies in the 'Glocal' Age: New Processes, Effects, and Principles of Organization* (Barcelona: Generalitat de Catalunya Institut d'Estudis Autonomics).

Baym, N.K. (1998) 'The emergence of on-line community', in S. Jones (ed), *CyberSociety 2.0. Revisiting Computer-Mediated Communication and Community* (London: Sage), pp. 35–68.

Baym, N. K. (2015) *Personal Connections in the Digital Age* (second edition) (Cambridge, Malden: Polity).

Beck, E. (1999) 'Language rights and Turkish children in Germany', *Patterns of Prejudice*, 33, 2, 3–12.

Benwell, B. and Stokoe, E. (2006) *Discourse and Identity* (Edinburgh: Edinburgh University Press).

Berns, M., Claes, M.-T., de Bot, K., Evers, R., Hasebrink, U., Huibregtse, I., Truchot, C., and van der Wijst, P. (2007) 'English in Europe', in M. Berns, K. De Bot, and U. Hasebrink (eds), *In the Presence of English: Media and European Youth* (New York: Springer) pp. 16–42.

Björkman, B. (2016a) 'English as a lingua franca in the business domain', in A. Linn (ed.), *Investigating English in Europe: Contexts and Agendas* (Amsterdam: Mouton de Gruyter), 89–92.

Björkman, B. (2016b) 'Policies in the European Higher Education Arena', in A. Linn (ed.), *Investigating English in Europe: Contexts and Agendas* (Amsterdam: Mouton de Gruyter), 145–52.

Bjornson, M. (2007) 'Speaking of citizenship: language ideologies in Dutch citizenship regimes', *Focaal—European Journal of Anthropology*, 49, 65–80.

294 Bibliography

Blommaert, J. (2003) 'Commentary: a sociolinguistics of globalization', *Journal of Sociolinguistics*, 7, 4, 607–23.

Blommaert, J. (2010) *The Sociolinguistics of Globalization* (Cambridge: Cambridge University Press).

Blommaert, J. and Rampton, B. (2011) 'Language and superdiversity', *Diversities*, 13, 2: 1–20.

Boyd, D. (2011) 'Social network sites as networked publics: affordances, dynamics, and implications', in Z. Papacharissi (ed.), *A Networked Self: Identity, Community, and Culture on Social Network Sites* (London, New York: Routledge), pp. 39–58.

Breiteneder, A. (2009) 'English as a lingua franca in Europe: an empirical perspective', *World Englishes*, 28, 2, 256–69.

Broersma, M., and de Bot, K. (2006). 'Triggered codeswitching: A corpus-based evaluation of the original triggering hypothesis and a new alternative', *Bilingualism: Language and Cognition* 9, 1, 1–13.

Callahan, L. (2005) '"Talking both languages": 20 perspectives on the use of Spanish and English inside and outside the workplace', *Journal of Multilingual and Multicultural Development*, 26, 4, 275–95.

Chanseawrassamee, S. and Shin, S. (2009). 'Participant and discourse-related code-switching by Thai-English bilingual adolescents', *Multilingua - Journal of Cross-Cultural and Interlanguage Communication* 28 (1, February), 45–78.

Claus, P., and Taeldeman, J. (1989) 'De infiltratie van Engelse (leen) woorden in het Nederlands en in Nederlandse woorden boeken', in S. Theissen and J. Vromans (eds), *Album Moors: Een bundel opstellen aangeboden aan Joseph Moors ter gelegenheid van zijn 75ste verjaardag* (Liège, Belgium: C.I.P.L.), pp. 11–30.

Clayman, S. E. and Gill, V. T. (2014) 'Conversation analysis', in J.P. Gee and M. Handford (eds), *The Routledge Handbook of Discourse Analysis* (London, New York: Routledge), pp. 120–134.

Clyne, M. (1967). *Transference and Triggering: Observations on the Language Assimilation of Postwar German-Speaking Migrants in Australia*. Den Haag: Martinus Nijhoff.

Coleman, J. A. (2006) 'English-medium teaching in European higher education', *Language Teaching*, 39, 1–14.

Coupland, N. (2010) 'Introduction: sociolinguistics in the global era', in N. Coupland (ed.), *The Handbook of Language and Globalization* (Malden, Oxford: Blackwell), pp. 1–28.

Bibliography   **295**

Coupland, N. and Jaworski, A. (2004) 'Sociolinguistic perspectives on metalanguage: reflexivity, evaluation and ideology', in A. Jaworski, N. Coupland, and D. Galasinski (eds), *Metalanguage: Social and Ideological Perspectives* (Berlin, New York: Mouton de Gruyter), pp. 15–51.

Crystal, D. (2006) *Language and the Internet* (second edition) (Cambridge: Cambridge University Press).

Cuonz, C. and Studler, R. (eds) (2014) *Sprechen über Sprache: Perspektiven und neue Methoden der Spracheinstellungsforschung* (Tübingen: Stauffenburg Linguistik).

Dailey-O'Cain, J. (2013) 'The use and the discursive functions of English in native-language online conversations among Dutch and German youth', *Sociolinguistica*, 27, (special issue *New Media Spaces, New Media Practices, and New Language Communities*), 147–67.

Dailey-O'Cain, J. and Liebscher, G. (2009). 'Teacher and student use of the first language in foreign language classroom interaction: functions and applications', in M. Turnbull and J. Dailey-O'Cain (eds), *First Language Use in Second and Foreign Language Learning* (Bristol, Buffalo, Toronto: Multilingual Matters), pp. 131–44.

Danet, B. (2001) *Cyberplay: Communicating Online* (Oxford: Berg).

Danet, B. and Herring, S.C. (2007) 'Introduction: welcome to the multilingual internet', in B. Danet and S.C. Herring (eds), *The Multilingual Internet: Language, Culture, and Communication Online* (Oxford: Oxford University Press), pp. 3–42.

de Bot, K. (1994) 'Waarom deze rede niet in het Engels is.' Speech given at the attainment of Professor of Applied Linguistics at the Catholic University of Nijmegen on Friday 9 December 1994. 's Hertogenbosch, Nijmegen: CJL De Bot.

De Swaan, A. (2000) 'Why this is in English (and not in German, nor in Dutch)', Schumann Lecture, Maastricht University, accessed 12 February 2016. http://deswaan.com/why-is-this-in-english-and-not-in-german-nor-in-dutch/

De Vries Jr., H. J. (2008) 'Dutch: is it threatened by English?', in J. Rosenhouse and R. Kowner (eds), *Globally Speaking: Motives for Adopting English Vocabulary in Other Languages* (Clevedon: Multilingual Matters), pp. 68–81.

del-Teso-Craviotto, M. (2006) 'Language and sexuality in Spanish and English dating chats', *Journal of Sociolinguistics*, 10, 4, 460–80.

Deumert, A. (2014) *Sociolinguistics and Mobile Communication* (Edinburgh: Edinburgh University Press).

296 Bibliography

Dodd, W. (2015) 'Under pressure? The Anglicisms debate in contemporary Germany as a barometer of German national identity today', *German Politics and Society*, 114, 33, 1/2 (Spring/Summer), 58–68.

DuBois, J.W. (2007) 'The stance triangle' in R. Englebretson (ed.), *Stancetaking in Discourse: Subjectivity, Evaluation, Interaction* (Amsterdam, Philadelphia: John Benjamins), pp. 139–82.

Dyson, K. (1980) *The State Tradition in Western Europe* (Oxford, New York: Oxford University Press).

Edwards, A. (2014) 'English in the Netherlands: functions, forms, and attitudes'. Unpublished Ph.D. dissertation, Cambridge University.

Entzinger, H. (2006) 'Changing the rules while the game is on: from multiculturalism to assimilation in the Netherlands', in Y.M. Bodemann, and G. Yurdakul (eds), *Migration, Citizenship, Ethnos* (London, New York: Palgrave Macmillan), pp. 121–44.

Erling, E.J. and Hilgendorf, S.K. (2006) 'English in the German university: a means of disadvantage or empowerment?', in A. Weideman and B. Smieja (eds) *Empowerment through Language and Education: Cases and Case Studies from North America, Europe, Africa and Japan* (Frankfurt am Main: Peter Lang), pp. 113–28.

Etzioni, A. (1991) 'Too many rights, too few responsibilities', *Society*, 28, 2, 41–8.

Extra, G. and Yağğmur, K. (eds) (2004) *Urban Multilingualism in Europe: Immigrant Minority Languages at Home and School* (Clevedon: Multilingual Matters).

Fialkova, L. (2005) 'Emigrants from the FSU and the Russian-language Internet', *Toronto Slavic Quarterly*, 32. Available at http://sites.utoronto.ca/tsq/12/fialkova12.shtml, retrieved 19 February 2016.

Gal, S., and Irvine, J. (1995) 'The boundaries of languages and disciplines: How ideologies construct difference', *Social Research*, 62, 4, 967–1001.

Garrett, P. (2005) 'Attitude measurement', in U. Ammon, N. Dittmar, K. J. Mattheier, and P. Trudgill (eds), *Sociolinguistics. An International Handbook of the Science of Language and Society* (Berlin: de Gruyter), pp. 1251–1260.

Gass, S. and Mackey, A. (2000) *Stimulated Recall Methodology in Second Language Research* (Mahwah, NJ: Erlbaum).

Geddes, A. (2001) *Ethnic Minorities in the Labour Market. Comparative Policy Approaches (Western Europe), Report commissioned by the Ethnic Minorities in the Labour Market Project of the Performance and Innovation Unit* (London: Cabinet Office).

Bibliography   297

Geddes, A. (2003) *The Politics of Migration and Immigration in Europe* (London, Thousand Oaks, New Delhi: Sage).

Gee, J.P. (2004) *Situated Language and Learning: A Critique of Traditional Schooling* (London, New York: Routledge).

Georgakopoulou, A. (1997) 'Self-presentation and interactional alignments in e-mail discourse: The style- and code switches of Greek messages', *International Journal of Applied Linguistics*, 7, 2, 141–64.

Georgakopoulou, A. (2007) *Small Stories, Interaction, and Identities* (Amsterdam, Philadelphia: John Benjamins).

Georgakopoulou, A. and Spilioti, T. (eds) (2016a) *The Routledge Handbook of Language and Digital Communication* (London, New York: Routledge).

Georgakopoulou, A. and Spilioti, T. (2016b) 'Introduction', in A. Georgakopoulou and T. Spilioti (eds) *The Routledge Handbook of Language and Digital Communication* (London, New York: Routledge), pp. 1–15.

Gerritsen, M. (1995) '"English" advertisements in the Netherlands, Germany, France, Italy, and Spain', in B. Machová and S. Kubátová (eds) *Sietar Europa 1995 Proceedings: Uniqueness in Unity: The Significance of Cultural Identity in European Cooperation* (Munich: Sietar Europa). pp. 324–41.

Gerritsen, M., Nickerson, C., Van Hooft, A., Van Meurs, F., Nederstigt, U., Starren, M., and Crijns, R. (2007) 'English in product advertisements in Belgium, France, Germany, the Netherlands, and Spain', *World Englishes*, 26, 3, 291–315.

Giles, H. and Ryan, E.B. (1982) 'Prolegomena for developing a social psychological theory of language attitudes', in E.B. Ryan and H. Giles (eds) *Attitudes Towards Language Variation. Social and Applied Contexts* (London: Edward Arnold), pp. 208–23.

Glahn, R. (2002) *Der Einfluss des Englischen auf gesprochene deutsche Gegenwartssprache* (Frankfurt am Main: Peter Lang).

Gnutzmann, C., Jakisch, J., Koenders, J., and Rabe, F. (2012) 'Englisch als Verkehrssprache in Europa—identitätsstiftendes Medium für junge Europäer?', *Fremdsprachen Lehren und Lernen*, 41, 2, 60–83.

Goffman, E. (1959) *The Presentation of Self in Everyday Life* (New York: Anchor Books).

Goffman, E. (1979) 'Footing', *Semiotica*, 25, 1–29.

Gramling, D. (2009) 'The new cosmopolitan monolingualism: on linguistic citizenship in twenty-first century Germany', *Die Unterrichtspraxis / Teaching German*, 42, 2, Fall, 130–140.

298 Bibliography

Grice, H.P. 1975 (1989) 'Logic and conversation', reprinted in H.P. Grice (ed), *Studies in the Way of Words*, (Cambridge, MA: Harvard University Press), pp. 22–40.

Guerini, F. (2006) *Language Alternation Strategies in Multilingual Settings—A Case Study: Ghanaian Immigrants in Northern Italy* (Frankfurt am Main: Peter Lang).

Gumperz, J.J. (1982) *Discourse Strategies* (Cambridge: Cambridge University Press).

Harré, R. and van Langenhove, L. (1991) 'Varieties of positioning', *Journal of the Theory of Social Behaviour*, 21, 4, 393–407.

Hasebrink, U. (2007) 'English, youth, and media environments', in M. Berns, K. De Bot, and U. Hasebrink (eds) *In the Presence of English: Media and European Youth* (New York: Springer), pp. 88–110.

Hasebrink, U., Berns, M., and de Bot, K. (2007) 'In the presence of English: a resume after step one of an international study', M. Berns, K. De Bot, and U. Hasebrink (eds) *In the Presence of English: Media and European Youth* (New York: Springer), pp. 111–119.

Heller, M. (2007a) 'Bilingualism as ideology and practice', in M. Heller (ed), *Bilingualism, A Social Approach* (London, New York: Palgrave Macmillan), pp. 1–22.

Heller, M. (2007b) 'Multilingualism and transnationalism', in P. Auer and W. Li (eds) *Handbook of Multilingualism and Multilingual Communication* (Berlin: Mouton de Gruyter), pp. 539–53.

Herring, S. C. (2001) 'Computer–mediated discourse', in D. Schiffrin, D. Tannen, and H. E. Hamilton (eds), *The Handbook of Discourse Analysis* (Maldon, MA: Blackwell), pp. 612–34.

Herring, S. C. (2004) 'Computer–mediated discourse analysis: an approach to researching online behavior', in S. Barab, R. King, and J. Grey (eds), *Designing for Virtual Communities in the Service of Learning* (New York: Cambridge University Press), pp. 338–376.

Herring, S.C. (2007) 'A faceted classification scheme for computer–mediated discourse', *Language@Internet*, 1, article 1.

Herring, S. C., Scheidt, L. A., Bonus, S., and Wright, E. (2004) 'Bridging the gap: a genre analysis of weblogs', in *Proceedings of the 37th Hawaii International Conference on Systems Science* (Los Alamitos: IEEE Press), pp. 1–11.

Herring, S. C., Paolillo, J.C., Ramos-Vielba, I., Kouper, I., Wright, E. L., and Stoerger, S. (2007) 'Language networks on LiveJournal', in *Proceedings of the*

40th Hawaii International Conference on System Sciences (Los Alamitos, CA: IEEE Press), pp. 79–90.

Hilgendorf, S.K. (2010) 'English and the global market: the language's impact in the German business domain', in: H. Kelly-Holmes and G. Mautner (eds) *Language and the Market* (London, New York: Palgrave Macmillan), pp. 68–80.

Hilgendorf, S.K. (2013). 'Transnational media and the use of English: the case of cinema and motion picture titling practices in Germany', *Sociolinguistica*, 27 (special issue *New Media Spaces, New Media Practices, and New Language Communities*), 167–86.

Hilgendorf, S.K. and Martin, E.A. (2001) 'English in advertising: update for France and Germany', in E. Thumboo (ed), *The Three Circles of English: Language Specialists Talk about the English Language* (Singapore: Unipress, National University of Singapore), pp. 217–40.

Hinchcliffe, D. (2006) 'The state of Web 2.0', *Web Services Journal*. Available at: http://web2.socialcomputingjournal.com/the_state_of_web_20.htm (accessed on January 24, 2010).

Hinrichs, L. (2006) *Codeswitching on the Web: English and Jamaican Creole in E-Mail Communication* (Amsterdam: Benjamins).

Holden, N. (2016) 'English in multilingual English economic space', in A. Linn (ed), *Investigating English in Europe: Contexts and Agendas* (Amsterdam: Mouton de Gruyter), 40–50.

Horst, H. A. and Miller, D. (eds) (2012) *Digital Anthropology* (London, New York: Berg).

House, J. (2003) 'English as a lingua franca, a threat to multilingualism?', *Journal of Sociolinguistics*, 7, 4, 556–78.

Jacquemet, M. (2005) 'Transidiomatic practices: language and power in the age of globalization', *Language and Communication*, 25, 257–77.

Jacquemet, M. (2010) 'Language and transnational spaces', in P. Auer and J.E. Schmidt (eds), *Language and Space: An International Handbook of Linguistic Variation*, (volume 1: Theories and Methods) (Berlin, New York: De Gruyter), pp. 50–69.

Jaspers, J. (2014) 'Interactional sociolinguistics and discourse analysis', in J.P. Gee and M. Handford (eds), *The Routledge Handbook of Discourse Analysis* (London, New York: Routledge), pp. 135–46.

Jaworski, A., Coupland, N., and Galasinski, D. (2004) 'Metalanguage: why now?', in A. Jaworski, N. Coupland, and D. Galasinski (eds), *Metalanguage: Social and Ideological Perspectives* (Berlin, New York: De Gruyter), pp. 3–8.

300 Bibliography

Jeeves, A. (2014) 'The relevance of English language instruction in a changing linguistic environment in Iceland: the L2 self of young Icelanders', *Multilingua*, 33, 3–4, 267–90.

Jenkins, J. (2009) 'English as a lingua franca: interpretations and attitudes', *World Englishes*, 28, 2, 200–7.

Jenkins, J. (2013) *English as a Lingua Franca in the International University: The Politics of Academic English Policy* (London, New York: Routledge).

Jewitt, C. (2016) 'Multimodal analysis', in A. Georgakopoulou and T. Spilioti (eds) *The Routledge Handbook of Language and Digital Communication* (London, New York: Routledge), pp. 69–84.

Jones, S.G. (1995) 'Understanding community in the information age', in S.G. Jones (ed.), *CyberSociety: Computer-Mediated Communication and Community* (Thousand Oaks, CA, London: Sage), pp. 10–35.

Jones, R.H. and Hafner, C.A. (2012) *Understanding Digital Literacies: A Practical Introduction* (London, New York: Routledge)

Jørgensen, J.N., Karrebaek, M.S., Madsen, L.M., and Møller, J.S. (2011) 'Polylanguaging in superdiversity', *Diversities*, 13, 2: 23–37.

Kachru, B.B. (1985) 'Standards, codification, and sociolinguistic realism: The English language in the outer circle', in R. Quirk and H.G. Widdowson (eds), *English in the World: Teaching and Learning the Language and Literatures* (Cambridge: The British Council), pp. 11–30.

Kachru, B.B. (1992) *The Other Tongue: English Across Cultures* (Champaign-Urbana: University of Illinois Press).

Kelly-Holmes, H. (2006) 'Multilingualism and commercial language practices on the Internet', *Journal of Sociolinguistics*, 10, 4, 507–19.

Kelly-Holmes, H. (2013) '"Choose your language!" Categorization and control in cyberspace', *Sociolinguistica*, 27 (special issue *New Media Spaces, New Media Practices, and New Language Communities)*, 132–45.

Kirkpatrick, A. (2006) 'Which model of English: native speaker, nativised or lingua franca?', in M. Saraceni and R. Rubdy (eds), *English in the World: Global Rules, Global Roles* (London: Continuum Press), pp. 71–83.

Kouper, I. (2010). 'The pragmatics of peer advice in a livejournal community'. *Language @Internet*, 7, article 1.

Koutsogiannis, D. and Mitsikopoulou, B. (2007) 'Greeklish and Greekness: trends and discourses of "glocalness"', in B. Danet and S.C. Herring (eds), *The Multilingual Internet: Language, Culture, and Communication Online* (Oxford: Oxford University Press), pp. 142–60.

Bibliography 301

Kress, G. (2010) *Multimodality: A Social Semiotic Approach To Contemporary Communication* (London, New York: Routledge).

Kress, G. (2014) 'Multimodal discourse analysis', in J.P. Gee and M. Handford (eds), *The Routledge Handbook of Discourse Analysis* (London, New York: Routledge), pp. 35–50.

Küppers, A. and Yağmur, K. (2014) 'Why multilingual matters: alternative language change agents in language education policy' (Istanbul: Istanbul Policy Center). Available at: http://ipc.sabanciuniv.edu/en/wp–content/uploads/2014/07/14580_IPMAlmutRaporWEB.07.07.14REV1.pdf

Kytölä, S. (2016) 'Translocality', in A. Georgakopoulou and T. Spilioti (eds) *The Routledge Handbook of Language and Digital Communication* (London, New York: Routledge), pp. 371–88.

Lambert, W.E., Hodgson, R., Gardner, R.C., and Fillenbaum, S. (1960) 'Evaluational reactions to spoken languages', *Journal of Abnormal and Social Psychology* 60, 1: 44–51.

Lee, C. (2016) 'Multilingual resources and practices in digital communication', in A. Georgakopoulou and T. Spilioti (eds) *The Routledge Handbook of Language and Digital Communication* (London, New York: Routledge), pp. 118–132.

Li, W. (1998) 'The "why" and "how" questions in the analysis of conversational code-switching', in P. Auer (ed), *Code-Switching in Conversation: Language, Interaction, and Identity* (London, New York: Routledge), pp. 156–176.

Li, W. (2011) 'Moment Analysis and translanguaging space: discursive construction of identities by multilingual Chinese youth in Britain', *Journal of Pragmatics*, 43, 1222–35.

Liebscher, G. and Dailey-O'Cain, J. (2004), 'Learner code-switching in the content-based foreign language classroom', *The Canadian Modern Language Review*, 60, 4, 501–25.

Liebscher, G. and Dailey-O'Cain, J. (2009), 'Language attitudes in interaction', *Journal of Sociolinguistics*, 13, 2, 195–222.

Liebscher, G. and Dailey-O'Cain, J. (2013) *Language, Space, and Identity in Migration* (London, New York: Palgrave Macmillan).

Maheux-Pelletier, G. and Golato, A. (2008) 'Repair in membership categorization in French', *Language in Society*, 37, 5, 689–712.

Martin, P.L. (2004) 'Germany: managing migration in the twenty-first century', in J. Hollifield, P. Martin, and P. Orrenius (eds), *Controlling Immigration: A Global Perspective* (2nd ed) (Stanford, CA: Stanford University Press), pp. 221–53.

302 **Bibliography**

McClure, E. (2001) 'Oral and written Assyrian codeswitching', in R. Jacobsen (ed.), *Trends in Linguistics: Studies and Monographs*, 126, pp. 157–91.

Meyerhoff, M. and Niedzielski, N. (2003) 'The globalisation of vernacular variation', *Journal of Sociolinguistics*, 7, 4, 534–55.

Miller, D. (2012) 'Social networking sites', in H.A. Horst and D. Miller (eds), *Digital Anthropology* (London, New York: Berg), pp. 146–61.

Muus, P. (2004) 'Dutch immigration policy: a pragmatic adjustment', in J. Hollifield, P. Martin, and P. Orrenius (eds), *Controlling Immigration: A Global Perspective* (2nd ed) (Stanford, CA: Stanford University Press), pp. 262–88.

Nickerson, C. (2000) *Playing the Corporate Language Game. An Investigation of the Genres and Discourse Strategies in English Used by Dutch Writers Working in Multinational Corporations* (Amsterdam, Atlanta: Rodopi).

Nishimura, Y. (2007) 'Linguistic innovations and interactional features in Japanese BBS communication', in B. Danet and S.C. Herring (eds), *The Multilingual Internet: Language, Culture, and Communication Online* (Oxford: Oxford University Press), pp. 163–83.

Nishimura, Y. (2016) 'Style, creativity, and play', in A. Georgakopoulou and T. Spilioti (eds) *The Routledge Handbook of Language and Digital Communication* (London, New York: Routledge), pp. 103–117.

Myers-Scotton, C. (1993) *Duelling Languages: Grammatical Structure in Code-switching* (Oxford: Oxford University Press).

O'Hara-Davies, B. (2010) 'The paradox of English', *Journal of Multilingual and Multicultural Development*, 31, 2, 107–18.

Onysko, A. (2007) *Anglicisms in German: Borrowing, Lexical Productivity, and Written Codeswitching* (Berlin, New York: De Gruyter).

Onskyo, A. (2009) 'Exploring discourse on globalizing English: a case study of discourse on anglicisms in German', *English Today*, 97, 25–36.

Page, R. (2016) 'Moving between the big and the small: identity and interaction in digital contexts', in A. Georgakopoulou and T. Spilioti (eds) *The Routledge Handbook of Language and Digital Communication* (London, New York: Routledge), pp. 403–11.

Pan, L. and Block, D. (2011) 'English as a "global language" in China: An investigation into learners' and teachers' language beliefs', *System*, 39, 3: 391–402.

Paolillo, J.C. (2007) 'How much multilingualism? language diversity on the internet', in B. Danet and S.C. Herring (eds), *The Multilingual Internet:*

Bibliography 303

Language, Culture, and Communication Online (Oxford: Oxford University Press), pp. 408–30.

Papacharissi, Z (ed). (2011) *A Networked Self: Identity, Community, and Culture on Social Network Sites* (London, New York: Routledge).

Park, J. S. and Wee, L. (2012) *Markets of English: Linguistic Capital and Language Policy in a Globalizing World* (London, New York: Routledge).

Parks, M. R. (2011) 'Social network sites as virtual communities', in Z. Papacharissi (ed.), *A Networked Self. Identity, Community, and Culture on Social Network Sites* (London, New York: Routledge), pp. 105–23.

Parmegiani, A. (2008) 'Language ownership in multilingual settings: exploring attitudes among students entering the University of KwaZulu-Natal through the Access Program', *Stellenbosch Papers in Linguistics*, 38, 107–24.

Penninx, R. (1996) 'Immigration, minorities policy and multiculturalism in Dutch society since 1960', in R. Bauböck, A. Heller, and A.R. Holberg (eds), *The Challenge of Diversity: Integration and Pluralism in Societies of Immigration* (Aldershot, Brookfield USA: Avebury), pp. 187–206.

Pennycook, A. (2007) *Global Englishes and Transcultural Flows* (London, New York: Routledge).

Peuronen, S. (2011) '"Ride hard, live forever": translocal identities in an online community of extreme sports Christians', in C. Thurlow and K. Mroczek (eds), *Digital Discourse: Language in the New Media* (Oxford: Oxford University Press). pp. 154–76.

Phillipson, R. (1992) *Linguistic Imperialism* (Oxford: Oxford University Press).

Phillipson, R. (2004) *English-Only Europe: Challenging Language Policy* (London, New York: Routledge).

Phillipson, R. (2006) 'English, a cuckoo in the nest of languages?', *European Journal of English Studies*, 10, 1, 13–32.

Poplack, Shana (1980): Sometimes I'll start a sentence in Spanish y termino en español: toward a typology of code-switching. In: Linguistics 18: 581–618.

Poplack, S. (1988) 'Contrasting patterns of code-switching in two communities', in M. Heller (ed.), *Codeswitching: Anthropological and Sociolinguistic Perspectives* (Berlin: de Gruyter), pp. 215–44.

Poplack, Shana., Sankoff, David., & Miller, Chris. (1988). The social correlates and linguistic processes of lexical borrowing and assimilation. Linguistics, 26 (1), 47–104.

Poplack, S. and Meechan, M (eds) (1998) *Instant Loans, Easy Conditions: The Productivity of Bilingual Borrowing. Special Issue of the International Journal of Bilingualism* (London: Kingston Press).

304 Bibliography

Potter, J. and Wetherell, M. (1987) *Discourse and Social Psychology* (London: Sage).

Pratt, M.L. (1987) 'Linguistic utopias', in N. Fabb, D. Attridge, A. Durant and C. MacCabe (eds), *The Linguistics of Writing* (Manchester: Manchester University Press). pp. 48–66.

Preisler, B. (1999) 'Functions and forms of English in a European EFL country', in T. Bex and R.J. Watts (eds), *Standard English: The Widening Debate* (London, New York: Routledge), pp. 239–67.

Preston, D. (1999) 'A language attitude approach to the perception of regional variety', in D. Preston (ed.), *Handbook of Perceptual Dialectology*, Volume 1 (Amsterdam, Philadelphia: Benjamins), pp. 359–73.

Pujolar, J. (2007) 'Bilingualism and the nation-state in the post-national era', in M. Heller (ed.), *Bilingualism: A Social Approach* (London, New York: Palgrave Macmillan), pp. 71–95.

Rampton, Ben (2005) *Crossing: Language and Ethnicity Among Adolescents* (second edition) (London: Longman).

Rettberg, J.W. (2008) *Blogging* (Cambridge, UK: Polity).

Rheingold, H. (1993) *The Virtual Community: Homesteading on the Electronic Frontier* (Reading, MA: Addison-Wesley).

Robertson, R. (1995) 'Glocalization: time-space and homogeneity-heterogeneity', in M. Featherstone, S. Lash, and R. Robertson (eds), *Global Modernities* (London: Sage), pp. 25–44.

Roudometof, V. (2005) 'Transnationalism, cosmopolitanism, and glocalization', *Current Sociology*, 53, 1, January, 113–35.

Safran, W. (2015) 'Reflections on states and the uses of language policy', in S. K. Sonntag and L. Cardinal (eds), *State Traditions and Language Regimes* (Montreal, Kingston: McGill-Queens University Press), pp. 253–68.

Saraceni, M. (2010) *The Relocation of English: Shifting Paradigms in a Global Era* (London, New York: Palgrave Macmillan).

Saraceni, M. (2015) *World Englishes: A Critical Analysis* (London, New Delhi, New York, Sydney: Bloomsbury).

Schelper, D. (1995) 'Anglizismen in der Pressesprache der BRD, der DDR, Österreichs und der Schweiz: eine vergleichende, typologische und chronologische Studie.' Unpublished Ph.D. dissertation, University of Laval.

Schneider, B. (2014) *Salsa, Language, and Transnationalism* (Bristol, Buffalo, Toronto: Multilingual Matters).

Bibliography   305

Sebba, M. (2003) '"Will the real impersonator please stand up?" Language and identity in the Ali G websites', *Arbeiten aus Anglistik und Amerikanistik*, 28, 2, 279–304.

Seargeant, P. (2009) 'Language ideology, language theory, and the regulation of linguistic behaviour', *Language Sciences*, 31, 345–59.

Seidlhofer, B. (2005) 'English as a lingua franca', *ELT Journal*, 59, 4, October, 339–41.

Sériot, P. (2013) 'Language and nation: two models', in V.-A. Vikman and K. Praakli, *Negotiating Linguistic Identity: Language and Belonging in Europe* (Frankfurt am Main: Peter Lang), pp. 255–72.

Silverstein, M. (1979) 'Language structure and linguistic ideology', in R. Cline, W. Hanks, and C. Hofbauer (eds), *The Elements: A Parasession on Linguistic Units and Levels* (Chicago: University of Chicago Press), pp. 193–247.

Skutnabb-Kangas, T. and Phillipson, R. (2010) 'The global politics of language: markets, maintenance, marginalization, or murder?', in N. Coupland (ed), *The Handbook of Language and Globalization* (Malden, Oxford: Blackwell), pp. 77–100.

Soler-Carbonell, J. (2016) 'English in the language ecology of Europe', in A. Linn (ed), *Investigating English in Europe: Contexts and Agendas* (Amsterdam: Mouton de Gruyter), 53–8.

Sonntag, S.K. and Cardinal, L. (2015) 'Introduction: state traditions and language regimes: conceptualizing language policy choices', in S.K. Sonntag and L. Cardinal (eds), *State Traditions and Language Regimes* (Montreal, Kingston: McGill/Queens University Press), pp. 3–28.

Spitzmüller, J. (2005) *Metasprachdiskurse: Einstellungen zu Anglizismen und ihre wissenschaftliche Rezeption* (Berlin, New York: De Gruyter).

Stevenson, P. (2015) 'The language question in contemporary Germany: the challenges of multilingualism', *German Politics and Society*, 114, 33, 1/2 (Spring/Summer), 69–83.

Stommel, W. (2008) 'Conversation analysis and community of practice as approaches to studying online community', *Language@Internet*, article 5.

Stroud, C. (2007) 'Bilingualism: colonialism and postcolonialism', in M. Heller (ed.), *Bilingualism: A Social Approach* (London, New York: Palgrave Macmillan), pp. 25–49.

Thelen, M. (2005) 'Translating into English as a non-native language: the Dutch connection', in G. Anderman and M. Rogers (eds), *In and Out of English: For Better, For Worse* (Clevedon, Buffalo, Toronto: Multilingual Matters), pp. 242–55.

306   Bibliography

Thurlow, C. and Mroczek, K. (eds) (2011) *Digital Discourse: Language in the New Media* (Oxford: Oxford University Press).

Tsiplakou, S. (2009) 'Doing (bi)lingualism: Language alternation as a performative construction of online identities', *Pragmatics*, 19, 3, 361–391.

Van Hoorde, J. (2013) 'Competing, complementary, or both? English as a lingua franca and the position of Dutch', *Sociolinguistica*, 28, 1, 9–24.

van der Sijs, N. (1998) *Geleend en uitgeleend: Nederlandse woorden in andere talen en andersom* (Amsterdam, Antwerpen: Het Taalfonds).

van der Sijs, N. (2012) 'Engelse leenwoorden revisited: hoeveel wordt het Nederlands gemixt met Engels?', *Onze Taal*, 5, 132–4.

van Leeuwen, T. (2004) 'Ten reasons why linguists should pay attention to visual communication', in P. Levine and R. Scollon Ron (eds), *Discourse and Technology: Multimodal Discourse Analysis* (Washington, DC: Georgetown University Press), pp. 7–19.

Varis, P. (2016) 'Digital ethnography', in A. Georgakopoulou and T. Spilioti (eds) *The Routledge Handbook of Language and Digital Communication* (London, New York: Routledge), pp. 55–68.

Varis, P. and Wang, X. (2011) 'Superdiversity on the internet: a case from China', *Diversities*, 13, 2, 71–83.

Vertovec, S. (1999) 'Conceiving and researching transnationalism', *Ethnic and Racial Studies*, 22, 2, 447–62.

Vertovec, S. (2007) 'Super-diversity and its implications', *Ethnic and Racial Studies*, 30, 6, 1024–54.

Vertovec, S. (2009) *Transnationalism* (London, New York: Routledge).

Vihman, V.-A. and Barkhoff, J. (2013) 'Introduction: the shaping of linguistic identity in Europe', in V.-A. Vikman and K. Praakli (eds), *Negotiating Linguistic Identity: Language and Belonging in Europe* (Frankfurt am Main: Peter Lang), pp. 1–31.

Waldinger, R. and Fitzgerald, D. (2004) 'Transnationalism in question', *American Journal of Sociology*, 109, 5, 1177–95.

Walsh, J. (2015) 'The Irish language regime and language ideology in Ireland', in S.K. Sonntag and L. Cardinal (eds), *State Traditions and Language Regimes* (Montreal, Kingston: McGill-Queens University Press), pp. 62–78.

Walther, J.B., Carr, C.T., Choi, S.S.W., DeAndrea, D.C., Kim, J., Tong, S.T., and Van Der Heide, B. (2011) 'Interaction of interpersonal, peer, and media influence sources online', in Z. Papacharissi (ed.), *A Networked Self: Identity, Community, and Culture on Social Network Sites* (London,New York: Routledge), pp. 17–38.

Bibliography 307

Warschauer, M., El Said, G.R., and Zohry, A. (2007) 'Language choice online: globalization and identity in Egypt', in B. Danet and S.C. Herring (eds), *The Multilingual Internet: Language, Culture, and Communication Online* (Oxford: Oxford University Press), pp. 303–18.

Wenger, E. (1998) *Communities of Practice: Learning, Meaning, and Identity* (Cambridge: Cambridge University Press).

Wilkinson, R. (2013) 'English-medium instruction at a Dutch university: challenges and pitfalls', in A. Doiz, D. Lasagabaster, and J.M. Sierra (eds), *English-Medium Instruction at Universities: Global Challenges* (Bristol, Buffalo, Toronto: Multilingual Matters), pp. 3–24.

Woolard, K.A. (1992) 'Language ideology: issues and approaches', *Pragmatics*, 2, 3, 235–49.

Woolard, K.A. and Schieffelin, B.B. (1994) 'Language ideology', *Annual Review of Anthropology*, 23, 55–82.

Wright, S. (2004) *Language Policy and Language Planning* (London, New York: Palgrave Macmillan).

Yağğmur, K. (2009) 'Language policy in the Netherlands', Working paper, *AMARAUNA World Languages Network*. Available at: http://amaraunalanguages.com/orokorra/artikuluak/eu/Bilbao_Yagmur.pdf. Retrieved 11 February 2016.

Yağğmur K. and Konak, Ö.A. (2009) 'Assessment of language proficiency in bilingual children. How revealing is the interdependence hypothesis?' *Turkic Languages*, 13, 274–84.

Yağğmur, K. and van de Vijver, F.J.R. (2012) 'Acculturation and language orientations of Turkish immigrants in Australia, France, Germany, and the Netherlands', *Journal of Cross-Cultural Psychology*, 43, 7: 1110–30.

Zenner, E., Speelman, D., and Geeraerts, D. (2012) 'Cognitive sociolinguistics meets loanword research: measuring variation in the success of anglicisms in Dutch', *Cognitive Linguistics* 23, 4, 749–92.

Zentella, A.C. (1997) *Growing Up Bilingual: Puerto Rican Children in New York* (Oxford, Malden, MA: Blackwell).

Index

A

Affinity spaces, 5, 13
Alfonzetti, G., 52, 93, 94, 104
Alvarez-Cáccamo, 50, 52
Ammon, U., 26, 27
Anders, 136
Androutsopoulos, J., 14, 43, 45–46, 48, 54–56, 63, 109
Anglicisms, 28, 31, 90, 146, 184
Angouri, J., 4
Arnaut, K., 39
Auer, P., 15, 48, 50–52, 66, 92–93, 96, 109

B

Bailey, B., 52, 53, 63, 110
Baker, C., 136
Barbour, S., 27, 28, 90
Barkhoff, J., 33
Baron, N. S., 45

Barrett, R., 24
Barton, D., 6, 10, 17–18, 39–40, 43–45, 47–49, 55, 58
Bastardas-Boada, A., 39
Baym, N. K., 4–5, 15, 42, 45–46
Beck, E., 36
Benwell, B., 15, 46, 55, 139
Berns, M., 30, 47, 87
Blogs, 3, 6, 7–9, 43, 65, 74, 84
Björkman, B., 26
Bjornson, M., 34, 36
Block, D., 137
Blog posts, 3, 6, 74
Blommaert, J., 39–41, 63, 88, 289
and Rampton, B., 39
Breiteneder, A., 27

C

Callahan, L., 25, 29, 289
Cardinal, L., 34, 37

© The Author(s) 2017
J. Dailey-O'Cain, *Trans-National English in Social Media Communities*, DOI 10.1057/978-1-137-50615-3

310 Index

Claus, P., 31
Clayman, S. E., 50
Code-switching, 49–51, 62, 76, 128, 271
  as a contextualization cue, 51, 128
  discourse-related, examples52, 93, 103, 109
  discourse-related vs. participant-related, 92, 109, 128, 131, 281
  participant-related, examples, 52, 109, 111
  problems with concept, 49
Communities
  computer-mediated, 4–14
  diasporic, 5, 12, 48
  face-to-face, 92, 94, 109, 132–132, 135
  of practice, 5
Contextualization cue, 15, 51, 93, 95, 96, 100, 107–108, 132
Conversation analysis, 50, 92, 138
Coupland, N., 39, 137
Crossing, 49, 52–53, 88, 110, 129, 245
Crystal, D., 44
Cuonz, C., 136

D

Dailey-O'Cain, J., 16–17, 52, 54, 109–110, 136
  and Liebscher, G., 16–17, 52, 54, 109–110, 136
Danet, B., 45, 47
  and Herring, S. C., 47
De Bot, K., 28, 90, 155
Del-Teso-Craviotto, M., 54, 72
De Swaan, A., 28, 90

Deumert, A.. 17, 41–42, 46–47, 50, 53–54, 58, 64–65, 129, 283
De Vries Jr., H. J., 28
Discourse-centred online ethnography, 21, 54
Dodd, W., 27–28, 90
Domain shift and loss in higher education, 28, 90
DuBois, J. W., 137
Duden: Das große Wörterbuch der deutschen Sprache, 14, 63
Dyson, K., 34

E

Edwards, A., 26, 28–31, 90
English
  amount on the internet, 47
  global, 22, 37, 52, 56–59, 65, 88, 279–280, 282–284, 289–290
  increasing use of, 90
  lexical borrowing from, 31
  as a lingua franca, 26–29, 283, 288–289
  as a neutral language, 27, 29, 53, 88
  proficiency in, 30, 66, 73, 76, 146
  role of, debate within public discourse, 146, 201
  role of, debate within academic discourse, 28
  role of, debate within sociolinguistics, 26, 27, 56–60, 61
English media, dubbing vs. subtitling practices, 287
Entzinger, H., 33, 36
Erasure, 138–139, 239

Index
311

Erling, E. J., 26, 30
Etzioni, A., 4
Extra, G., 36

F

Facebook, 2, 5–6, 13, 43, 55, 118
Fialkova, L., 48
Fitzgerald, D., 36
Footing, 52, 103, 108

G

Gal, S., 137–138
Garrett, P., 136
Gass, S., 16
Gee, J. P., 5
Georgakopoulou, A., 43, 46, 51, 54
Gerritsen, M., 26
Giles, H., 136
Gill, V. T., 50
Glahn, R., 31
Globalization, 4, 22–23, 27, 38–40, 48–49, 56–60, 61, 63, 289
Glocalization, 39
Gnutzmann, C., 29, 30
Goffman, E., 46, 52
Golato, A., 139
Gramling, D., 36
Grice, H. P., 137
Guerini, F., 110
Gumperz, J. J., 15, 51

H

Harré, R., 17, 53, 138
Hasebrink, U., 26, 30, 88
Heller, M., 50, 131

Herring, S. C., 5, 6, 7, 43, 45, 47, 111
Herring, S. C., 6
Herring, S. C., 7
Heteroglossia, 53, 54
and heteroglossic repertoires, 53
Hilgendorf, S. K.., 26, 30
Hinchcliffe, D., 43
Hinnenkamp, V., 54
Hinrichs, L., 15, 55
Holden, N., 26
House, J., 289
Hyperlinks, 8

I

Iconicity, 137, 139, 239
Icons, 6, 15, 76–77, 80, 84–85, 98, 139, 146, 191, 234, 236
Identity, 9, 15, 24, 29, 39, 41, 51–52, 55, 59, 87, 109–110, 235, 237, 250, 280–281
in social media discourse, 59
Ideological stance, 31–32, 35, 137–139, 181
Indexicality, 41, 46, 53, 54, 137
and indexical field, 41
Interactional sociolinguistics, 50
Interview, 3–4, 11–14, 16–17, 20–21, 22, 25, 32, 44, 54, 57, 65, 135–136, 138–141, 150, 152, 161, 163, 16172, 174, 176–177, 180, 185, 188, 201–202, 207, 209, 212, 214, 216–217, 220, 222, 224–225, 227, 235, 240, 242, 245–248, 250–251, 255, 256–258, 261, 263, 266–267, 272, 275, 277, 290
Irvine, J., 137–138

312 Index

J

Jacquemet, M., 40, 42, 45, 49, 54
Jaspers, J., 50
Jaworski, A., 137
Jeeves, A., 30
Jenkins, J., 26, 27
Jewitt, C., 55
Jones, S. G., 4, 45

K

Kachru, B. B., 27, 38
Kelly-Holmes, H., 25–26, 29, 47
Kirkpatrick, A., 27
Kouper, I., 6, 7
Koutsogiannis, D., 39
Kress, G., 55
Küppers, A., 36
Yağğmur, K., 36

L

Lambert, 136
Langenhove, L., 17, 53, 138
Language attitudes, 16–17, 22, 25,
        57, 133, 136–139, 281, 283
    in interaction, 16, 17
Language ideology
    and language policies, 21, 23, 34,
        37, 61, 89, 285 (Language
        policies)
    and nationalism, 37, 277, 287
        (Nationalism, civic and n;
        Nationalism, ethnic)
    and state institutions, 37–38, 285
    changes under increased
        globalization, 38
    definition, 24

language and commodity
    model, 34
    relationship with language
        practice, 13, 25, 34, 38, 42, 58,
        62, 87, 90, 285, 287
Language policies
    and language ideologies, 21, 23,
        34, 37, 61, 89, 285 (Language
        ideology)
    in Germany, 35–37, 284
    in the Netherlands, 35–37, 284
    overt vs covert, 37, 38
Language power blocs, 38
Language regime, 34–35, 37, 283,
        285
Language regulation scenario, 35
Lee, C., 6, 10, 17–18, 39–40, 43–45,
        47–49, 55, 58
Li, W., 49
Liebscher, G., 16–17, 52, 54,
        109–110, 136
    Dailey-O'Cain, J., 16–17, 52, 54,
        109–110, 136
Linguistic imperialism, 26, 47
Linguistics of contact, 40
Livejournal.com, 6, 102
    demographics of, 11

M

Mackey, A., 16
Maheux-Pelletier, G., 139
Martin, E. A., 26
Martin, P. L., 35
McClure, E., 48
Membership categorization, 139
Meyerhoff, M., 53
Mitsikopoulou, B., 39

Mroczek, K., 42–43
Multimodality, 15, 55
Muus, P., 36
Myers-Scotton, C., 50

N

Nationalism
civic, 33, 35, 37, 277, 285
ethnic, 33, 35, 37, 277, 285
Nation-state
changed role of under increased
globalization, 38
vs. state nation, 33, 285
(Nationalism, civic and;
Nationalism, ethnic)
Nickerson, C., 26
Niedzelski, N., 53
Nishimura, Y., 46, 53

O

O'Hara-Davies, B., 16
Onysko, A., 27, 31, 90

P

Page, R., 55
Pan, L., 137
Paolillo, J. C., 47
Park, J. S., 5, 25, 27, 29, 41, 42,
56–58
Parks, M. R., 5
Parmegiani, A., 16
Penninx, R., 36
Pennycook, A., 27, 38, 39, 41, 50,
63, 108

Peuronen, S., 30, 32, 48, 52, 53, 65,
108, 110, 121, 124, 131
Phillipson, R., 26
Pillarization, 33, 35, 37, 285
Polylanguaging, Transidiomatic
practices
Poplack, S., 50, 62, 67, 76, 82
Positioning, 16, 53–54, 92, 110,
118, 120, 130, 135–277, 281
Pratt, M.-L., 40
Preisler, B., 26
Preston, D., 136
Pujolar, J., 38

R

Rampton, B., 39, 52, 88, 110, 129
Recursiveness, 138, 139, 236
Research ethics, 17, 18
Rettberg, J. W., 6
Rheingold, H., 5
Robertson, R., 38, 39
Roudometof, V., 39
Ryan, E. B., 136
Safran, W., 34
Saraceni, M., 27
Schelper, D., 31
Seargeant, P., 24, 25, 26, 35, 138
Sebba, M., 54
Seidlhofer, B., 27
Sériot, P., 33
Silverstein, M., 24, 138
Skutnabb-Kangas, T., 26
Social media language, distinctive
features of, 46
Soler-Carbonell, J., 30
Sonntag, S. K., 34, 37
Spitzmüller, J., 27, 28, 90, 184

314   **Index**

Stance, 32, 35, 140, 144, 147, 148,
153, 154, 156, 165, 166, 168,
170, 171, 175, 176, 181–189,
191–195, 198, 199, 201, 202,
205–207, 209, 211, 212, 217,
219–222, 224, 227, 234,
245–247, 250, 251, 255, 256,
258, 260, 263, 266, 269–271,
274–276
Stokoe, E., 15, 46, 55, 139
State traditions, 25, 34, 57, 279, 284,
285
Stevenson, P., 34, 36
Stommel, W., 54
Stroud, C., 34, 285
Studler, R., 136
Superdiversity, 39, 40, 44, 46, 48,
49, 50, 53, 56, 57

T

Taeldeman, J., 31
Thelen, M., 31
Threads, in blogging, 7
Thurlow, C., 42–43
Transidiomatic practices, 40–42, 44,
47–49, 51, 52, 54–58, 64–67,
76, 82–87, 89, 92, 94, 103,
105, 108, 110, 115, 120, 124,
125, 128, 130, 139, 140, 144,
146, 147, 152, 153, 155, 156,
163, 166–168, 170–177, 179,
180, 182, 183, 185–187,
191–195, 197–199, 201, 202,
206, 207, 209, 216–221,
223–227, 229, 231, 234, 236,
237, 239, 240, 242, 245–247,
249–251, 254–256, 259, 262,
267, 271, 276, 279–284, 289

Translanguaging, Transidiomatic
practices
Translingual practices,
Transidiomatic practices
Translocal communities,
Communities, computer-
mediated
Translocal and transcultural flows, 41
Transnationalism, 40, 56, 124–130,
132, 192, 281
Tsiplakou, S., 55

U

Unserekleinestadt (the German
community), 7, 79, 81, 85, 86,
280
Userpics, Icons

V

*Van Dale groot woordenboek van de
Nederlandse taal*, 14, 63
Van der Sijs, N., 28, 31
Van Hoorde, J., 28, 90
Van Leeuwen, T., 15
Varis, P., 39, 42, 53, 58, 64, 65
Vertovec, S., 39
Vihman, V.-A., 33
Virtual communities, Communities,
computer-mediated
Vraagvrije vrijdag, 7, 102, 123, 125,
127–130, 172, 174, 179, 189,
191, 234, 240, 241, 270
Vragenuurtje (the Dutch
community), 80, 82, 86, 95,
98, 103, 108, 280

Index **315**

W
Waldinger, R., 36
Walsh, J., 34, 37
Walther, J. B., 43
Wang, X., 39, 42, 53, 64, 65
Warschauer, M., 48
Web 2.0, 6, 43, 44, 45, 47
Wee, L., 25, 27, 29, 41–42, 56, 57, 58
Wenger, E., 5
Wilkinson, R., 26, 30
Woolard, K. A., 25, 137
  and Schieffelin, B. B., 24
World Englishes, 27

Wright, S., 33
Writing spaces online, 43

Y
Yagğmur, K.
  and Konak, Ö. A., 36
  and van de Vijver, F. J. R., 37

Z
Zenner, E., 31
Zentella, A. C., 52, 94, 104

CPSIA information can be obtained
at www.ICGtesting.com
Printed in the USA
LVOW13*0355130917
548436LV00015B/387/P